I0803201

IMAGES
of America

JACKSONVILLE

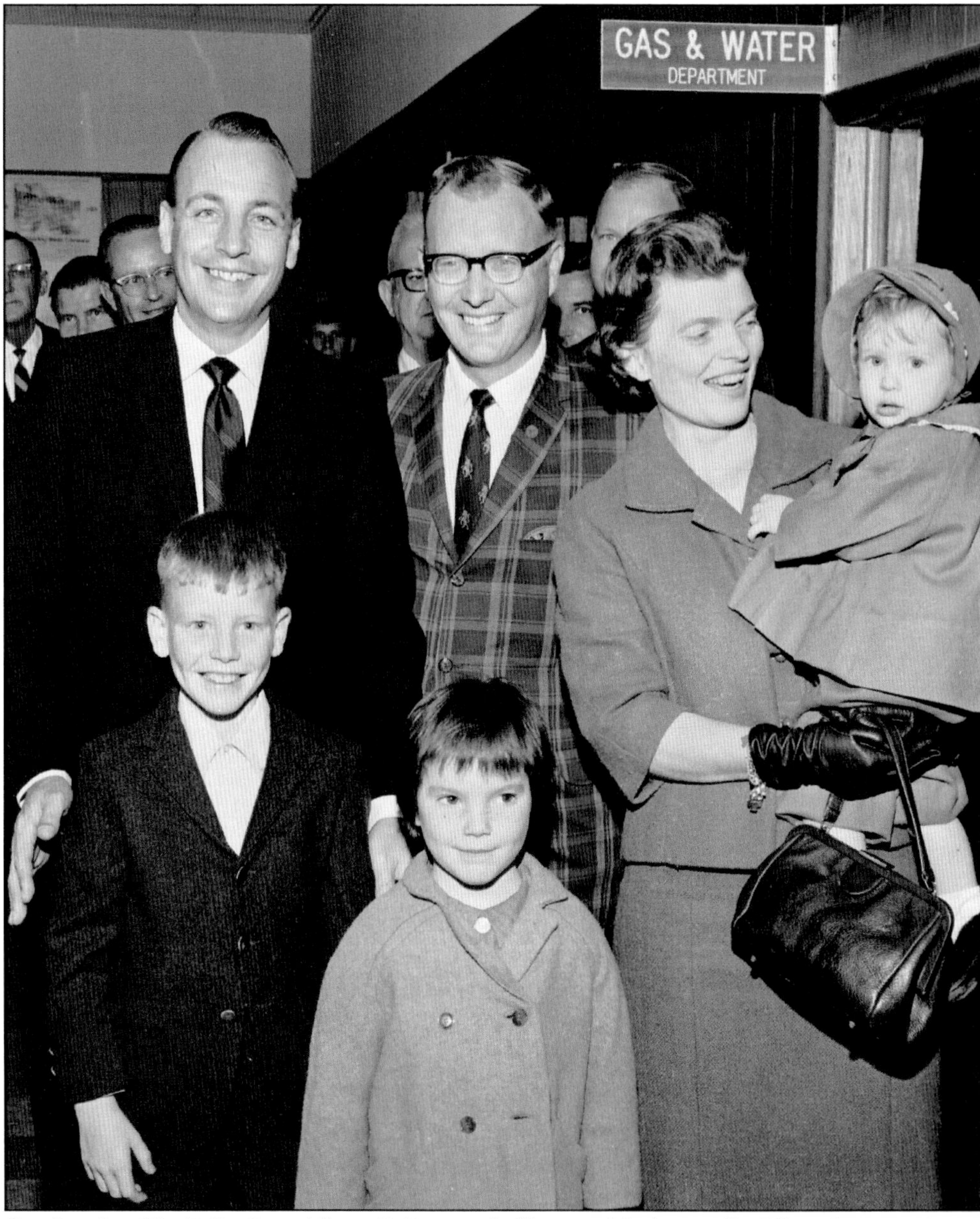

On October 30, 1968, Gov. Albert P. Brewer (left) visited Jacksonville. This photograph was taken in City Hall (today, the police station). Posing with Gov. Brewer are Mayor John B. Nisbet Jr., Dorothy Jane Warren Nisbet (holding Virginia), Nancy Nisbet (front, center), and John B. Nisbet III. Dorothy Jane sewed virtually all of the clothes the Nisbets are wearing. (Nisbet family collection.)

On the Cover: Curtis Clifford "Curt" Powell stands behind the counter of his City Café. Powell later ran a taxicab stand out of this building and gave numerous children rides to school in his cabs. It was in the City Café that a young Reba Irene Tillery met the man who would become her husband of 60 years, Homer Barnwell. (Courtesy of Mrs. Homer Barnwell.)

IMAGES
of America

JACKSONVILLE

John B. Nisbet III and Dorothy Jane Nisbet

ARCADIA
PUBLISHING

ISBN 978-1-4671-1353-3

Published by Arcadia Publishing
Charleston, South Carolina

Printed in the United States of America

Library of Congress Control Number: 2014948118

For all general information, please contact Arcadia Publishing:
Telephone 843-853-2070
Fax 843-853-0044
E-mail sales@arcadiapublishing.com
For customer service and orders:
Toll-Free 1-888-313-2665

Visit us on the Internet at www.arcadiapublishing.com

To my Dad, I miss you

To Diane, what a wonderful adventure through this life I am having with you

To Will, Matthew, and Sarah, my hope is that you come to understand your history without being overwhelmed by it

Contents

ACKNOWLEDGMENTS

My father, John B. Nisbet Jr., and my maternal great aunt, Miss Ella Mills McCutchen, made me my generation's family historian. My dad was my touchstone for everything in our hometown of Jacksonville, Alabama. With a few sentences ("Sure you know who that is, Johnny. His mother worked at the Winn Dixie; they lived up on Fourth Avenue by the Prichards. He was in Nancy's grade, was in Troop 147"), he could immediately place a person in my mind precisely. Rick Bragg, who grew up in Jacksonville and was a year or two ahead of me in high school, brought these "homing" instincts back to me in his first book, *All Over but the Shoutin'*. In one story, he recalls that the only person he let drive his hot rod was the prettiest girl in school. Before my eyes got to the words "Patrice Curry," I had already named her and pictured her in my mind. Rick has written richly about our hometown. I hope to achieve some semblance of that tradition in this book through photographs. Any errors and/or omissions are solely mine.

I want to thank Barbara Rowell, Christie Wallace, Arnetha Turner, and the rest of the staff at the Jacksonville Public Library for making this book possible. I would also like to thank Jacksonville State University president Dr. William A. Meehan for his generous approval of my use of JSU images in this book, as well as the staff at the Houston Cole Library for their help in acquiring images from the Alabama room. The following people played a part in producing this book, and I want to thank them: Angel Sircy, David Brady, Jetta Manners (she lit the match that started me thinking about a book with Arcadia), Dr. Calvin Dickinson, Dr. Michael "Birdie" Birdwell, Carolyn West, Eric Wayne Key, Secolina "Jeanie" Levell Morris, Jennifer Snow Sims, Emily Lipscomb, Debra Deering-Barrett, Denise Rucker, Lynn Causey, Leighton Kittleman, Floyd "Buddy" Tredaway, Worden Weaver, Dr. Ouida Susie Francis Dempsey, Sarah Griffith Byrne, Jarrod Simmons, John Curtis Powell, Thomas Michael O'Mara, and Linda Cain.

I would also like to thank John Prichard, Frances Prichard, Flint Patterson, Martha Patterson, Thomas Ficklen, Giles Herb, Carolyn Jernigan, Sue Vondracek, and Francis Adkins.

This book could not have been written without Jack Boozer's University of Alabama master's thesis and his "History of Jacksonville" articles in the *Jacksonville News*.

I owe Mrs. Homer Barnwell a special debt of gratitude.

I am eternally grateful and indebted to Diane Lander Mount Nisbet for her advice and editing skills.

Unless otherwise noted, all images appear courtesy of the Jacksonville Public Library.

The authors' after-tax profits and royalties from this book will be donated to the Jacksonville Public Library.

Introduction

Not much has been written about the history of Jacksonville, Calhoun County, Alabama. Jacksonville is one of the oldest towns in northeast Alabama, having been founded in 1834, incorporated by the legislature in 1836, and selected the county seat of Benton County. Modern-day Jacksonville, in Jeffersonian land language, comprises Township 14-E, Range 8-E, sections 11, 12, 13, 14, 23, 24, 25, and 26. In 1834, Jacksonville was formed in the northern half of section 14; Church Street forms the dividing line between sections 11 and 12, 14 and 13, and 23 and 24. Originally named Drayton, the town's name was changed to Jacksonville in 1836. There can be no doubt that Jacksonville was named in honor of Pres. Andrew Jackson, largely for his success in the Creek War of 1813–1814 and his adroit handling of the Creeks by removing them from northeastern Alabama in the Trail of Tears. Benton County was named for Thomas Hart Benton, a US senator from Missouri who had fought with Jackson in the Creek War (and who later fought a gunfight against Jackson). Benton County was renamed Calhoun County in honor of John C. Calhoun in 1858.

One way to think of the history of Jacksonville is as a series of invasions. Hernando de Soto passed through the Choccolocco Valley about three miles east of Jacksonville around 1540. This invasion resulted in the death of 90 percent of the Native Americans in the areas he traveled. A second invasion occurred when other Native Americans repopulated the area. Andrew Jackson organized the third invasion in 1813 by declaring war on the Creek Nation. The fourth invasion was in the 1830s, by white settlers (often with slaves) into former Creek Indian property ceded to the US government in the 1832 Treaty with the Creeks (also known as the Third Treaty of Washington and the Treaty of Cusseta). In the 1860s, the fifth invasion began with "Yankees" (persons born outside of the states that composed the Confederate States of America) arriving in Jacksonville initially as combatants and then as investors. Several Yankee soldiers came through Jacksonville during the Civil War and returned after the war to rebuild their lives. After the war, and until the 1870s, a US Army unit was stationed in Jacksonville. This added a great many European names to the 1870 census.

The final "invasion" occurred when Federal Mogul Corporation, headquartered in Southfield, Michigan, located a distribution plant in Jacksonville in 1974, and Parker Hannifin, based in Mayfield Heights, Ohio, opened a plant in 1980.

Interspersed with these invasions were other migrations of people that revolved around the growing town of Jacksonville. Among these migrations, four stand out: the cotton mill; the evolution of the State Normal School at Jacksonville; the haphazard development of primary and secondary schools in Jacksonville (and the pride that came with those schools); and Camp/Fort McClellan.

Ide/Profile Cotton Mill

The Ide Cotton Mill began operation in October 1905 with Northern investors George P. Ide, Henry Ide, L.K. Quimby, and J.E. Henry. Local stockholders included H.L. Stevenson, J.W. Hawke, and numerous others. The Ide Cotton Mill constructed 40 "operative" houses early in 1905, and in 1908, it built an additional 90. In 1911, the mill changed ownership, as J.E. Henry became the principle stockholder, and William I. Greenleaf was named vice president and secretary. The facility's name was changed to Profile Cotton Mill. Pulitzer Prize–winning author and Jacksonville native Rick Bragg described the situation in a 2010 interview with the *Anniston Star*:

> Yankee investors needed cotton, which of course was all over the place, but they also needed a source of labor—an inexhaustible source—so they sent flyers into the mountains, into the hill country, to the little farms and valleys, and the people came walking. Half of them were half-starved. They were scraping by as sharecroppers. They traded their mules and their little houses in the mountains for these company houses. It was their salvation. But it also just chewed them up. They gave their fingers, hands and arms to those machines. It filled their lungs full of cotton fiber. It shortened their lives. But at the same time, it was survival.

In his book *The Most They Ever Had*, Bragg recounts a story from Homer Barnwell, who remembered "a day, just another day, his father had sunk down on the porch, exhausted after walking home from his shift. Something made Homer look up the street, then down the street, and there he saw the same scene on porch after porch, as women and men made it only as far as that and melted onto the stoops." Albert B. Moore, an early-1900s historian, pointed out in *History of Alabama and Her People* what attracted these Northern investors to the South (and Jacksonville) in the first place:

> Experience has demonstrated that the native white people, taken largely from the foothills and mountain country, possess a high order of latent talent for textile pursuits. They not only possess unusual technical acumen but they are also psychologically fit for the work. They are industrious, reliable, responsive, practical-minded and possessed of the power of gratitude. Their individualism and their gratitude for the better life that the factory affords have made them practically immune to trade unionism. . . . Labor is not only intelligent and dependable, but it is also cheap.

The mill closed in 1955, and in 1956, Union Underwear purchased the mill and reopened it under the name Union Yarn Mill. The mill operated until 1999, when Union Underwear went bankrupt; the mill closed forever in 2001.

State Normal School

Jacksonville State University traces its origins to the Jacksonville Male (1836) and Female (1837) Academies, because those primary schools, or their successors, were absorbed by the State Normal School when it opened in 1883. The State Normal School absorbed several other schools or colleges that operated in Jacksonville: John H. Forney's polytechnic school (1867), Calhoun College (1871) and Calhoun Grange College (1878). Calhoun College and Calhoun Grange College were not really "colleges" as they are thought of today. They were closer to modern-day high schools. Jacksonville Male and Female Academies, and, presumably, the polytechnic school, merged with Calhoun College in 1873. What connects these "colleges" are their land and buildings. Both colleges used a brick building on 15 acres of land west of Spring Street, between College and Francis Streets. The building would eventually be called Hames Hall. Today, Kitty Stone Elementary stands on a portion of the property.

Unquestionably, the State Normal School at Jacksonville was created in 1882 by the Alabama Legislature as a two-year teacher training school. The Normal School opened in the fall of 1883 and held classes in the building formerly used by Calhoun College and Calhoun Grange College. The 1883 catalog states that the course of study is a primary department, intermediate department, collegiate department, and a normal professional course. The primary department served "as a model and training school for the Normal pupils." The 1883 catalog lists all of the students at the school, among them children as young as eight years old. According to the school's 1902 "announcement" (catalog), the courses at the school were "directed mainly towards fitting teachers for the ungraded schools of the State, and special stress will be laid upon the preparation for the successful organizing, simplifying, controlling and enriching of the 'one teacher' schools." Applicants for the "normal course must be at least fifteen years of age, be of good moral character and sound constitution, and must stand such an examination as the Faculty of the school may require." Successful normal course graduates were "entitled to teach in the public schools of this State."

In 1897, the Alabama Legislature created the Jacksonville public school district, named the State Normal School board of directors the board of trustees for the Jacksonville public school district, and gave control to the trustees to establish the appropriate number of schools for both "white" and "colored" students. The legislature stated that "the public schools for the white children shall constitute a model training school for the State Normal School, Jacksonville, Alabama and shall be established a part of the State Normal School." In 1902, the State Normal School announcement stated that "the Normal School is by law the Public School of the town of Jacksonville." Although this would seem to settle the issue, in the early 1900s, there were four primary schools operating in Jacksonville: Jacksonville City Schools (grades one through twelve); State Normal School primary department; Jacksonville Colored School (grades one through eight until 1948, when grades nine through twelve were added); and Profile Mill Village School (grades one through six). Further complicating the picture was that, in 1925, the State Normal School added a boarding high school named, appropriately, the State Normal School High School.

In addition to the numerous schools in existence, the buildings the schools used changed frequently. In 1883, the State Normal School met in the building in which Calhoun (Grange) College met on College Street. In 1900, the normal school moved to the old courthouse just off the square on Ladiga Street, calling it Atkins Hall. In 1908, after renovations to Hames Hall, the school moved back. Starting prior to 1905, Jacksonville City School met in a building on Francis Street, moved to the old courthouse in the 1920s, and moved back to the building on Francis in the 1930s, when renovations on that building had been completed.

In 1929, the Alabama Legislature made the State Normal School a four-year college and changed the name to State Teachers College. Around that same time, and in order to settle any dispute over the legal title to the real estate and buildings that the Normal School had used, the City of Jacksonville, the city's board of education, and the state board of education entered into an agreement on March 26, 1929, that "sold" certain real estate and buildings to the state board. In 1943, the City of Jacksonville conveyed legal title to the real estate and buildings that comprised Eastwood School to the State of Alabama. Portions of the State Normal School campus buildings on Spring Street, as well as the Jacksonville City School building across Francis Street and Eastwood School, had been built and repaired on land purchased with money from the City of Jacksonville and its citizens.

In 1957, the legislature added graduate degrees to the school and changed the name to Jacksonville State College. In 1966, the legislature made the Teacher's College a university and changed the name to Jacksonville State University.

Primary Schools

Between 1897 and 1968, there were as many as four primary schools operating inside the city limits: Jacksonville City schools; the training/demonstration school for the State Normal School; the

Profile Mill Village School (1911 to 1942); and Jacksonville Colored School, eventually renamed Eastwood School (1895 to 1968).

Jacksonville Colored School in the Eastwood neighborhood of the city was a separate and unequal product of Jim Crow Alabama. The school opened in 1885 to provide some level of education to the black children in and around Jacksonville. A school for black children was started around 1895 in Rabbit Town (or Rocky Hollow). In 1901, the school moved to Vann Street between St. Paul CME and First Baptist churches. Around 1920, the school moved to its final location, off of East Vann Street. The original building on East Vann Street was a frame structure. A rock building was constructed in the 1940s by the Works Progress Administration and paid for, at least partially, by the City of Jacksonville. As late as 1952, the diplomas from the high school in Eastwood read "Jacksonville Colored High School." At some point, the diplomas were changed to read "Eastwood High School." In 1945, the Jacksonville Colored School expanded to include a senior high school, which was accredited in 1954. In 1968, Jacksonville State University closed the Colored High School (Eastwood), and the black students from the Eastwood neighborhood "went to the other side," as one Eastwood resident put it. These students went to the other side of town, to the other side of the color line, and to the other side of their world.

In 1911, the Profile Mill Village School opened, with Mrs. J.R. Alexander as principal. In order to accommodate the children's work schedule (child labor laws had yet to be enacted), there were two sessions: 6:00 a.m. to noon, and 1:00 p.m. to 6:00 p.m. In 1919, and after the child labor laws went into effect, the school held one session, from 8:00 a.m. to 4:00 p.m. In 1924, Ethel Posey became principal and operated the school 12 months a year. The school opened a lunchroom in 1932 and, eventually, operated a night school for adults. The Mill Village School closed in 1942, and the children went to the State Teachers College demonstration or laboratory school.

Camp McClellan

Camp Shipp was the first federal installation on a large tract of land south of Jacksonville. It would become part of Fort McClellan. Starting in 1898, Camp Shipp trained soldiers for the Spanish-American War. The location was used sporadically by the military until the nation's entry into World War I dramatically increased the need for training space. Although plans for a federal facility south of Jacksonville had begun prior to war being declared in April 1917, work began in earnest at Camp McClellan in July 1917. Named in honor of Union major general George B. McClellan, the camp housed 27,000 men from the 29th Division by November 1917. The division was ordered to France in June 1918 and suffered 5,570 casualties in the Meuse-Argonne offensive. On July 1, 1929, Camp McClellan was designated Fort McClellan. For the next 70 years, the facility was home to a World War II prisoner-of-war camp, a chemical corps school and training center, the Women's Army Corps training center, and a military police school. The federal government closed Fort McClellan on May 20, 1999.

One

Antebellum Jacksonville

Andrew Jackson organized the third invasion in 1813 by declaring war on the Creek Nation. The Battle of Talluschatchee took place about five miles west of Jacksonville, just outside of Alexandria. Davy Crockett, who participated in the massacre of 189 Creek Indian warriors, wrote that "we now shot them like dogs; and then set the house on fire and burned it up with the forty-six warriors in it." Jackson's troops returned the next day and ate the potatoes that had cooked in the fire. Another soldier wrote, "I cannot imagine, much less describe a more horrid spectacle." Jackson wrote Tennessee's Governor Blount that "We have retaliated for the destruction of Ft. Mims." The Creek War of 1813–1814 culminated in Jackson's victory at Horseshoe Bend, where at least 800 Creek warriors died.

With the fourth invasion, white settlers bought land from the US government, Chief Ladiga, and other Native American chiefs and headmen. According to land records from 1830, the original investors in Jacksonville purchased the land from a Creek Indian named Hobithtustunnuckee (who lived at Talluschatchee Town); Hobithtustunnuckee owned the land through a reservation authorized by the Treaty of Cusseta. The area's Indians were eventually forced into relocating to Oklahoma on the Trail of Tears. The whites proceeded to make a town by building homes, schools, churches, and businesses.

Almost immediately after arriving in Drayton/Jacksonville, settlers set about establishing churches and schools. The first church chartered was First Presbyterian Church, with the Baptist, Methodist, and Episcopal congregations following in close order. Jacksonville Male Academy was incorporated by the State of Alabama in 1836, and the Jacksonville Female Academy was incorporated in 1837.

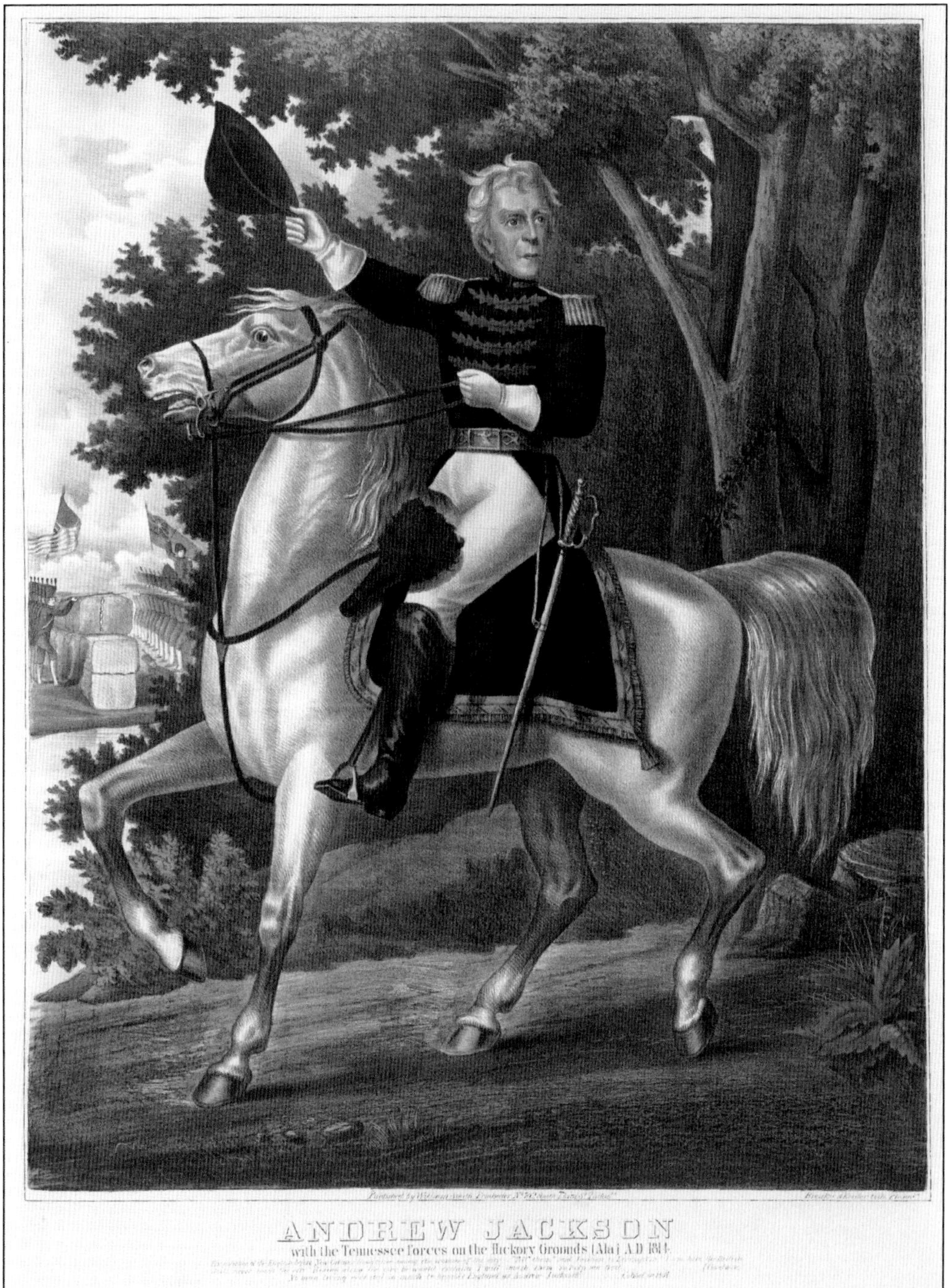

This 1814 etching displays Andrew Jackson on "the Hickory Grounds, Alabama" during the Creek War of 1813–1814. Contrary to local tradition, it is unlikely that Jackson came to or camped in Jacksonville; the closest he came was Fort Strother, near Neely Henry Dam in Ohatchee. (Library of Congress, Prints and Photographs Division.)

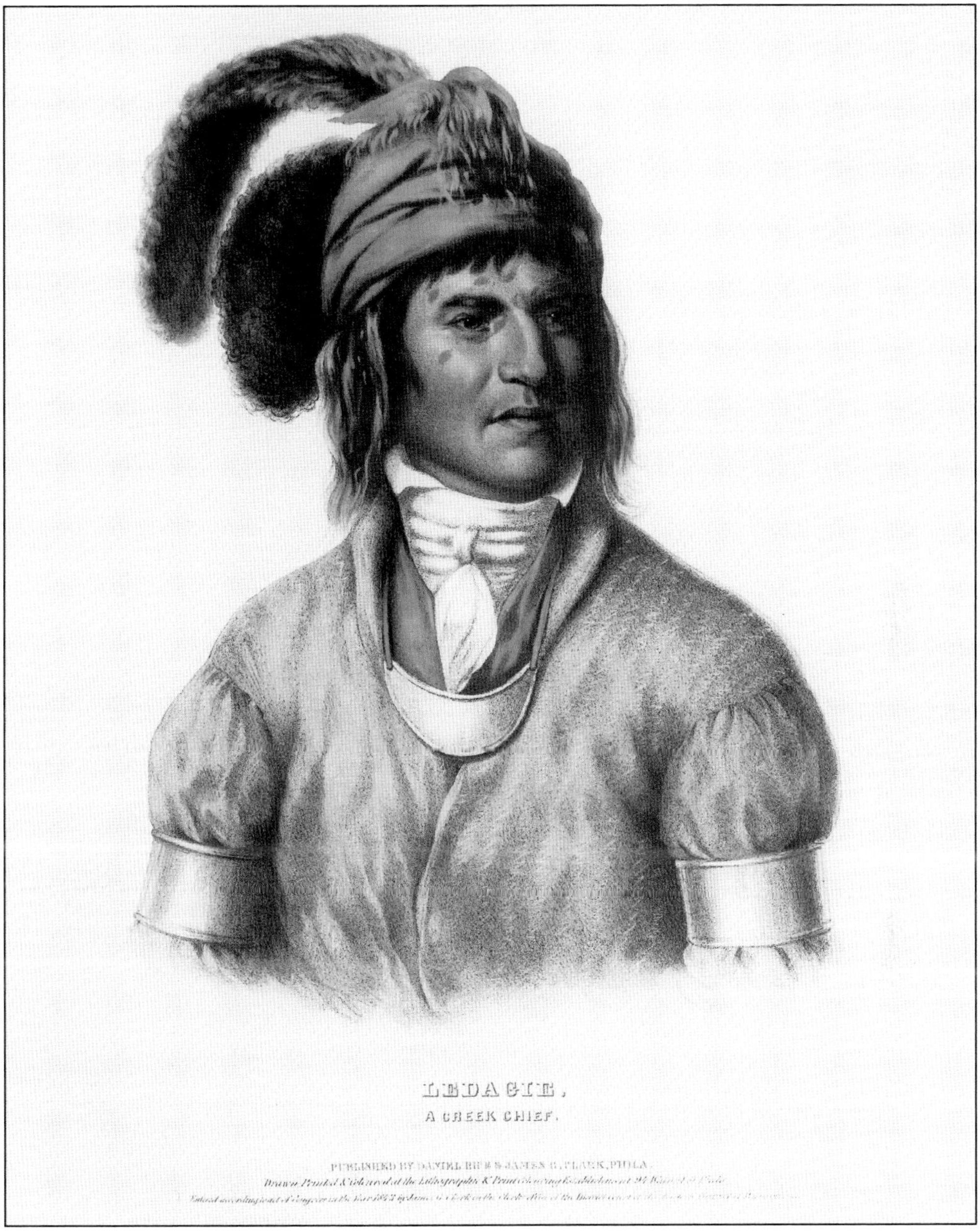

This image is of Chief Ladiga (sometimes spelled Ledagie). The earliest known observation of Jacksonville is from an account that appeared in 1885 in the *Jacksonville Republican*: "I saw Jacksonville in 1831, when Ladiga and family was the entire population of the town. Ladiga was an Indian chief." This image is from *History of the Indian Tribes* by Thomas L. McKenney and James Hall, published in 1844. The inscription states that the image was "published by Daniel Rice and James G. Clark." The original painting was probably done by Charles Bird King in 1825, when Ladiga was in Washington to contest the recently signed Treaty of Indian Springs and to negotiate and sign the Treaty of the Creeks (1826), which ceded Creek land in western Georgia to the United States. The original painting was destroyed in a fire at the Smithsonian Institution in 1865. (Tennessee State Library and Archives.)

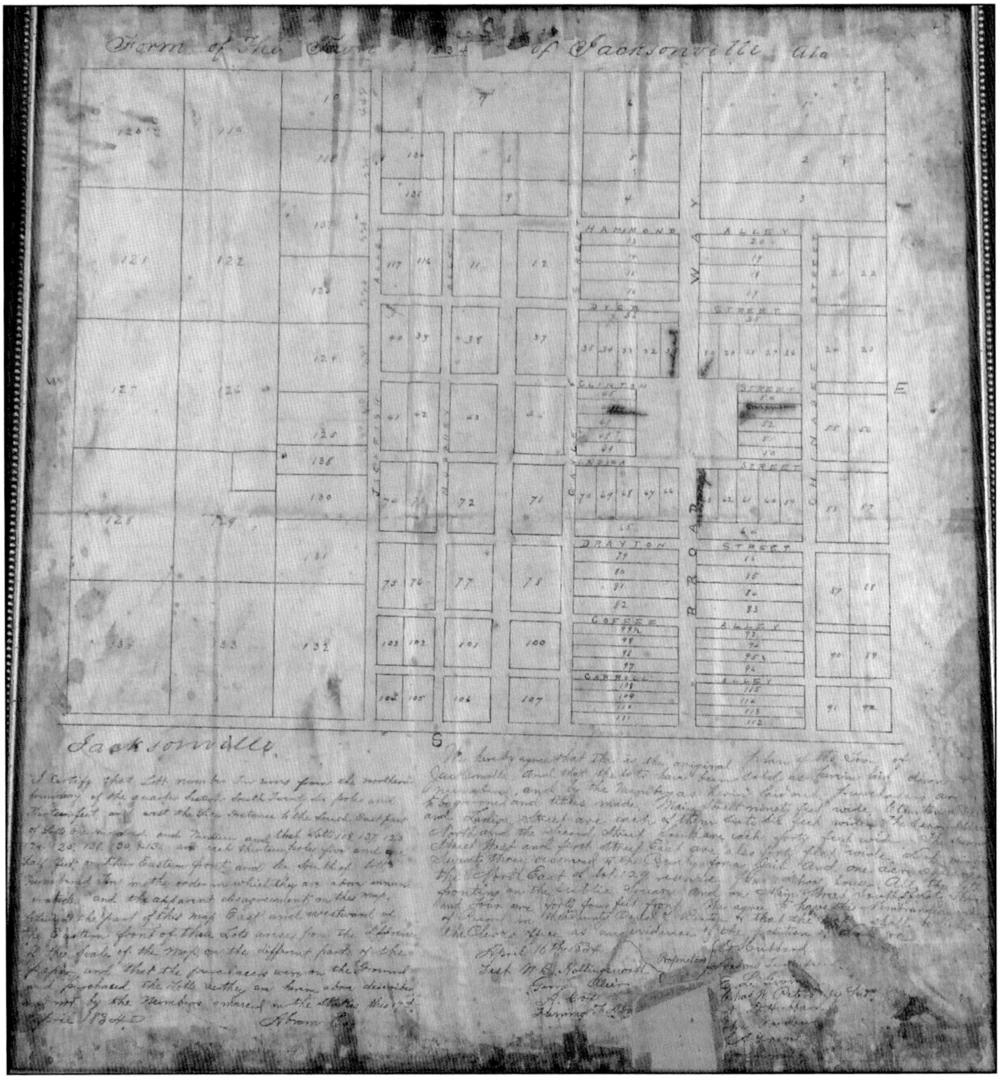

This previously unpublished map is the first map of Jacksonville. Created by surveyor Abram Cox, it was signed on April 16, 1834, by the original investors of Jacksonville: David Hubbard, Andrew Turnipseed, Edward L. Givens, Charles W. Peters (by his agent D. Hubbard), John Gooden, Christopher Green, and William Arnold. The lots were sold at auction on the same day the map was signed by the investors. The land depicted here, purchased by the investors from the Creek Indian named Hobithtustunnuckee, forms the northern half of Section 14 of Township 14-S, Section 8-E. (Private collection of Grant Paris.)

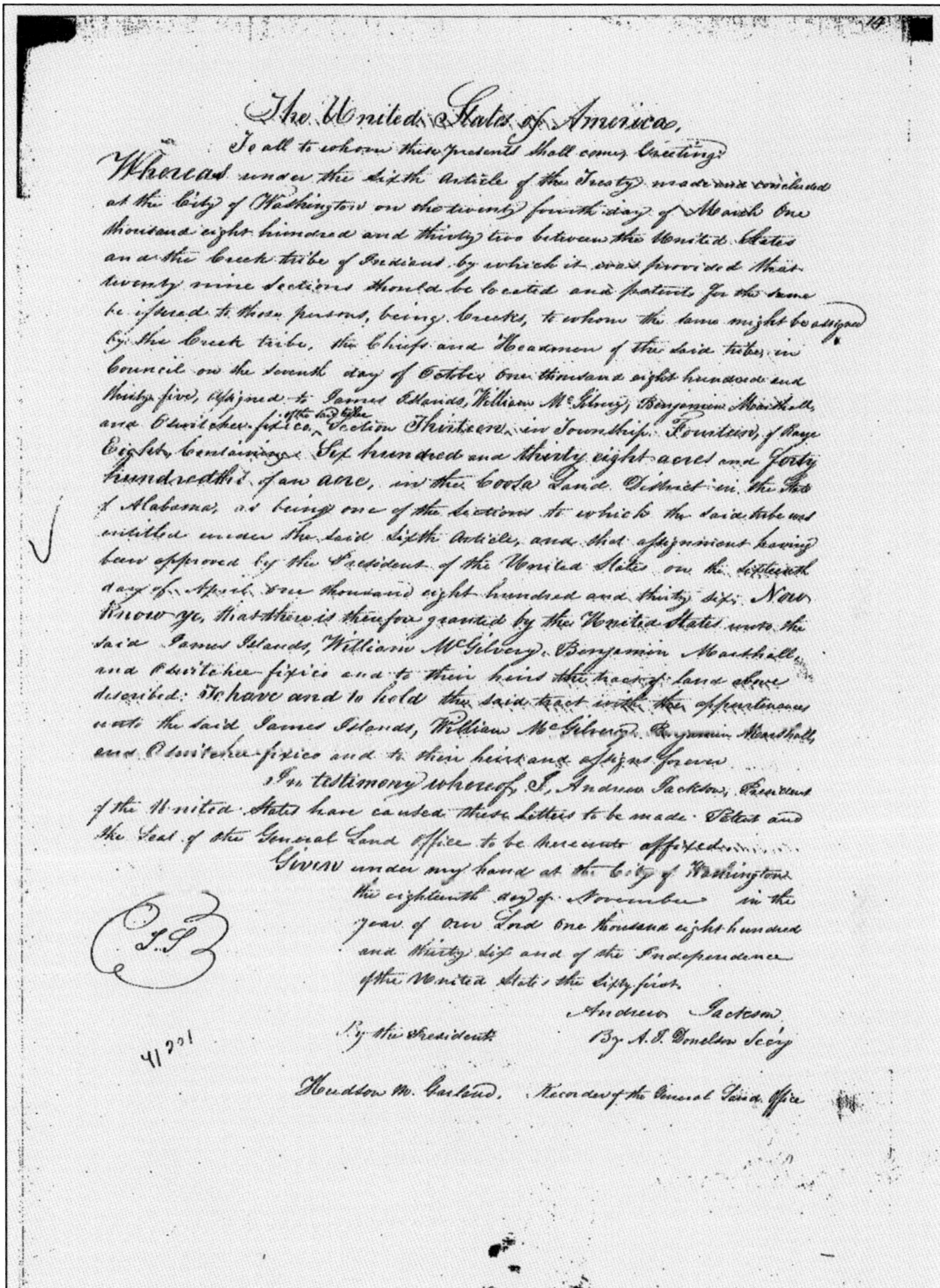
The United States of America,

To all to whom these presents shall come Greeting:

Whereas under the sixth Article of the Treaty made and concluded at the City of Washington on the twenty fourth day of March One thousand eight hundred and thirty two between the United States and the Creek tribe of Indians by which it was provided that twenty nine sections should be located and patents for the same be issued to those persons, being Creeks, to whom the same might be assigned by the Creek tribe, the Chiefs and Headmen of the said tribe in Council on the seventh day of October One thousand eight hundred and thirty five, assigned to James Islands, William McGilvery, Benjamin Marshall, and Oswitchee fixico, of the said tribe, Section Thirteen in Township Fourteen, of Range Eight, Containing Six hundred and thirty eight acres and Forty hundredths of an acre, in the Coosa Land District in the State of Alabama, as being one of the sections to which the said tribe was entitled under the said Sixth Article, and that assignment having been approved by the President of the United States on the fifteenth day of April One thousand eight hundred and thirty six: Now Know ye, that there is therefore granted by the United States unto the said James Islands, William McGilvery, Benjamin Marshall, and Oswitchee fixico and to their heirs the tract of land above described: To have and to hold the said tract with the appurtenances unto the said James Islands, William McGilvery, Benjamin Marshall and Oswitchee fixico and to their heirs and assigns forever.

In testimony whereof, I, Andrew Jackson, President of the United States have caused these Letters to be made Patent and the Seal of the General Land Office to be hereunto affixed.

Given under my hand at the City of Washington the eighteenth day of November in the year of our Lord One thousand eight hundred and thirty six and of the Independence of the United States the Sixty first.

L.S.

Andrew Jackson

By the President By A. J. Donelson Secy

Hudson M. Garland, Recorder of the General Land Office

This 1836 deed, signed by Pres. Andrew Jackson's designee, his nephew, Andrew Jackson Donelson, conveyed the entire Section 13 to four Creek Indians: James Islands, William McGilvery, Benjamin Marshall, and Oswitch Fixico. Section 13 is the eastern section of Jacksonville, bounded on the west by Church Street and on the north by Mountain Street. These four men also bought sections 1, 10, 11, 12, and 15. Benjamin Marshall was a Creek Indian who interpreted for the agents of the United States during treaty negotiations. (Bureau of Land Management.)

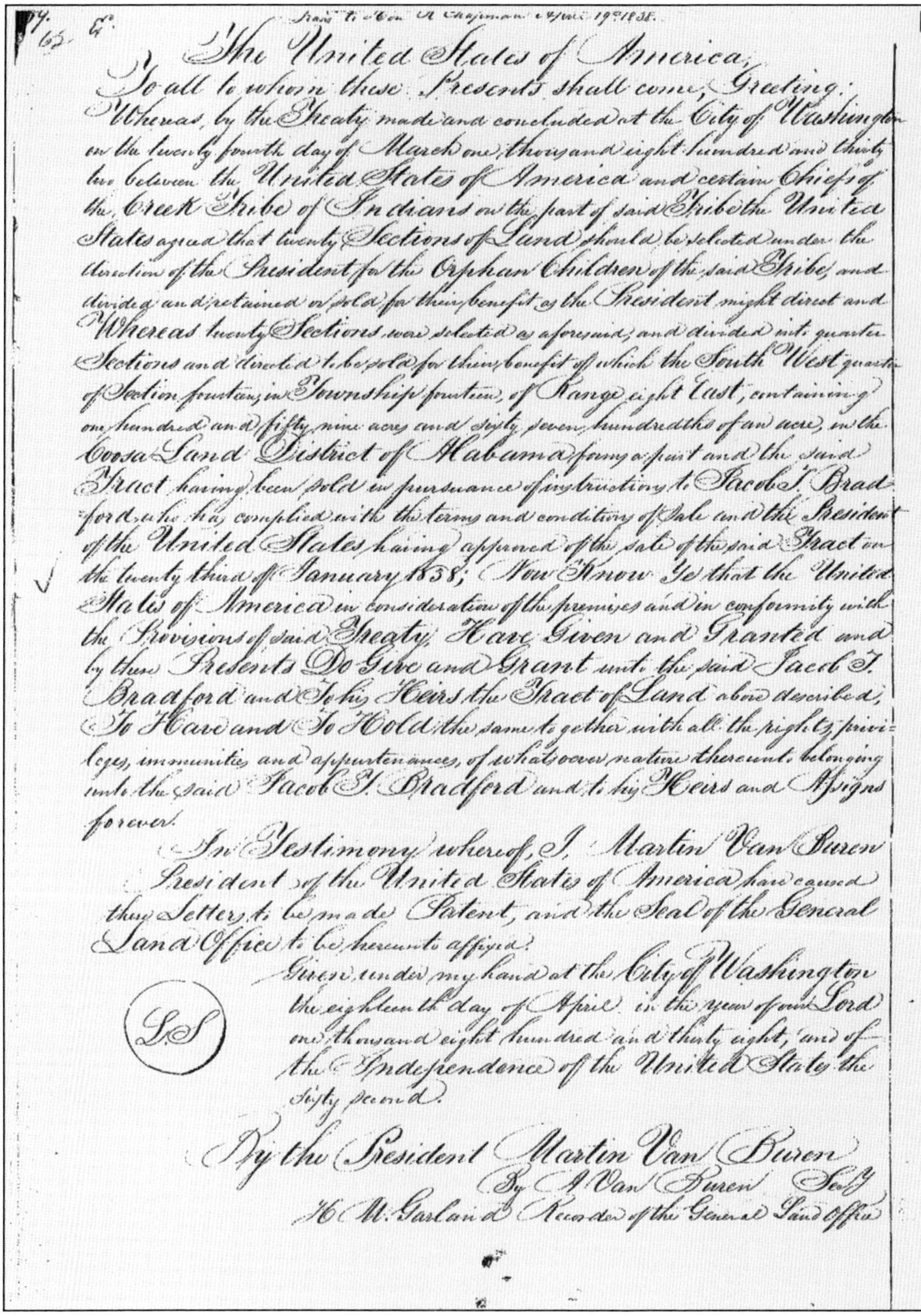

The United States of America,

To all to whom these Presents shall come, Greeting:

Whereas, by the Treaty made and concluded at the City of Washington on the twenty fourth day of March one thousand eight hundred and thirty two between the United States of America and certain Chiefs of the Creek Tribe of Indians on the part of said Tribe the United States agreed that twenty Sections of Land should be selected under the direction of the President for the Orphan Children of the said Tribe, and divided and retained or sold for their benefit as the President might direct and Whereas twenty Sections were selected as aforesaid, and divided into quarter Sections and directed to be sold for their benefit of which the South West quarter of Section fourteen in Township fourteen, of Range eight East, containing one hundred and fifty nine acres and sixty seven hundredths of an acre, in the Coosa Land District of Alabama forms a part and the said Tract having been sold in pursuance of instructions to Jacob T. Bradford who has complied with the terms and conditions of sale and the President of the United States having approved of the sale of the said Tract on the twenty third of January 1838; Now Know Ye that the United States of America in consideration of the premises and in conformity with the Provisions of said Treaty, Have Given and Granted and by these Presents Do Give and Grant unto the said Jacob T. Bradford and to his Heirs the Tract of Land above described; To Have and To Hold the same together with all the rights, privileges, immunities and appurtenances, of whatsoever nature thereunto belonging unto the said Jacob T. Bradford and to his Heirs and Assigns forever.

In Testimony whereof, I, Martin Van Buren President of the United States of America have caused these Letters to be made Patent, and the Seal of the General Land Office to be hereunto affixed.

L.S.

Given under my hand at the City of Washington the eighteenth day of April in the year of our Lord one thousand eight hundred and thirty eight, and of the Independence of the United States the sixty second.

By the President Martin Van Buren

By A Van Buren Secy

H. M. Garland Recorder of the General Land Office

This 1838 deed from the US government to Jacob T. Bradford, along with a second deed to Christopher A. Green, transferred one half of the southern half of Section 13. These deeds conveyed the property that now comprises Jacksonville from Coffee Street to Greenleaf Street. The deed is signed by Martin Van Buren. (Bureau of Land Management.)

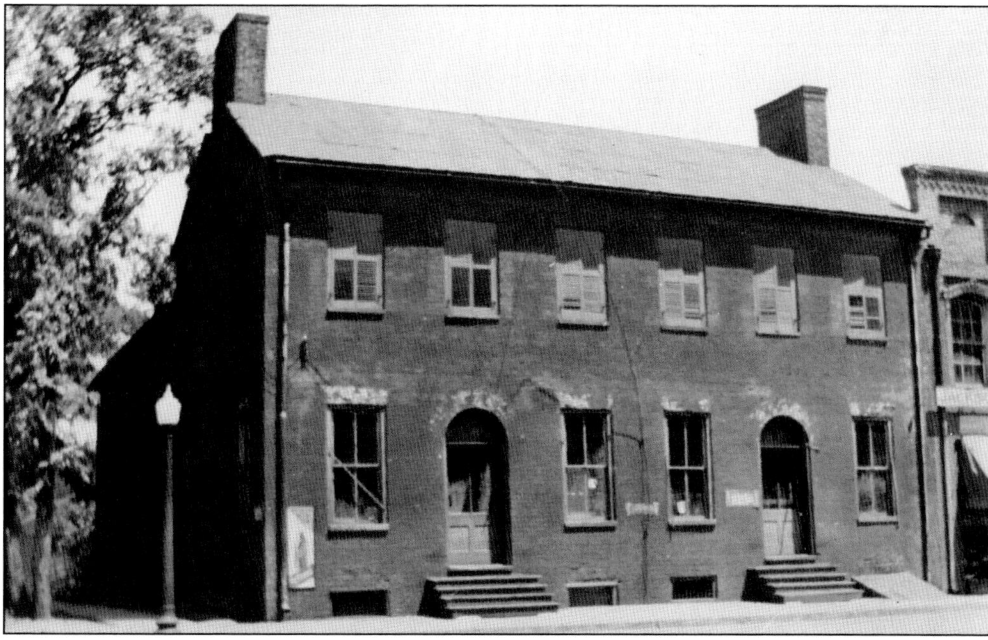

Originally known as "The Brick Tavern," this building was erected in 1838 and survived the great fire of 1883. The first floor had a lobby in the northern half and a dining room and saloon in the southern half. The second floor was divided into eight rooms for lodgers. Aaron Haynes built the tavern at a cost of $2,507.60. Haynes advertised in the *Jacksonville Republican* on May 10, 1838, that "he has lately opened a House of Entertainment . . . and hopes to merit and secure a liberal share of public patronage." The exterior brickwork is in the Flemish bond pattern. (Library of Congress, Prints and Photographs Division.)

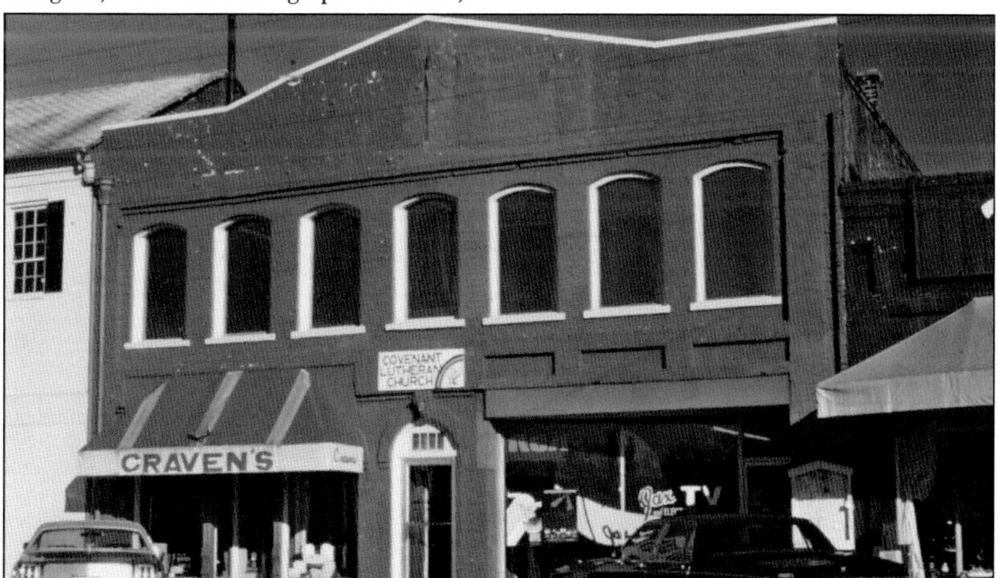

This building, seen here in the 1970s, was constructed around 1850. Due to its thick brick walls and lead-lined roof, it survived the 1883 fire that started in the building just to the right of this building.

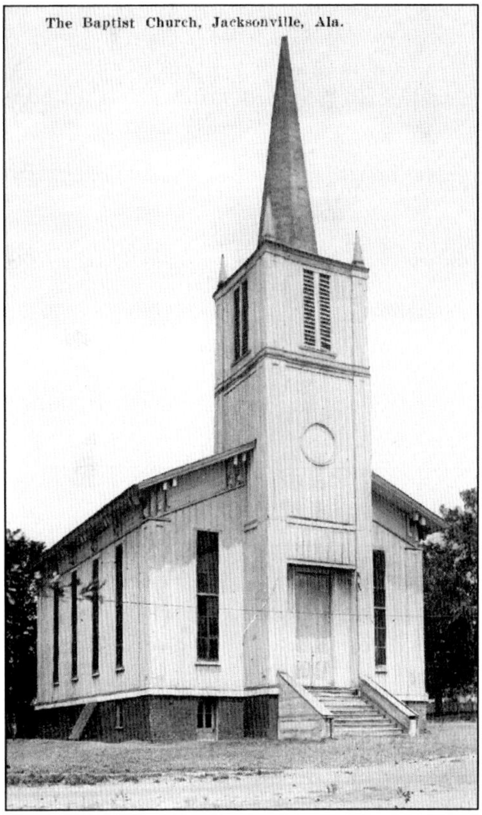

The First Baptist Church, seen here in a 1900 postcard, was constructed between 1855 and 1857. The congregation was established on March 27, 1836, as the United Baptist Church of Jacksonville. This building was the fifth structure of the congregation. Maj. John Pelham's funeral was held in the church in 1863. The building was torn down in the 1960s.

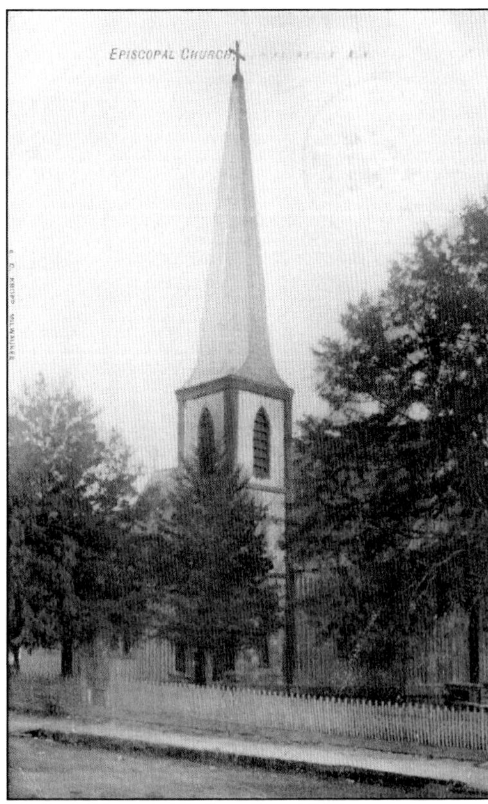

Shown here in a 1900 postcard, the Episcopal Church building was constructed in the English Gothic style and consecrated in 1856. It is one of the oldest surviving structures in Jacksonville. The congregation began worshipping in members' homes. The first official church service with an Episcopal priest in Jacksonville was held by the congregation in 1844. The building is still in use by the congregation.

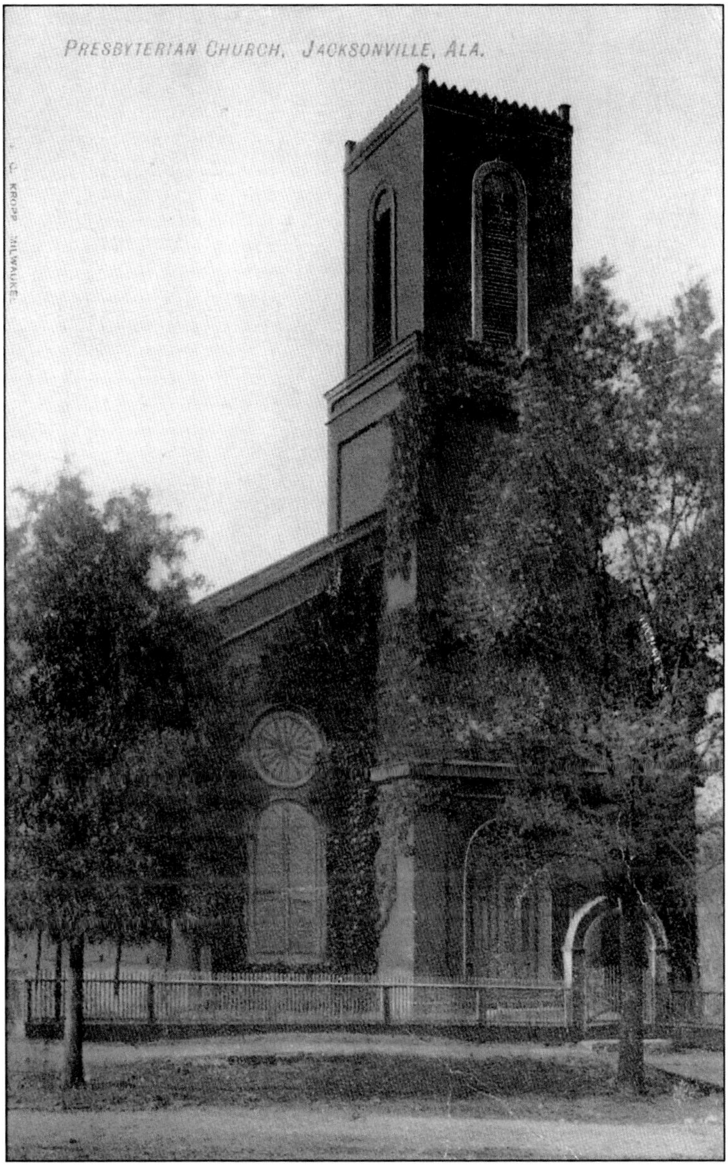

This 1900 postcard depicts the First Presbyterian Church. The initial plans for the building were drawn in 1858; construction proceeded slowly, and the exterior was completed in 1861. The bricks were made on-site by slave labor. Work was suspended on the building during the Civil War. The unfinished structure was used as a temporary hospital after the battles at Chattanooga and Lookout Mountain. After the war, the interior of the building was completed, and the congregation began using the building in April 1865. It is still in use by the congregation. In May 1865, the session examined W.J. Amberson about rumors of his recent intoxication. Amberson "acknowledged the truth of certain rumors in relation to his christian conduct . . . and promised by the help of God to avoid the temptation to such sins in time to come." It was the custom, and requirement, of the session to "examine" every member of the congregation prior to the congregant's receiving communion once a quarter. In this way, the congregant's fitness to receive communion could be determined. If the congregant "passed" the examination, he or she received a communion token, which they in turn gave to the elder prior to receiving communion.

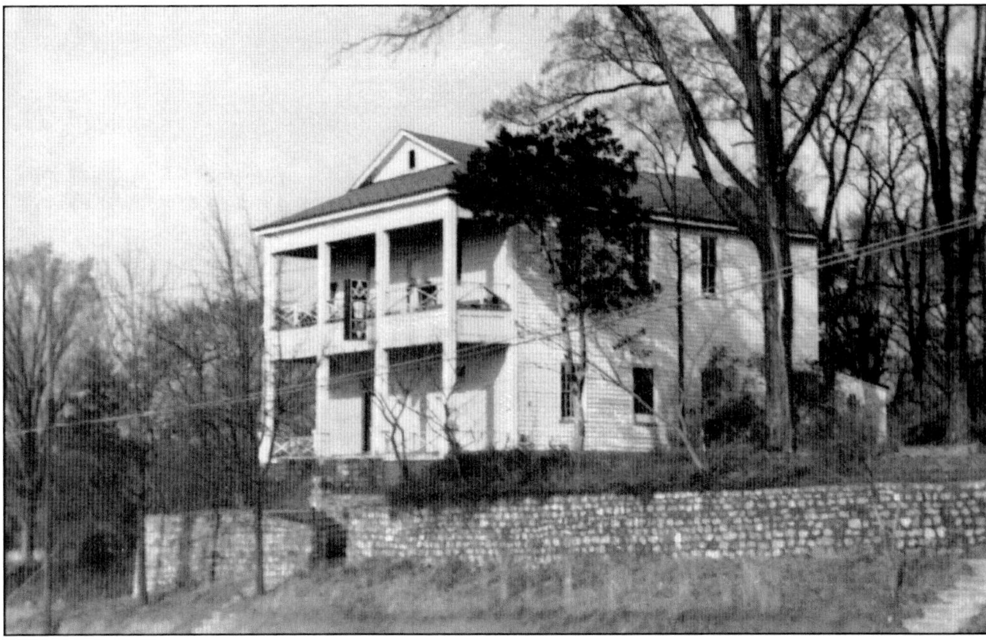

This 1839 structure was unique, in that the first floor served as the Methodist Church, and the second floor served as the hall for Hiram No. 42 Masonic Lodge. The congregation was organized in 1832–1833 as part of the Episcopal Methodist Church denomination. The Methodists worshiped in this structure until 1887–1888.

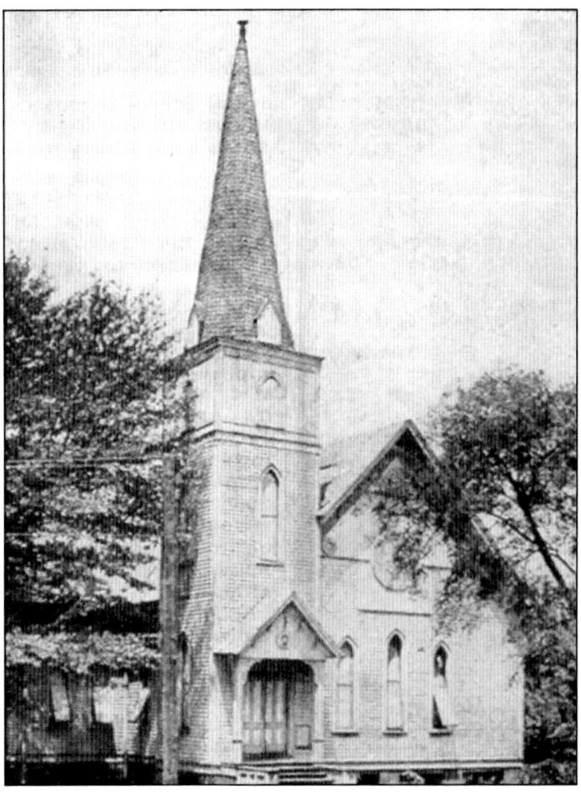

Shown in a 1905 postcard, this Gothic frame building was erected by the Methodist congregation on Lot 9 in 1887. The structure did not have Sunday school rooms; the sanctuary was divided by curtains for classes, with the boys in the amen corner and the girls in the choir loft. Although virtually destroyed by fire in 1993, the building was restored close to its original state with a few alterations. It is still in use by the congregation. (Courtesy of Floyd "Buddy" Tredaway.)

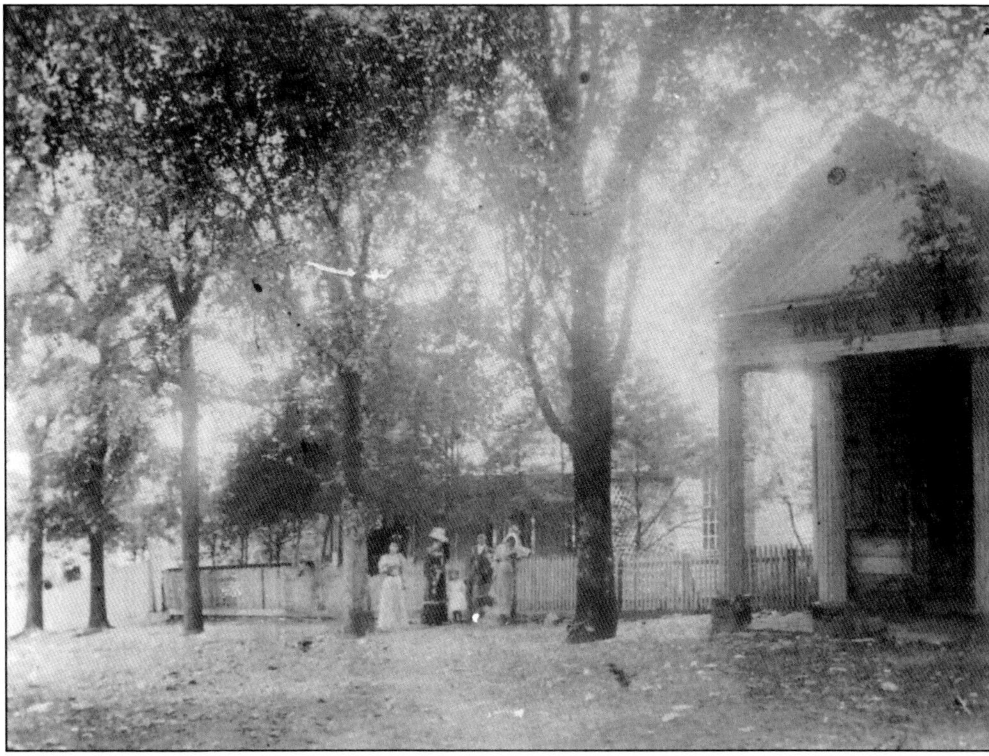

This building was erected in 1850 by Dr. James Carrington Francis on the north side of the public square, on Lot 32 or 33. Dr. Francis, trained as a medical doctor in Knoxville, Tennessee, moved to Jacksonville in 1837, practicing medicine there for the next 50 years. The building, of the Carpenter Gothic style, was moved about 100 feet west from its original site in 1970. Today, the building is owned by the Alabama Historical Commission and is operated as a museum.

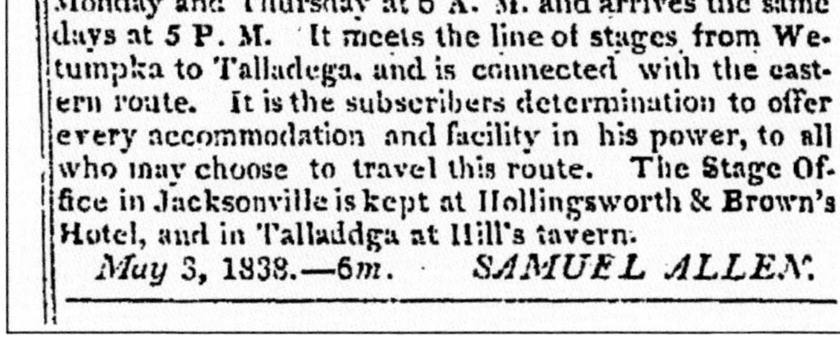

Talladega & Jacksonville

STAGE LINE.

LEAVES Jacksonville every Wednesday and Friday, at 6 A. M. and arrives at Talladega the same days at 5 P. M. Leaves Talladega every Monday and Thursday at 6 A. M. and arrives the same days at 5 P. M. It meets the line of stages from Wetumpka to Talladega, and is connected with the eastern route. It is the subscribers determination to offer every accommodation and facility in his power, to all who may choose to travel this route. The Stage Office in Jacksonville is kept at Hollingsworth & Brown's Hotel, and in Talladdga at Hill's tavern.

May 3, 1838.—6m. *SAMUEL ALLEN.*

This advertisement appeared in the May 3, 1838, issue of the *Jacksonville Republican*. The stage, operated by Samuel Adams, offered an 11-hour service between Jacksonville and Talladega, the neighboring county seat. In 1835, postal service was started, with mail being carried by horseback. There was no passenger service until the stagecoach line was started. (Courtesy of Jacksonville State University.)

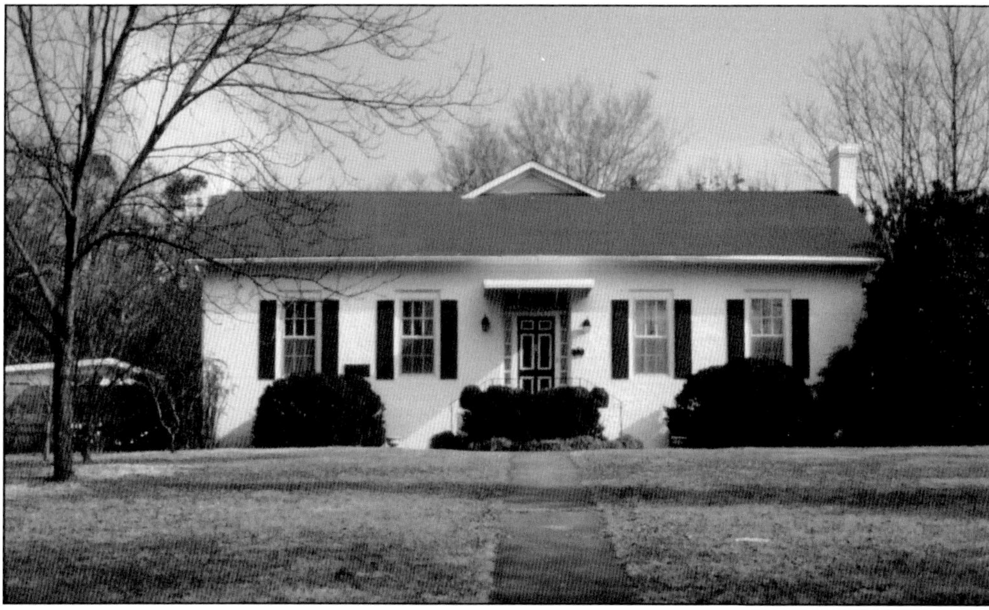

Known as the Female Academy Building, this home was built in 1837 when the Alabama Legislature chartered the Jacksonville Female Academy. Classes were held in this brick building until the late 1850s. In an advertisement in the February 15, 1838, *Jacksonville Republican*, the board of trustees for the Jacksonville Female Academy stated that the academy "will commence its spring session, under the supervision of Miss Thompson, on the first Monday of March next—usual terms of tuition as before published."

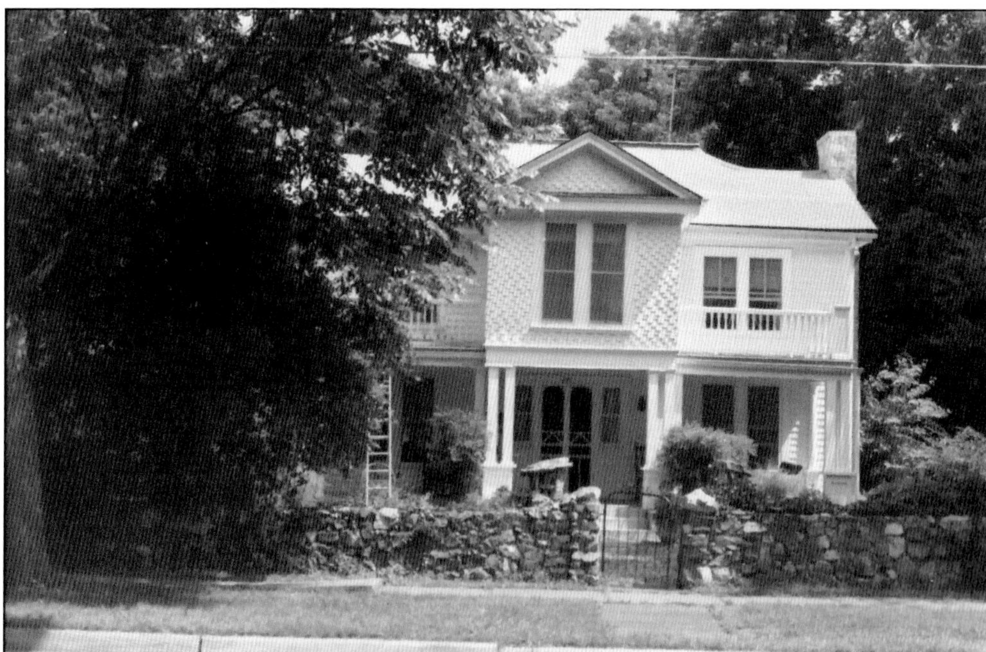

This house was built in 1850 by Jacob Forney for his sister Mary Forney Reinhardt. Note the unusual architectural feature of a room over the front porch. In 1884, Gen. John H. Forney moved into this house.

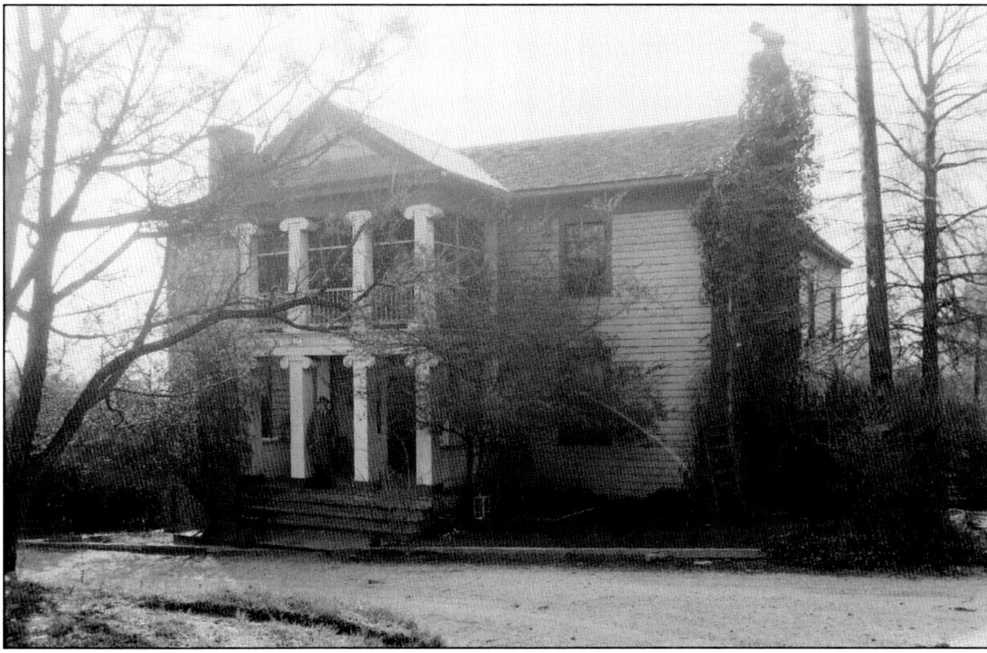

Fielding Snow built the original frontier structure in the 1830s. The house has three stairwells. The front columns are square and topped with Ionic capitals. Note that both the first- and second-floor porches have columns topped with Ionic capitals. Prior to 1917, Drs. Arnold and Rowan had their medical offices in the basement. (Library of Congress, Prints and Photographs Division.)

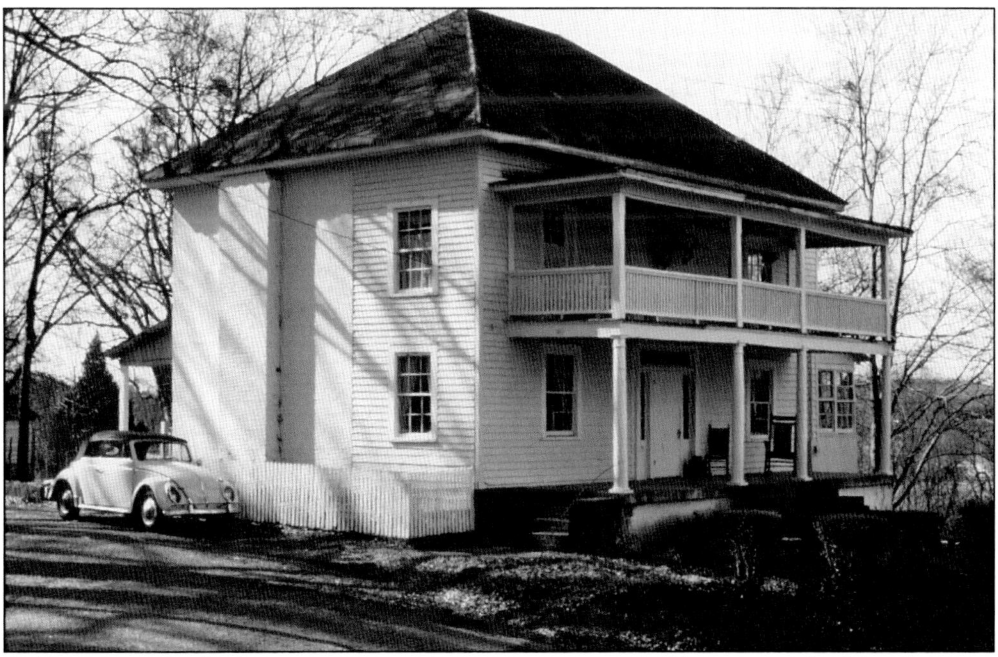

Fielding Snow built this structure in 1840 for use as a jail. The original building had two stories with brick walls 16 inches thick. In 1883, J.D. McCormick bought the building for his residence, adding the front porches and front rooms seen here. (Library of Congress, Prints and Photographs Division.)

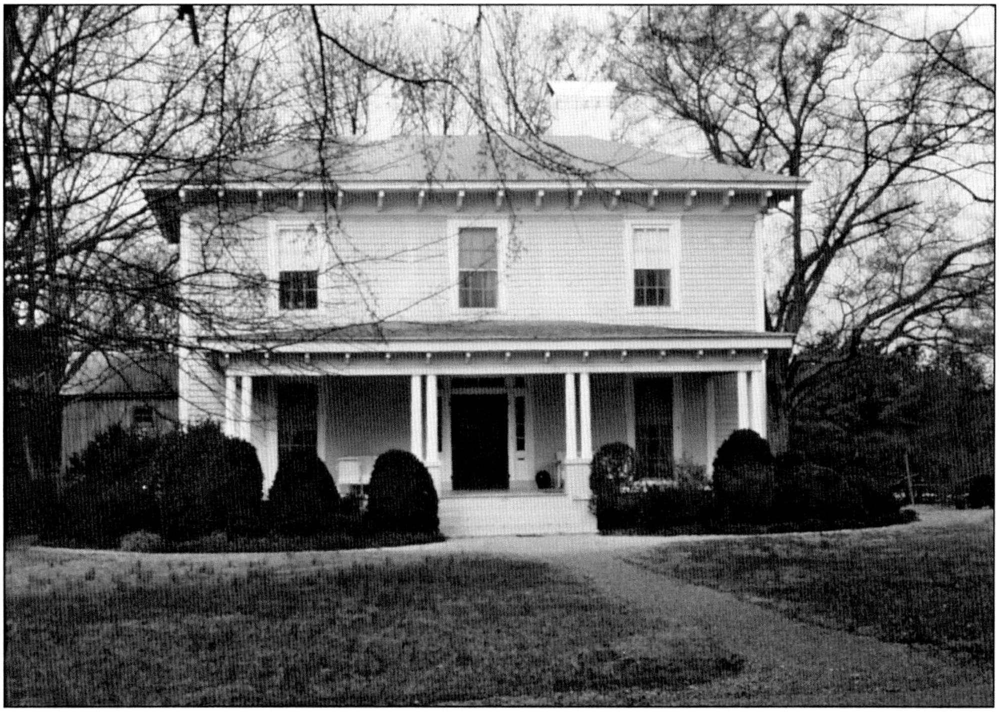

This home, named 80 Oaks for the oak trees that lined its carriage drive, was built by Col. George Craghn Whatley before 1850. This two-story Colonial farmhouse originally had six large rooms and a large central hallway on each floor. The remnants of the avenue of oak trees still remain. A lawyer, Whatley was elected to the Alabama House of Representatives in 1849 and to the convention that passed the Ordinance of Secession in 1861. A member of the 10th Alabama Infantry Regiment, Colonel Whatley was killed at the Battle of Sharpsburg (Antietam) on September 17, 1862. He had recently written a dispatch to the *Jacksonville Republican*, published on September 11, 1862.

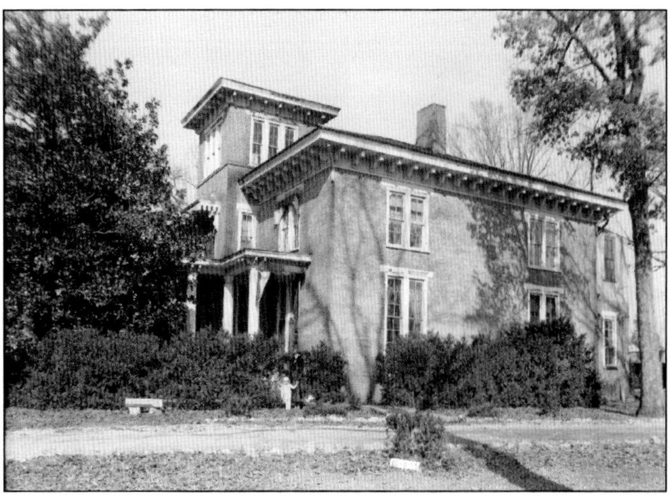

Thomas A. Walker built the Magnolias, an Italianate home, between 1850 and 1856. The building reflects a unique architectural style, with sliding double windows as a design element on both floors on three sides. On the front porch, the windows extend all the way to the floor, permitting easy access between the porch and the house, as well as ventilation. (Library of Congress, Prints and Photographs Division.)

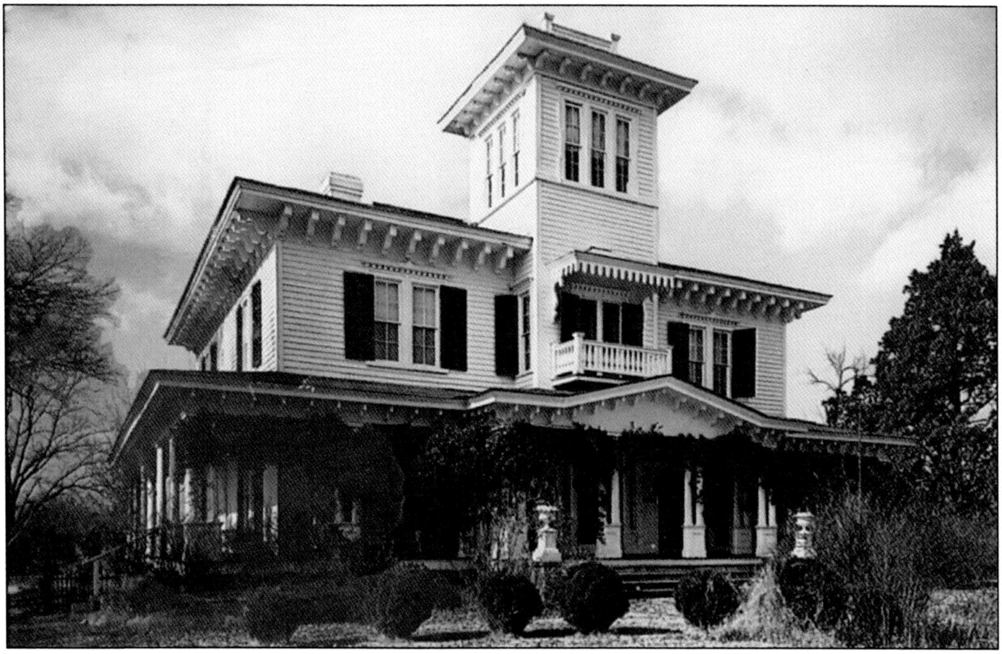

This Italianate home was built in 1850 by James Crook and named Ten Oaks. In 1864, the home was used for several weeks as the headquarters for Gen. P.G.T. Beauregard. (Library of Congress, Prints and Photographs Division.)

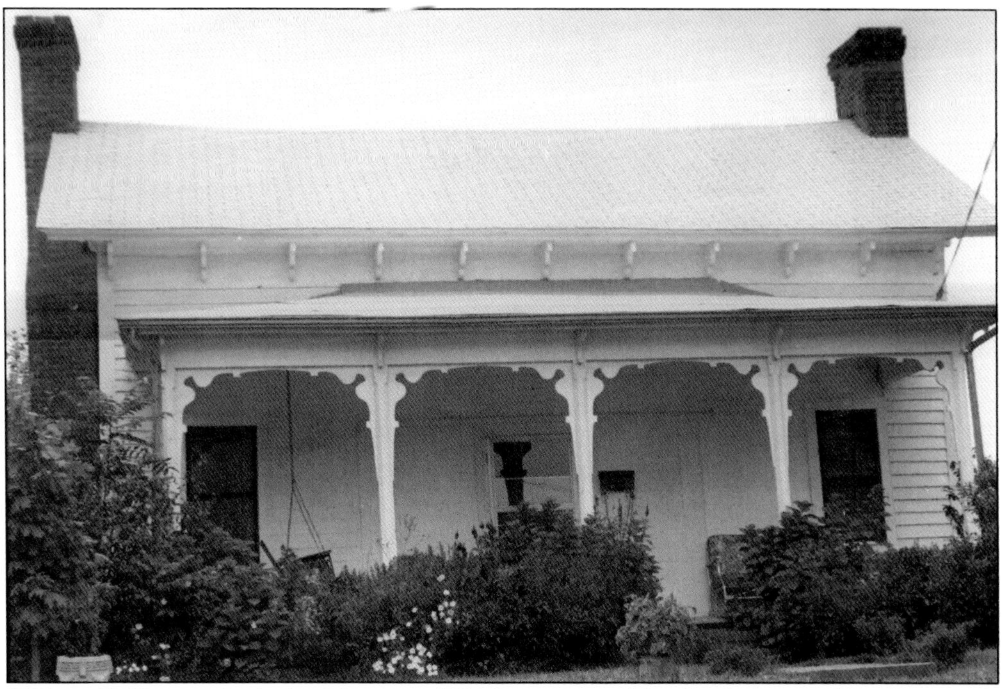

William H. Fleming built this I-house in 1836. It was one of the first houses on Broadway south of the square. Fleming's carriage shop was located across Broadway (Pelham) from his house.

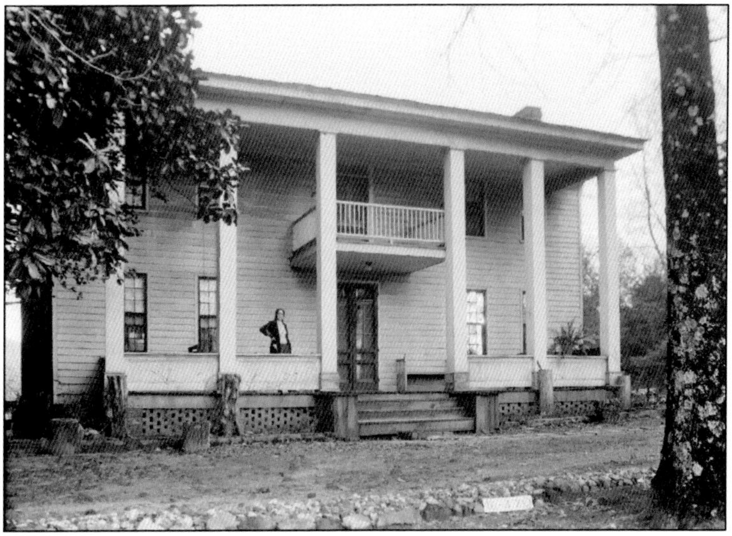

John Nisbet built this two-story I-house in 1837 on top of a hill just east of the square. Nisbet purchased the land from the Creek Indians listed in the 1836 Jackson deed. Local lore has it that Nisbet bought "80 acres and a wigwam" and built his house. (Library of Congress, Prints and Photographs Division.)

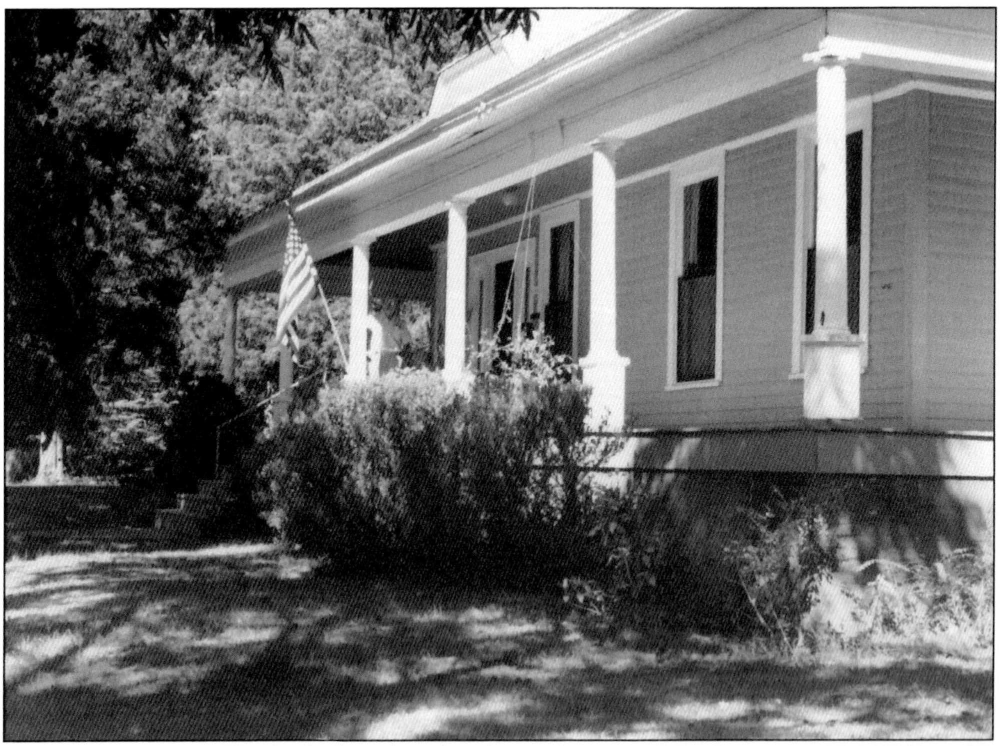

Judge Thomas A. Walker built the cabin that forms the core of this house in 1836. William H. Forney purchased the house in 1855. John Ramagnano purchased the house from Forney's estate in 1905 and gave it to his daughter, Mary Ramagnano, as a wedding gift when she married Z. "Lee" Leland Burton.

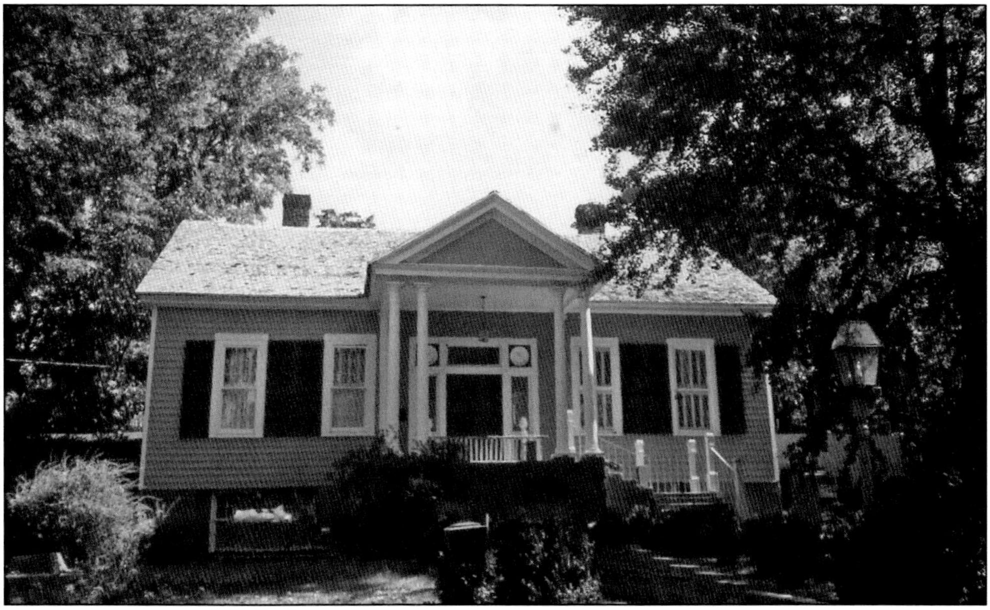

John H. Thomas built this raised Greek revival house in 1836 on land he had purchased from the four Creek Indians listed in the 1836 Jackson deed. During World War II, the owners of this house kept a cow and supplied milk for neighbors. It is reported that in one family of Presbyterians (who could not read the "funny papers" before church on Sunday) there were many volunteers to fetch the milk on those mornings in order to have the opportunity to read the comics.

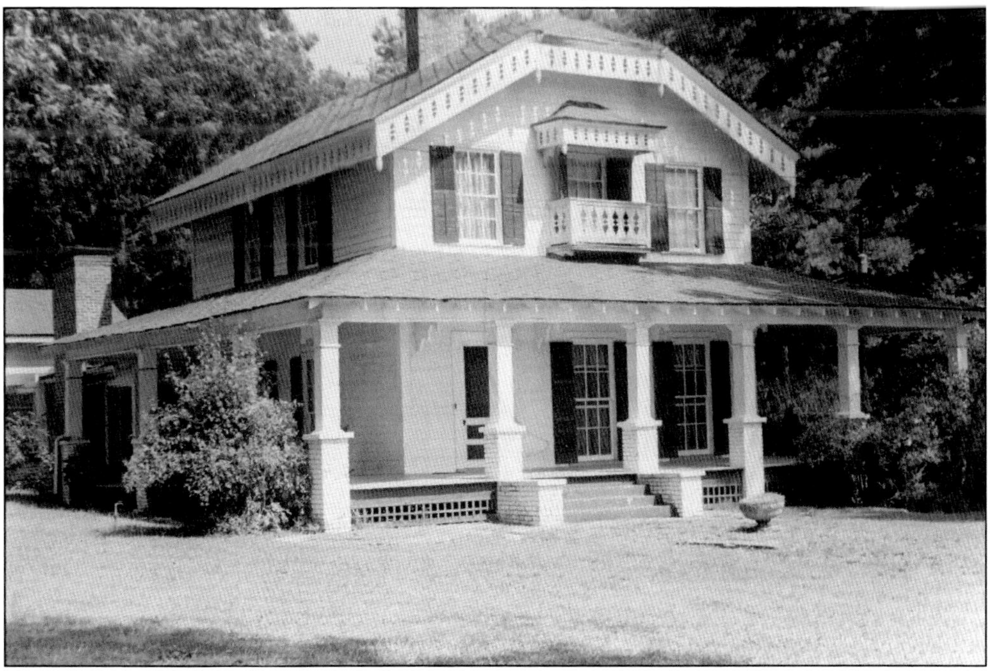

The original house was built in a Swiss chalet style, and the surrounding porch was added later. The house was built by Judge Robert Foster, who gave the "chaste and beautiful and feeling" eulogy at John Pelham's funeral at First Baptist Church. In 2014, the building serves as the Alumni House for Jacksonville State University.

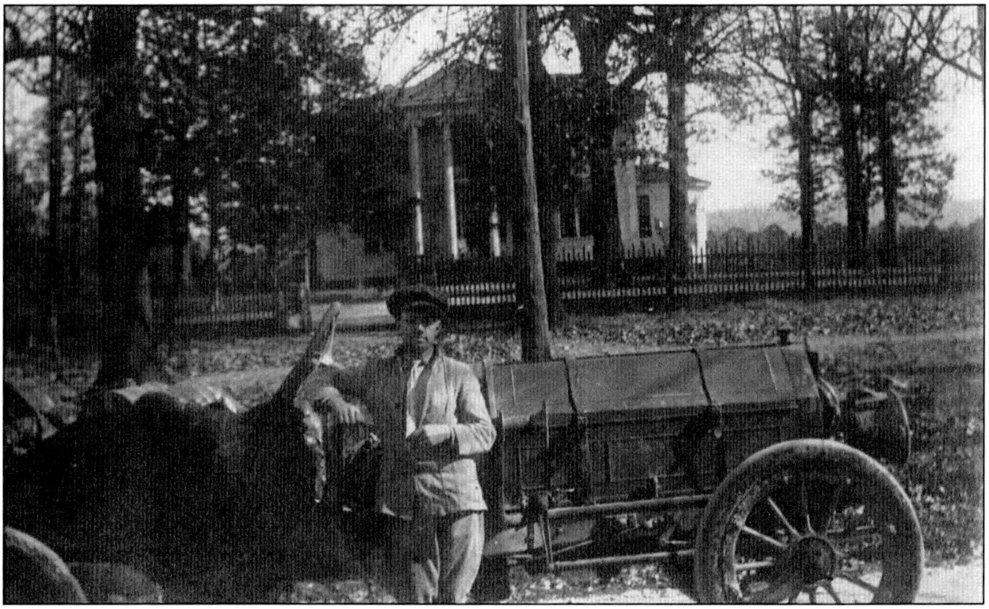

J. Thomas Martin stands in front of his family home in 1918. Tom was the Jacksonville postmaster from 1934 to 1956. The Martin house was built around 1850. In the 1960s, Jacksonville State University purchased the home and built Martin Hall on the site. (Nisbet family collection.)

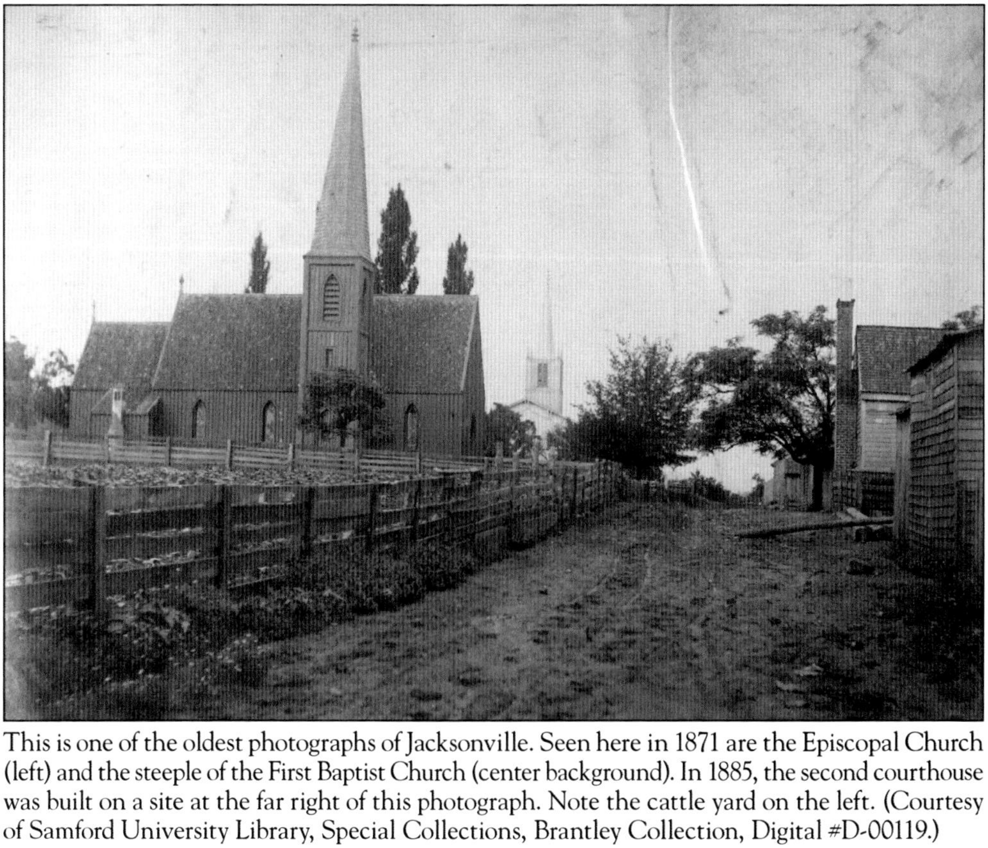

This is one of the oldest photographs of Jacksonville. Seen here in 1871 are the Episcopal Church (left) and the steeple of the First Baptist Church (center background). In 1885, the second courthouse was built on a site at the far right of this photograph. Note the cattle yard on the left. (Courtesy of Samford University Library, Special Collections, Brantley Collection, Digital #D-00119.)

Two

1860 TO 1890

Although many Jacksonville citizens fought in the Civil War, as Jack Boozer stated in his February 19, 1952, *Jacksonville News* "History of Jacksonville" column, "the Civil War did not become an actual reality to Jacksonville until 1862" with the Battle of Dranesville, in Virginia. "In this battle, Jacksonville lost one of its most prominent citizens, Lt. Col. James B. Martin, and saw many of its sons wounded, including Colonel John Forney and Captain William Forney." Immediately after the war, a unit of federal troops was stationed in Jacksonville to maintain the peace while the civil government was being rehabilitated and became an integral part of the community.

By the late 1860s, Northern investors came to Jacksonville and the immediate vicinity and built railroads. The Selma, Rome & Dalton Railroad (SR&D) was completed through Jacksonville in 1868 on the west side of town, with a depot where Mountain Street intersected the railroad. In 1870, just north of Jacksonville, the village of Cross Plains (now Piedmont) was on track to become a major railway hub for the SR&D, because several railroads intersected there. The investment fervor quickly soured, however, with an event in Cross Plains in July 1870. As set out in Gene Howard's book *Death at Cross Plains*, on July 11, 1870, the Ku Klux Klan seized and lynched five men. Among the victims was a white man, William Luke, who was employed by the railroad as a teacher for the children of the black railroad workers. The Northern railroad investors' plans quickly changed.

An early-morning fire on September 14, 1883, destroyed all the wooden structures on the east side of the square and 23 structures in all. Only the brick tavern and the Walker building immediately south survived. The fire started in William Milo Nisbet's drugstore (today, the northern half of Crow Drug Store). The fire spread south on the east side of the square, jumped Ladiga Street, and consumed "office row." It destroyed two stores, including Harper's dry goods, as well as Maj. John M. Wyly's corner residence. The blaze then headed south on Main Street. The *Jacksonville Republican* reported that "the Banner County Hose Company (white) and the Hook and Ladder Company (colored) were quickly on the ground at the ringing of the bell" and that "the water works have again saved the town more than they lost." After the fire, the town council declared that all future construction had to be of brick.

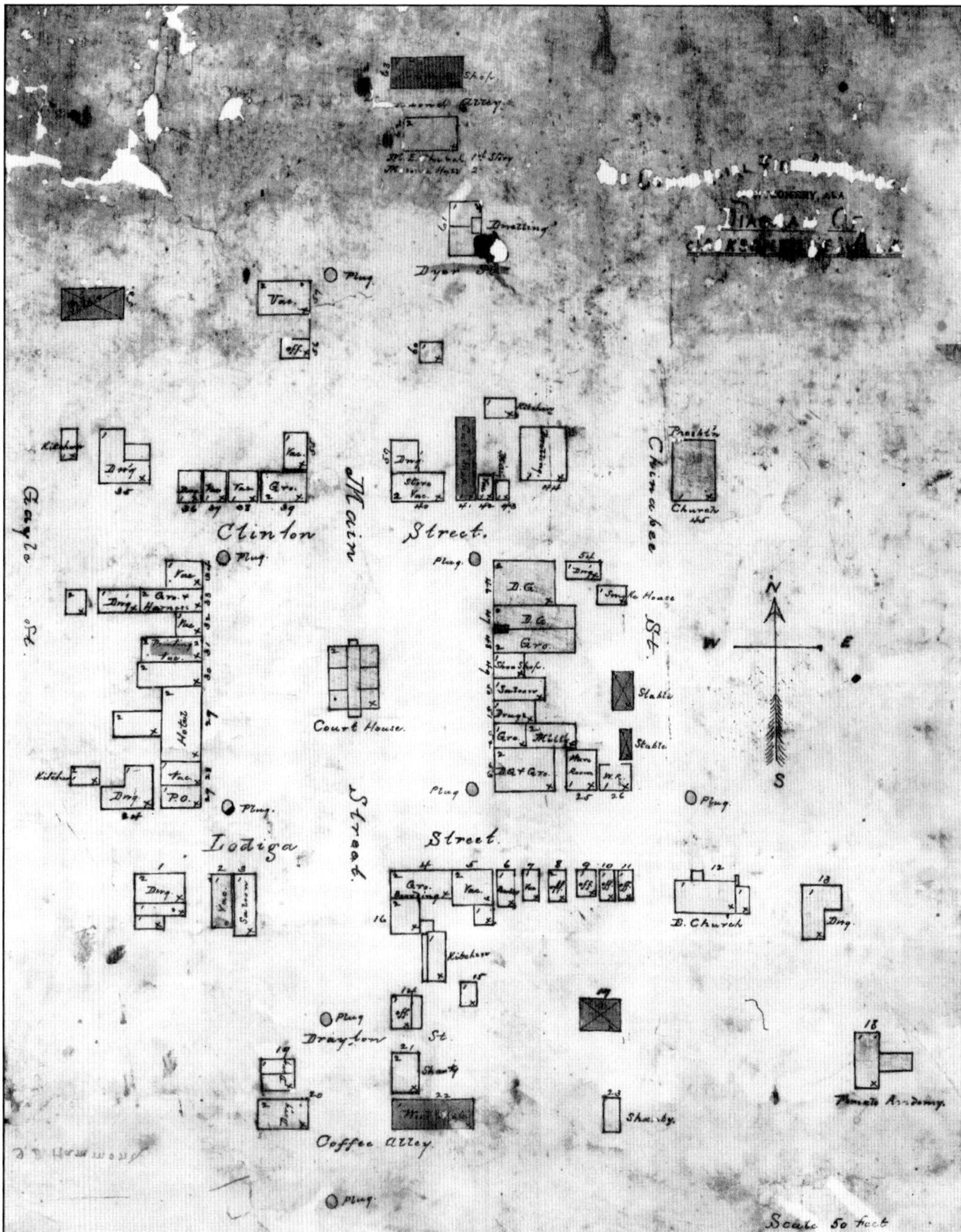

This early fire insurance company map, dating to about 1870, shows the six-room courthouse in the center of the growing square. Note the "plugs" on the map—part of the early water system. There are two saloons, a barbershop, a hotel, and several dry-good stores on the square. The Episcopal, Methodist, and Presbyterian churches are shown. The Baptist Church would be just south and west of the Female Academy.

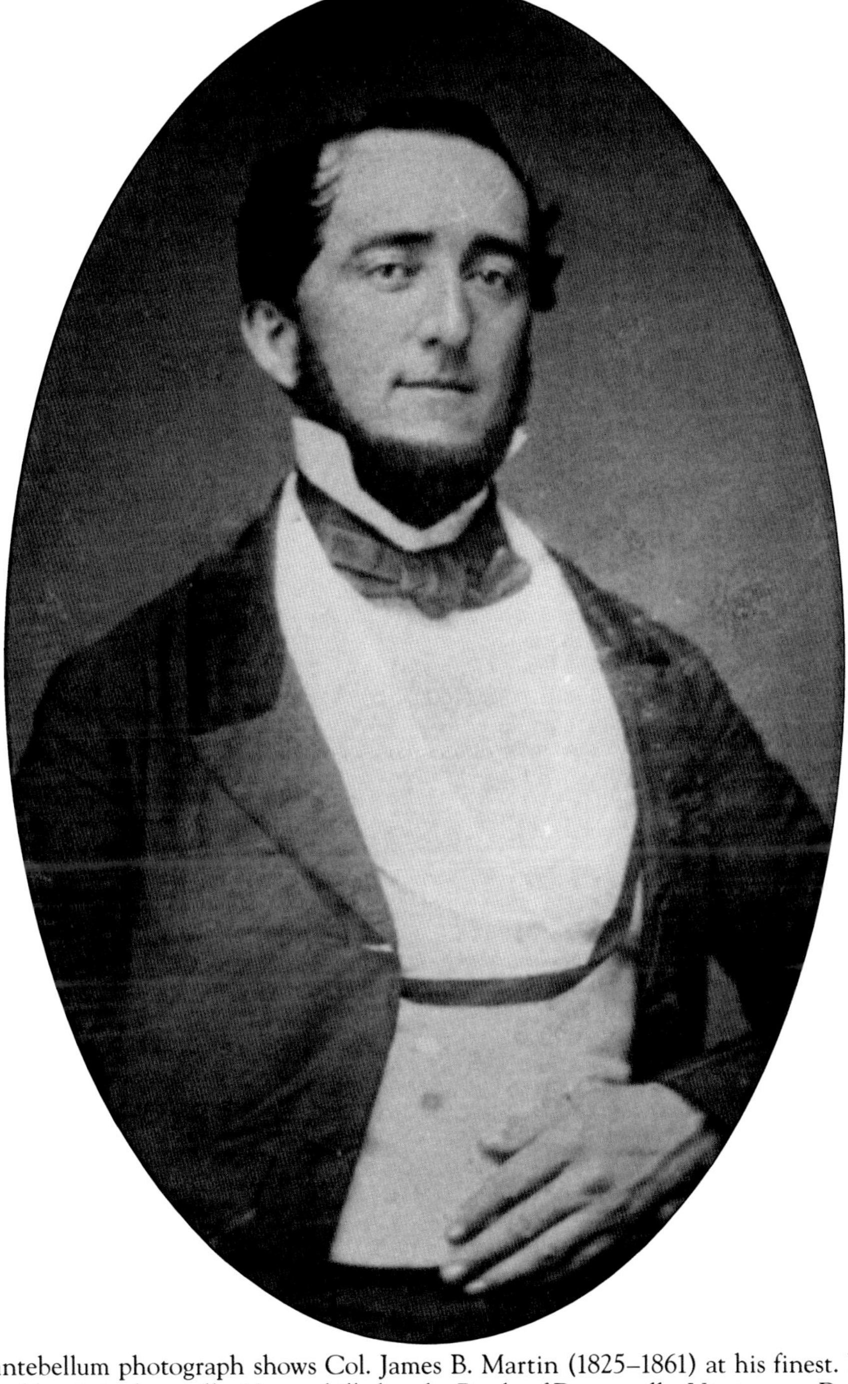

This antebellum photograph shows Col. James B. Martin (1825–1861) at his finest. Martin practiced law in Jacksonville. He was killed at the Battle of Dranesville, Virginia, on December 20, 1861, while rushing forward "in a shower of bullets." On December 31, 1861, Martin's funeral was held in the First Presbyterian Church, and he was buried in the Jacksonville City Cemetery with full military and Masonic honors. (Public Library of Anniston-Calhoun County, Russell Brothers Collection.)

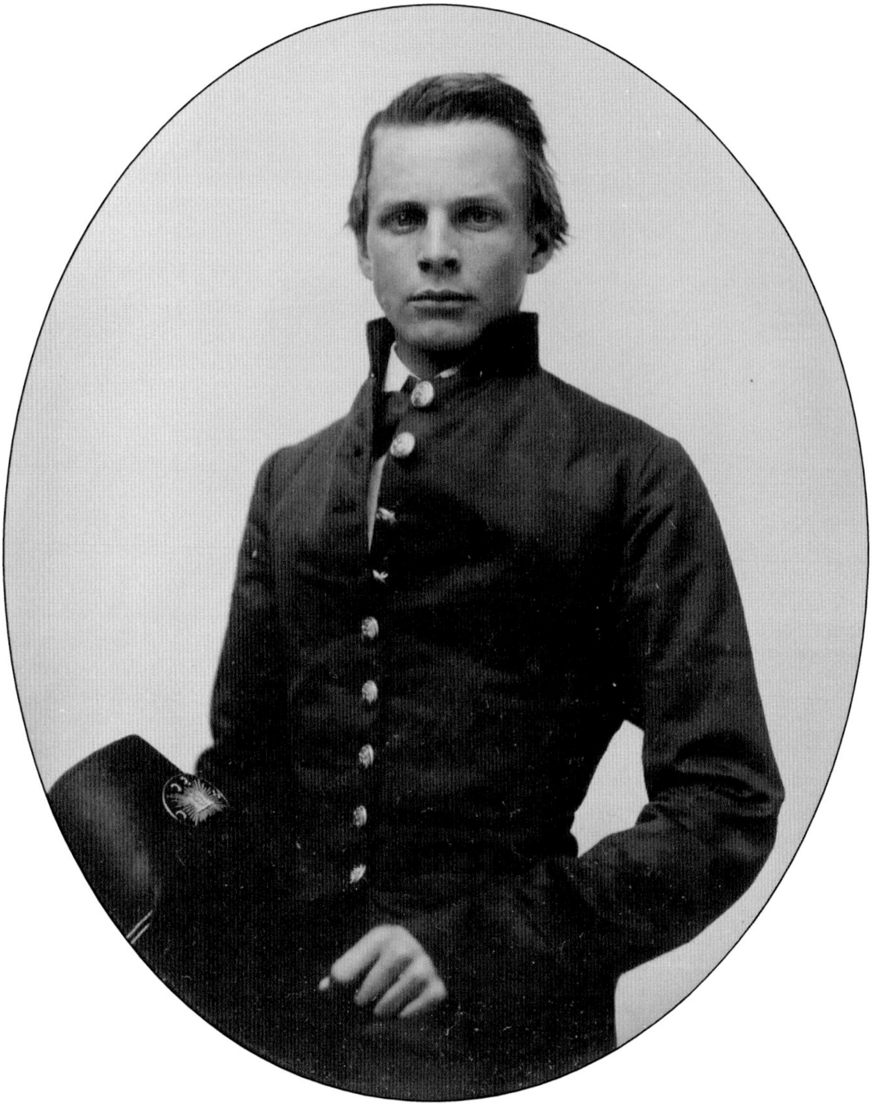

Matthew Brady made this ambrotype image of John Pelham (1838–1863) in 1858, while Pelham was enrolled at the US Military Academy at West Point, New York. In the original image, Pelham's cheeks have been painted blush red. Pelham was part of the only five-year class at the academy; he resigned his US military commission in April 1861, just a few weeks prior to graduating. Robert E. Lee observed Pelham's skills at Fredericksburg, where he used two small cannons to disrupt the entire Federal formation for almost an hour. Lee said, "It is glorious to see such courage in one so young." Union officer George Armstrong Custer, Pelham's West Point classmate, wrote directly to Pelham that "I rejoice, dear Pelham, in your success" after the Battle of Fredericksburg. Pelham was killed at Kelly's Ford, Virginia, on March 17, 1863. After learning of Pelham's death, Maj. Gen. J.E.B. Stuart wrote, "The noble, the chivalric, the gallant Pelham is no more. . . . He was killed in action yesterday. How much he was beloved, appreciated and admired, let the tears of agony we have shed, and the gloom of mourning throughout my command bear witness. . . . His loss to the country is irreparable." Stuart also wrote to Pelham's father that John was like a younger brother to him, a hero "so noble . . . so chivalrous . . . so pure . . . so beloved." (Courtesy of National Portrait Gallery, Smithsonian Institution/Art Resources, NY.)

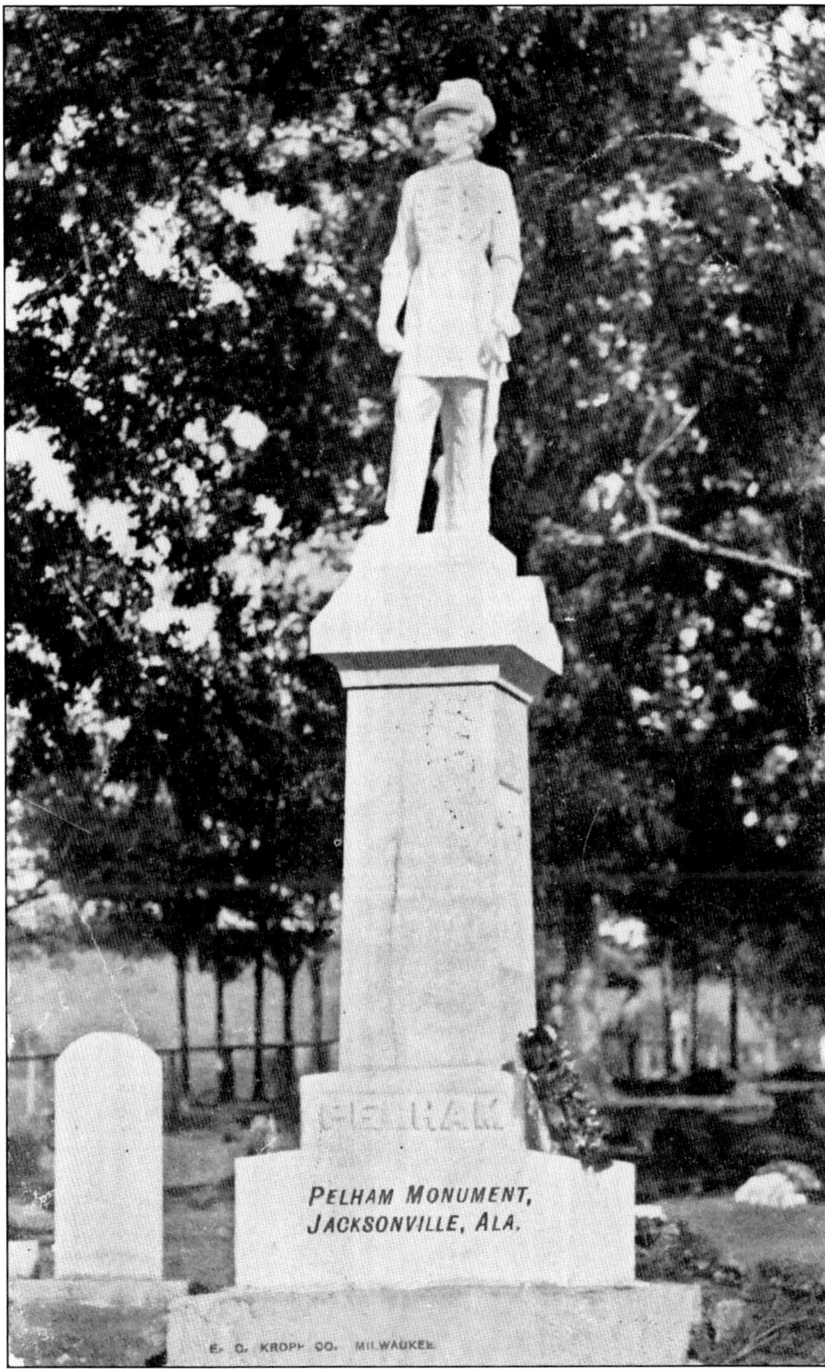

Erected in 1908 by the John H. Forney Chapter of the United Daughters of the Confederacy, this statue replaced a "melay [oyster] shell mound with a plain marble shaft" that previously marked Pelham's grave. The statue is a likeness of Pelham. Although a Presbyterian, to accommodate the large crowd, Pelham's lavish funeral, planned by the city leaders, was held at the First Baptist Church in Jacksonville. A procession followed the funeral the few blocks south to the city cemetery, where this monument marks his grave. (Nisbet family collection.)

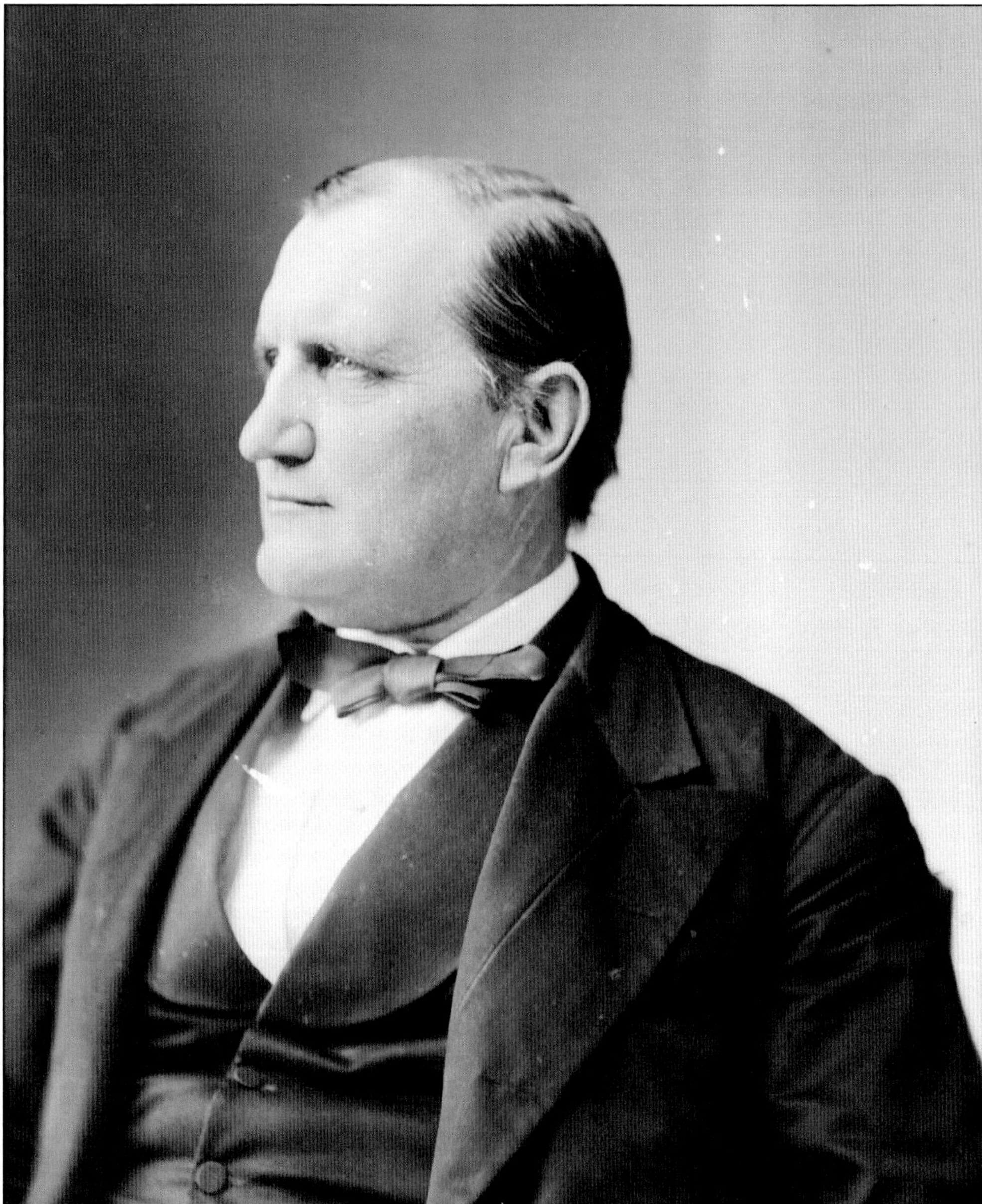

Raised and educated in Jacksonville, Gen. William H. Forney (1825–1894) was the older brother of John Horace Forney. William graduated from the University of Alabama and then studied law in Jacksonville with his brother Peter. Forney volunteered for the Mexican-American War and served for 12 months before returning to a law practice with James B. Martin. When the Civil War began, Forney again volunteered. He was severely wounded in the leg during the Battle of Dranesville, and he was left for dead on the battlefield at Gettysburg. Forney was twice taken prisoner; he served 12 months as a prisoner of war after being captured a second time. When he was released, he returned to his regiment and was promoted to brigadier general. He surrendered with Gen. Robert E. Lee at Appomattox. After the war, Forney was elected to the Alabama State Senate and then to nine successive terms in the US Congress (1874–1892). (Library of Congress, Prints & Photographs Division)

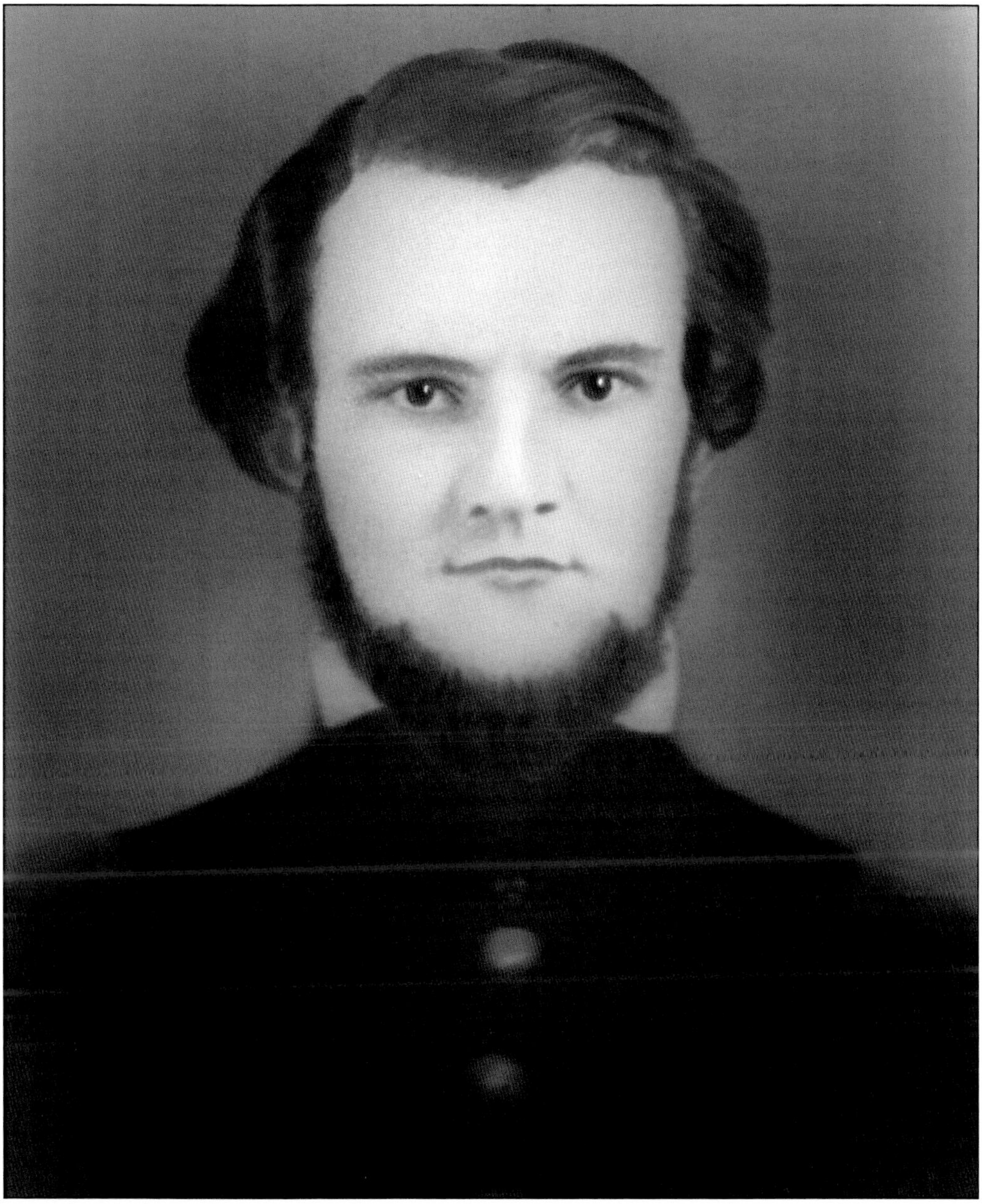

Raised and educated in Jacksonville, Gen. John H. Forney (1829–1902) graduated from the US Military Academy at West Point in 1852. After time on active duty in the US Army, Forney accepted a position back at West Point. At the beginning of the Civil War, John resigned his position as an instructor there and "hurried to Alabama," where secessionist governor Andrew Barry Moore commissioned him as a colonel. When the 10th Alabama Regiment was organized in June 1861, Col. Forney was in command. He was severely wounded in his arm during the Battle of Dranesville. In 1862, Forney was promoted to brigadier general and, later that year, to major general. There is a bronze statue by Steffen Thomas of Forney at the Vicksburg National Military Park in recognition of his bravery at the Battle of Vicksburg, Mississippi. Forney spent his years after the war working on the Selma, Rome & Dalton Railroad, and, as a civil engineer, he laid out the plans for Anniston, Alabama. This image shows Forney in his US Army uniform.

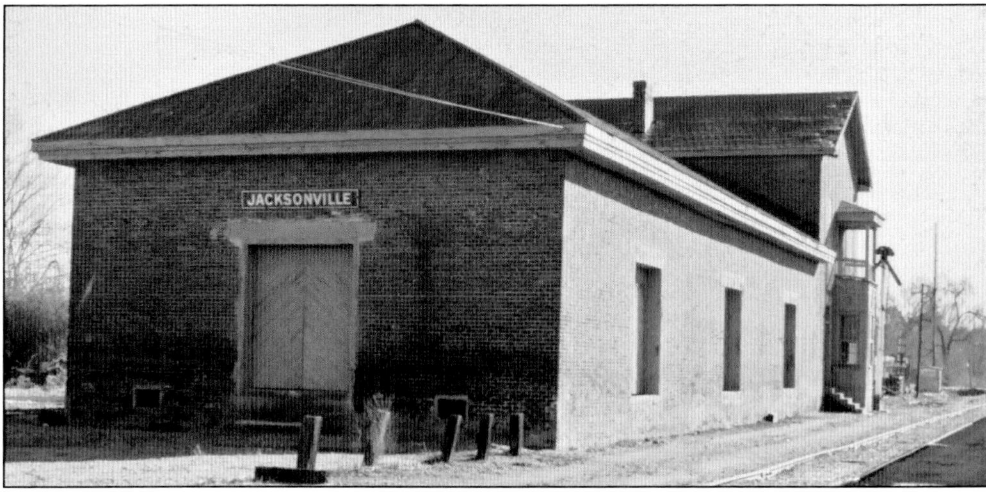

This building was opened for business on September 1, 1868, as a depot for the Selma, Rome & Dalton Railroad. A.R. Smith was the depot agent, accepting "all freight (both receiving and forwarding) and for passengers." Prior to and during the Civil War, the Alabama & Tennessee River Railroad came only as far north as Blue Mountain (outside what would become Anniston). The depot building was constructed only after the railroad changed names and was completed north toward Rome, Georgia. Beautifully restored in 2010, the depot now serves as a rest stop on the Chief Ladiga Trail, the office for Retired Senior Volunteer Program, and a rental hall for special occasions.

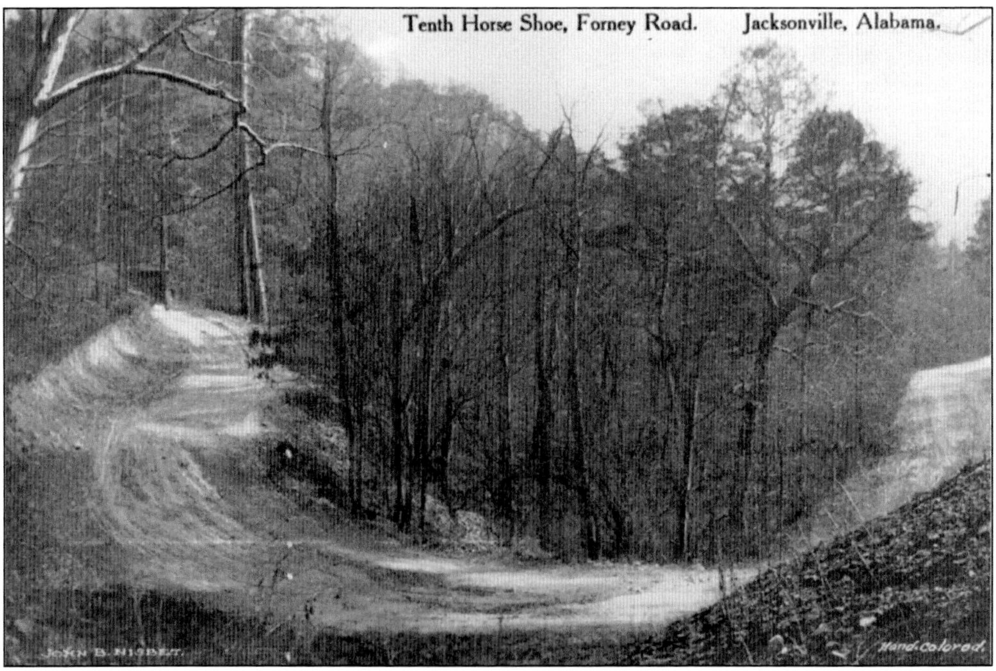

Completed in July 1868, this road, known as Forney Road, extended Ladiga Street eastward over the Blue Mountains to Rabbittown and White Plains. On June 6, 1868, the *Jacksonville Republican* stated that "the grades are so light as not to require the locking of a wagon at any point, and not so steep at any place, but what a horse may trot down with a buggy with ease and safety." Although the unpaved road still exists, it is not being maintained, and there is limited access to it.

The original name of the congregation that met in this building on Vann Street was First Baptist Church, Colored. This congregation traces its origins to the other (white) First Baptist Church. After emancipation, the black members of First Baptist requested to be allowed to form their own congregation. The mother church granted that request on February 16, 1867, and the congregation called Ned Wyley to be its first pastor. In 1869, the original building was constructed under the supervision of Mr. Bush. Destroyed around 1900 in a windstorm, it was rebuilt on the same foundation using much of the original material. The original 1869 pews are still in use today. (Courtesy of Secolina "Jeanie" Levell Morris.)

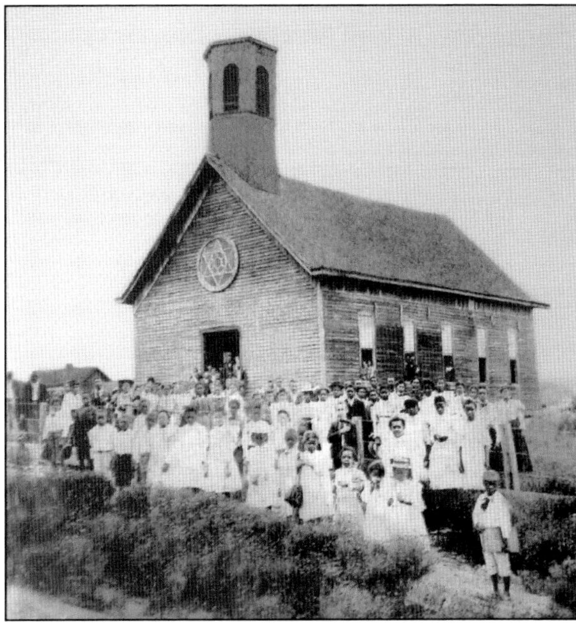

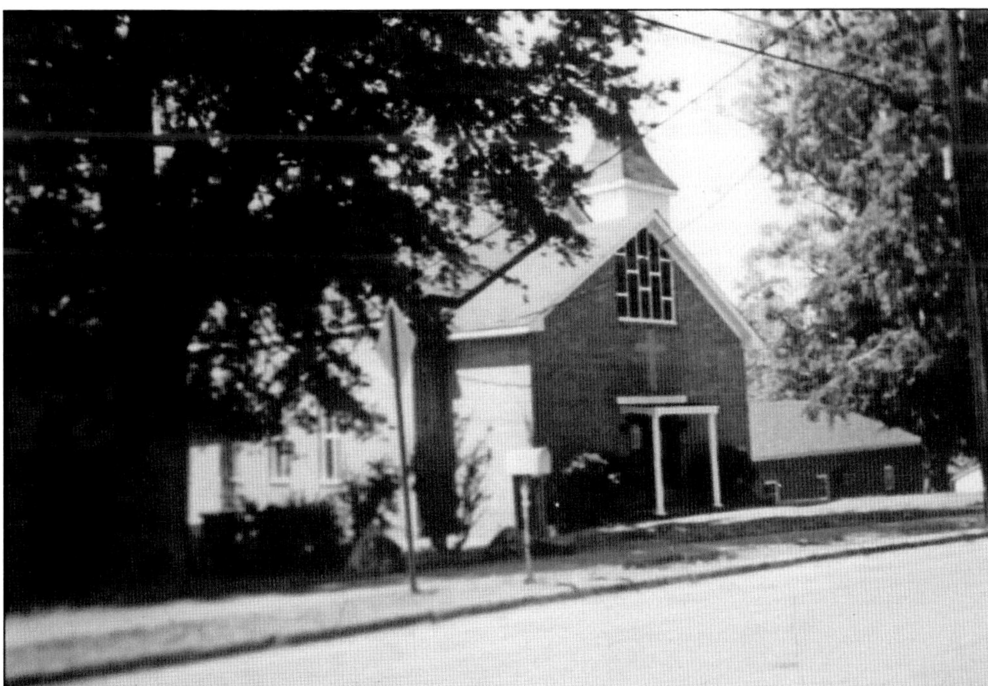

This photograph is of St. Paul's CME Church. The congregation, organized in 1867, was founded as an independent congregation, but, in 1870, it joined the Colored Methodist Episcopal Church denomination. In 1954, the denomination changed its name to Christian Methodist Episcopal Church. (Nisbet family collection.)

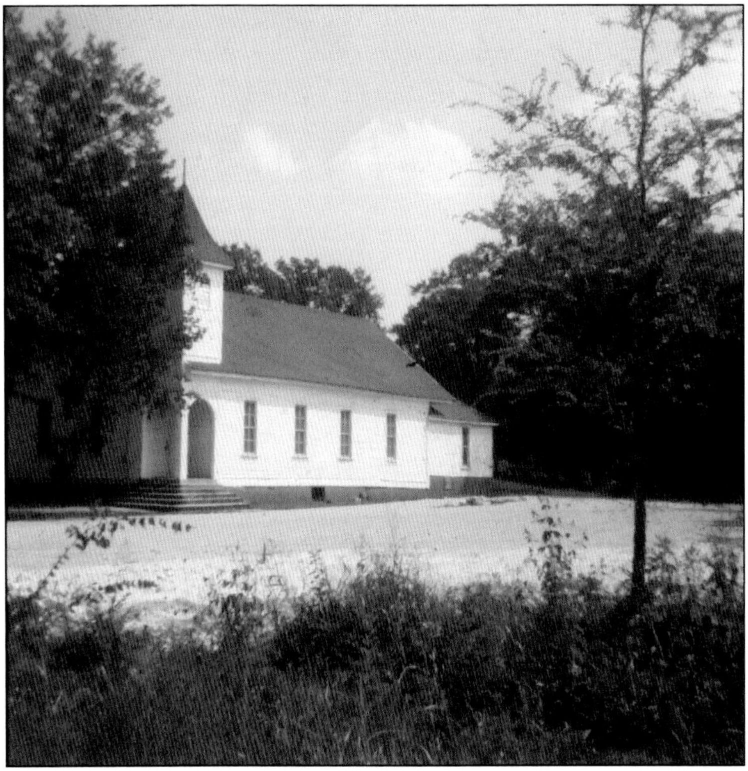

New Hope Baptist Church was organized in 1872. The congregation built the structure in this photograph the same year. (Nisbet family collection.)

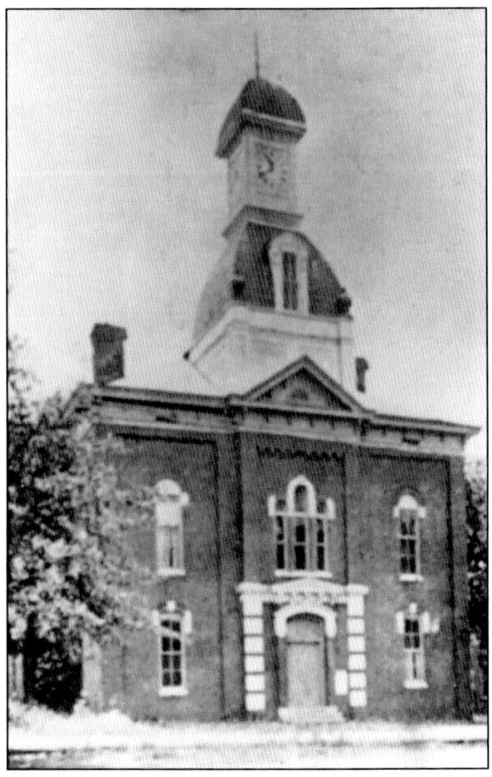

This courthouse was built in 1885 to replace the original courthouse, which stood in the middle of the square and had survived the 1883 fire. Even before construction on this building, the new editor for the *Anniston Hotblast* began a campaign to move the county seat to Anniston. A bitter debate broke out between the *Jacksonville Republican* and the *Hotblast*. An election was held to settle the dispute, and Anniston won: 3,840 votes were cast for Anniston, and 2,236 votes were for Jacksonville. After a series of unsuccessful lawsuits, the county seat (and its official courthouse) moved to Anniston. This building burned down in 1925. (Public Library of Anniston–Calhoun County Alabama Room.)

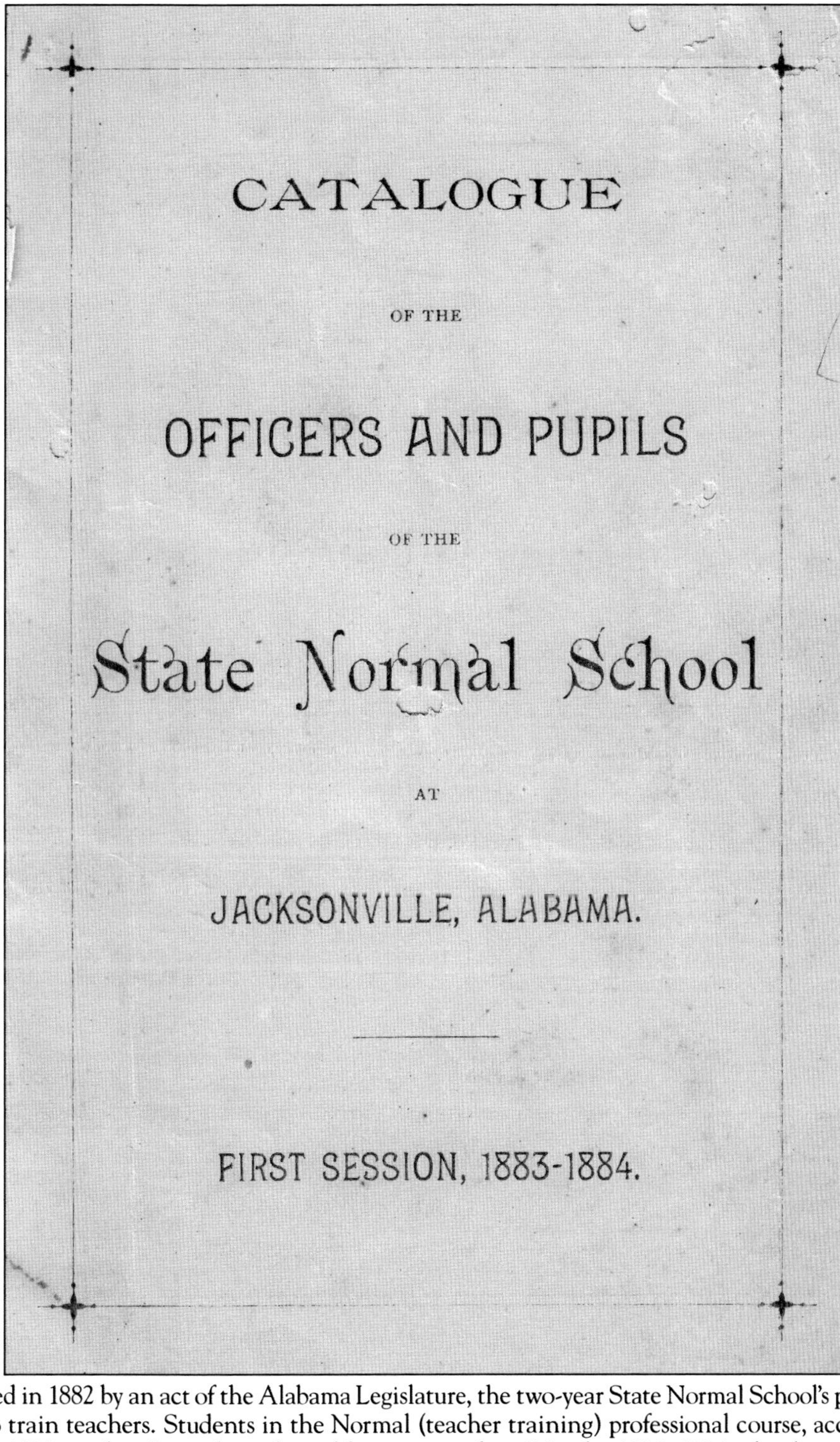
CATALOGUE

OF THE

OFFICERS AND PUPILS

OF THE

State Normal School

AT

JACKSONVILLE, ALABAMA.

FIRST SESSION, 1883-1884.

Created in 1882 by an act of the Alabama Legislature, the two-year State Normal School's purpose was to train teachers. Students in the Normal (teacher training) professional course, according to the 1883 catalog, "must be at least fifteen years of age." In the 1883–1884 school year, there were 247 students in the primary, intermediate, and collegiate departments, and 25 students in the Normal training program. (Courtesy of Jacksonville State University.)

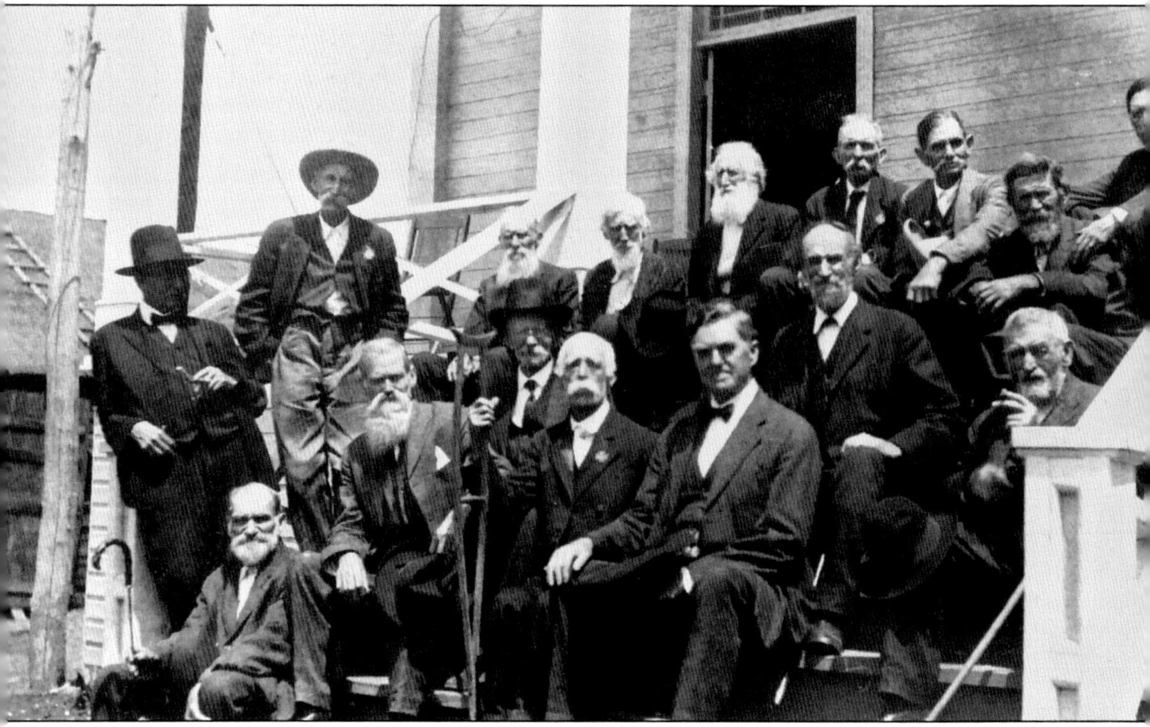

This undated photograph, probably taken around 1900, shows members of Camp Col. James B. Martin, Chapter 292 of the United Confederate Veterans sitting on the front steps of the Masonic lodge. In the photograph (in no particular order) are Col. H.L. Stevenson (holding crutch), D.W. Warlick, B.H. Denman, C.D. McHarq, G.J. King, T.J. Nance, D.D. Wilkins, R.D. Bradley, D.J. Craig, J.C. Aderholt, M.J. Weaver, E.C. Lusk, C.C. Bray, D.F. Weaver, T.R. Weaver, T.R. Ward, Rev. S.H. Bennett, and Rev. T.D. Cartledge. All of the men were from Jacksonville except C.D. McHarg (Alexandria) and D.F. Weaver (Weaver). (Nisbet private collection.)

Three

1890 to 1920

By 1890, the next round of "Yankee investors" had appeared. The first of these investors, George P. Ide, opened the Tredegar National Bank and then built the Ide Cotton Mill and associated cotton gin and cotton oil mill. Other Northern investors built on what George Ide had started at the bank and cotton mill.

In the late 1880s, Gen. Joseph W. Burke, J.A. Gaboury, James Crook, E.D. Ross, and L.W. Grant formed the Jacksonville Mining & Manufacturing Company and bought land on speculation that the company could create a whole town (Anniston was experiencing a similar event). The company named the town Tredegar and printed an elaborate map to publicize the town and its opportunities. As drawn, Tredegar touched Jacksonville and then spread north and west from the square. Later maps changed the name to Jacksonville, indicating that Tredegar would be a part of the town of Jacksonville. The Ide Cotton Mill was built on land purchased from the company. The company never took off, and it eventually went out of business.

After the county seat (and its courthouse) moved to Anniston, Jacksonville settled into its new status.

The newly established State Normal School began to thrive, requiring many new buildings on its campus.

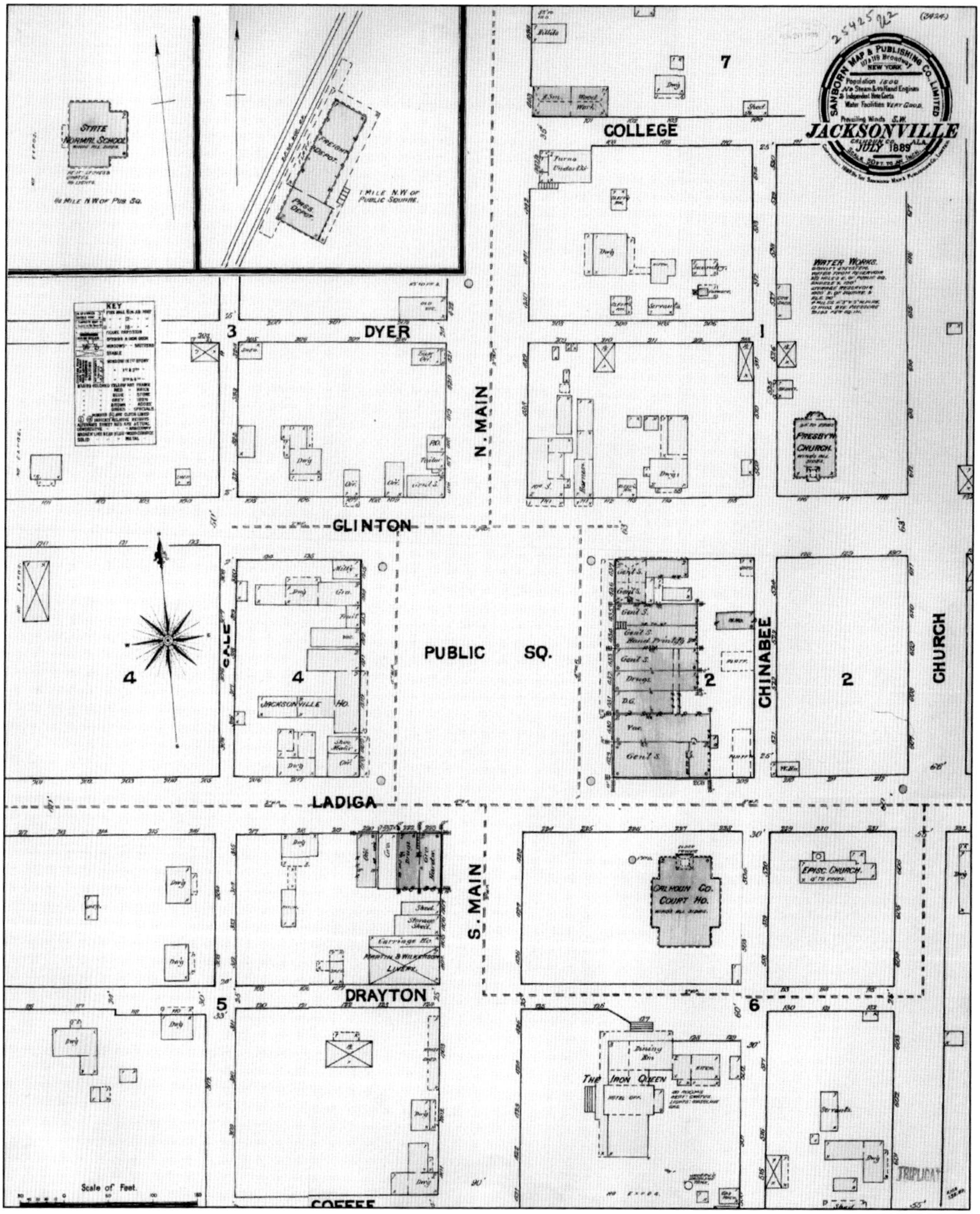

This 1889 Sanborn map of the Jacksonville square depicts the heart of the town at the time. The newly built courthouse is shown on East Ladiga Street, next to the Episcopal Church, but the original courthouse is no longer on the square. The original courthouse appeared on the 1885 Sanborn map.

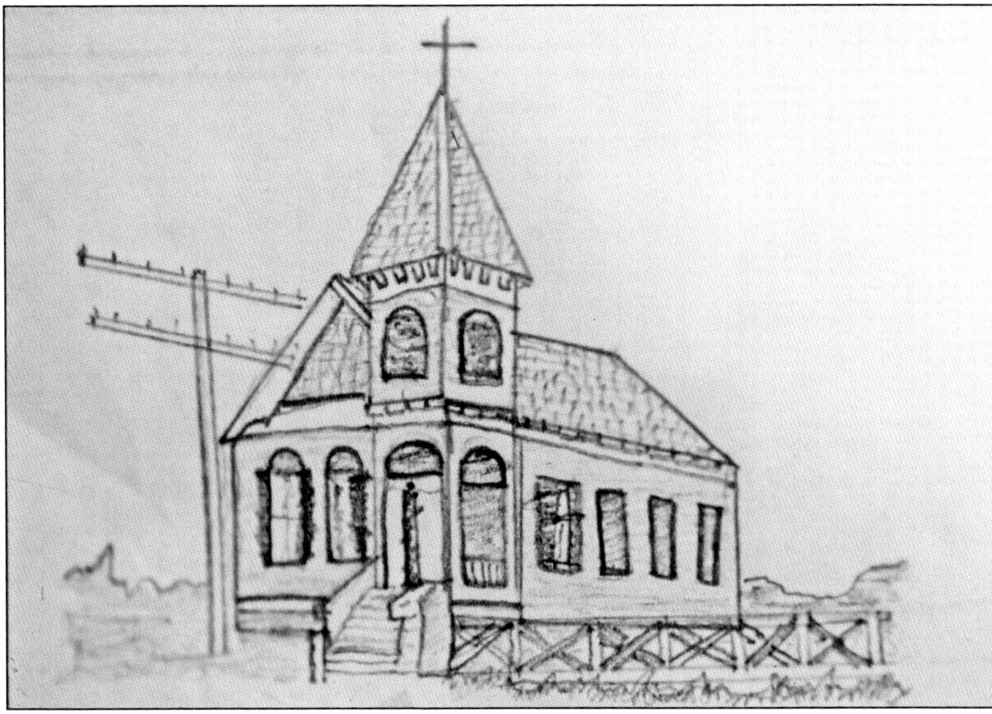

On February 7, 1891, St. Rose of Lima Roman Catholic Church was dedicated by Bishop O'Sullivan, bishop of the Diocese of Mobile. The Jacksonville Mining & Manufacturing Company and its president, General Burke, donated the land to the diocese. The building's modern address would be 706 West Francis Street. The structure was built by J.A. Gaboury, and the altar was donated by one of his brothers, Rev. Father Gaboury. This building was destroyed by 1940, and the land was eventually sold to Profile Mill.

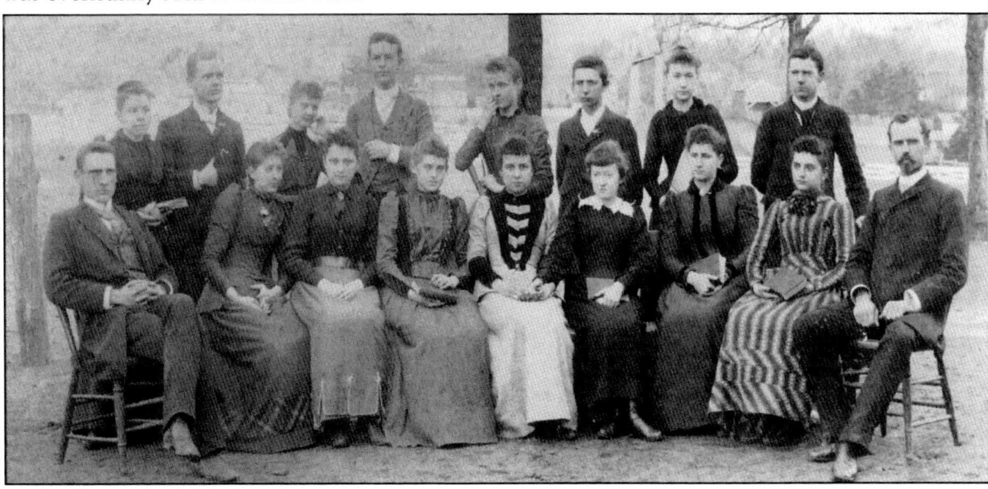

The State Normal School graduation class of 1892 poses for a photograph. Pictured here (in no particular order) are Maggie Woodruff, Maria Ward, Matamoras "Mattie" Wharton, Lucy Woodruff, Lizzie Prevett, Annie Bates, Annie L. Stevenson, Ida G. Woodward, "Bessie" Adams, George P. McClurkin, W.B. Bowling, Curtis B. Haley, John Hames, Woodson J. Martin, Mary Ramagnano, and Sunnie M. Henderson. In the front row, seated at far right, is Prof. C.B. Gibson. (Nisbet family collection.)

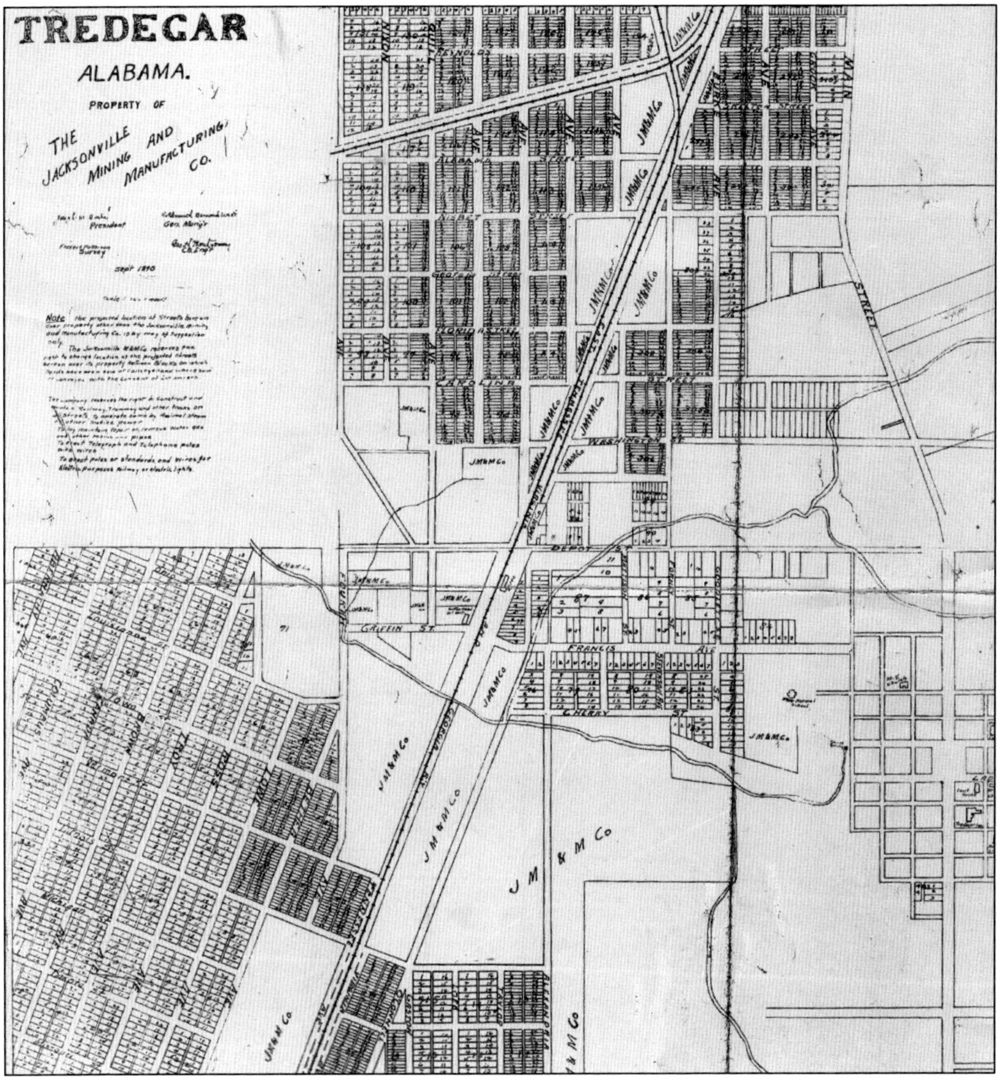

This map shows the ambitious plans that the Jacksonville Mining & Manufacturing Co. had for the town of Tredegar, Alabama, a suburb of Jacksonville. A later version of this map changes the name of the town to Jacksonville. (Private collection of Lynn Causey.)

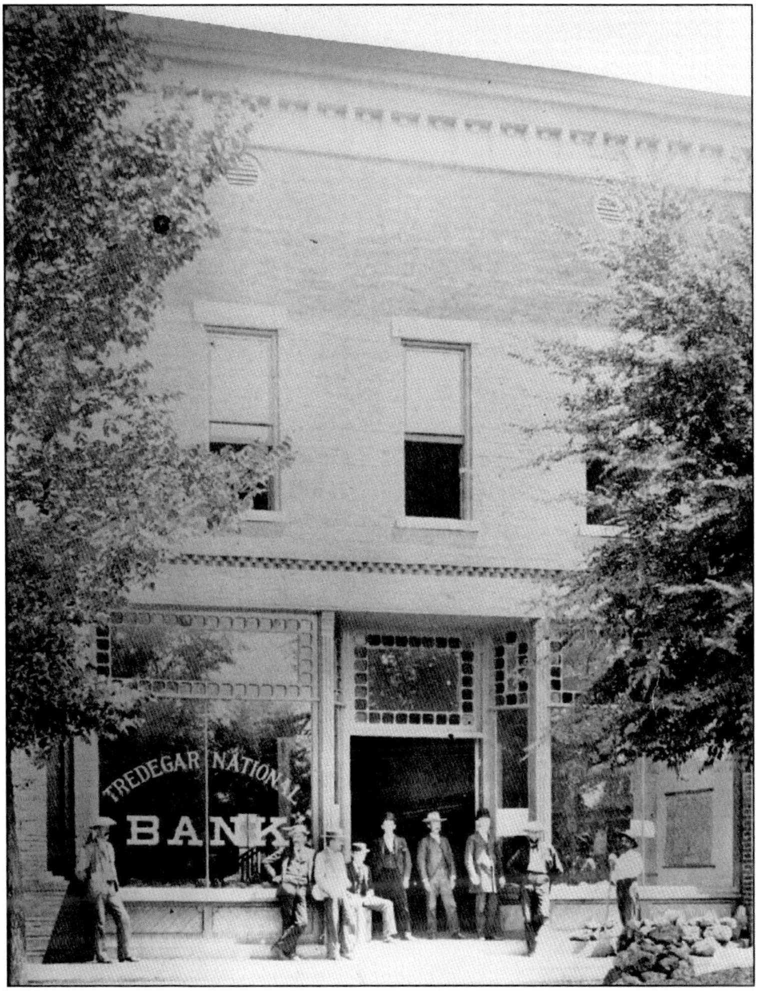

George P. Ide (pictured seated in the photograph below) founded Tredegar National Bank in 1891 with money he had raised in Vermont and New Hampshire. In his autobiography, Knox Ide, George's adopted son, wrote that the Northern investors "insisted that George become cashier to watch their money and a prominent resident, George Rowan, was elected President to keep his eye on that 'damn Yankee.'" The Jacksonville Mining & Manufacturing Co. occupied the upper floor of this building in 1890.

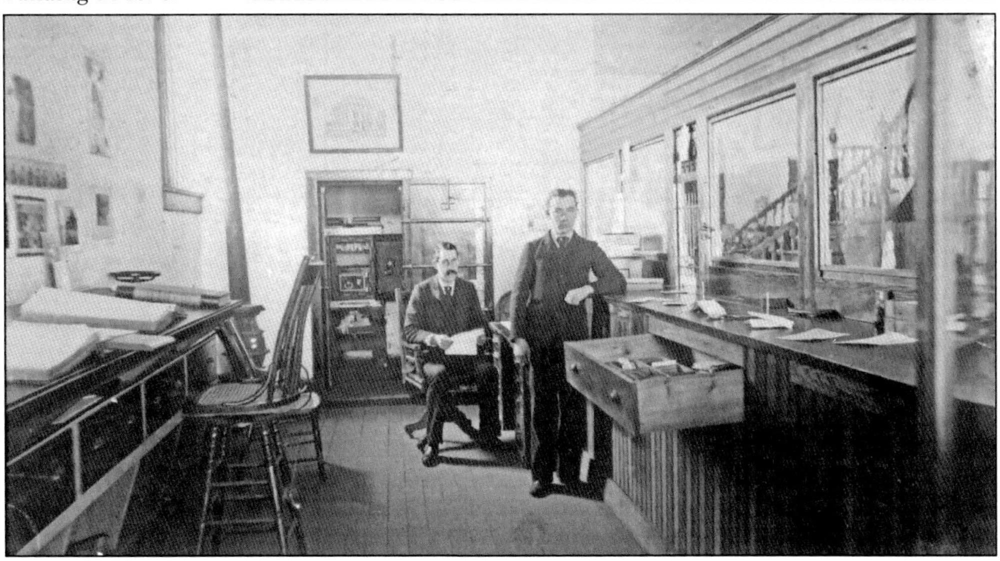

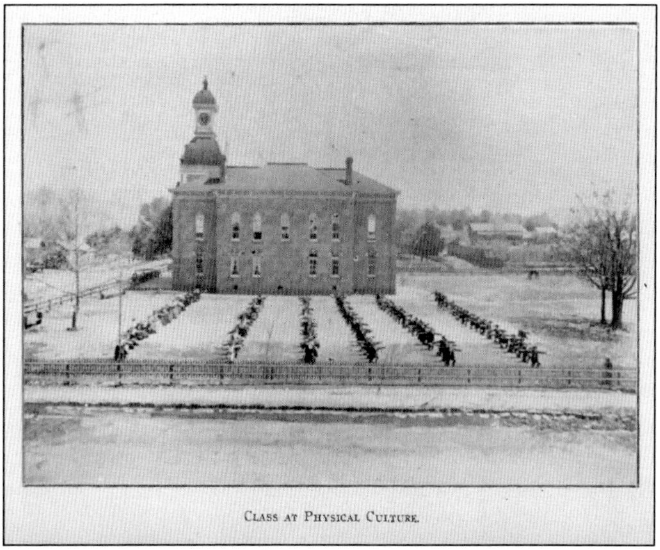

This 1907 photograph, looking east from across Main (Pelham) Street, shows one of the State Normal School's classes practicing "physical culture," an early form of physical education. The students are in front of the old courthouse, then called Atkins Hall. (Courtesy of Jacksonville State University.)

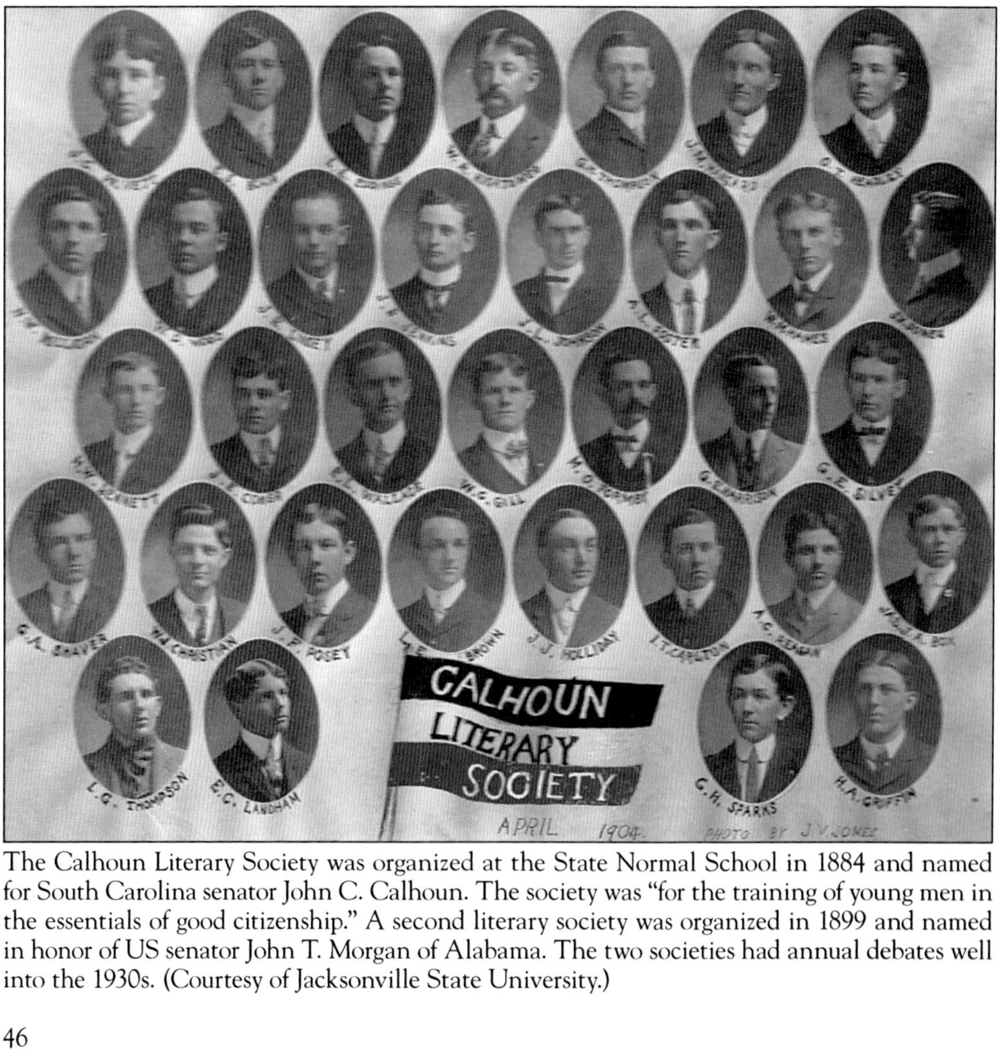

The Calhoun Literary Society was organized at the State Normal School in 1884 and named for South Carolina senator John C. Calhoun. The society was "for the training of young men in the essentials of good citizenship." A second literary society was organized in 1899 and named in honor of US senator John T. Morgan of Alabama. The two societies had annual debates well into the 1930s. (Courtesy of Jacksonville State University.)

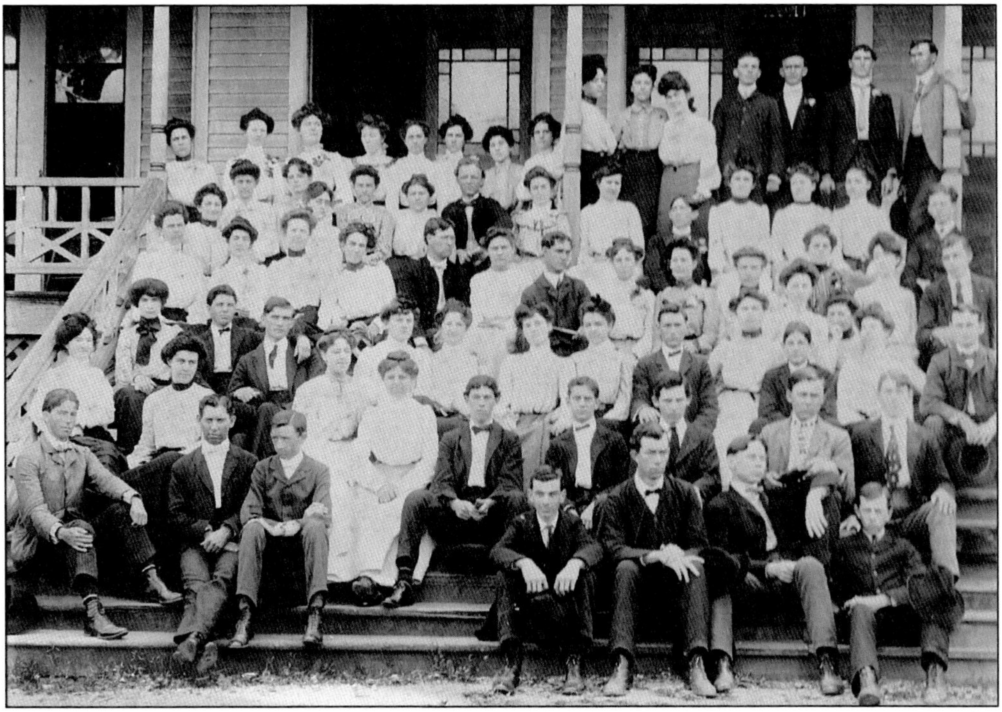

The hotel featured in the below photograph had at least two names during its existence. On this postcard, it is called the Alleghany Hotel. The hotel also went by the name the Iron Queen. Written on the back of the photograph above, dating from the early 1900s, is the following: "Front steps of old Iron Queen, run by Mr. Gasser. First operated as a hotel, later as dormitory or boarding house for school." Photographed above are the State Normal School dormitory residents. The Alleghany/Iron Queen/dormitory burned down in the 1910s. (Above, Nisbet family collection; below, courtesy of Jacksonville Public Library.)

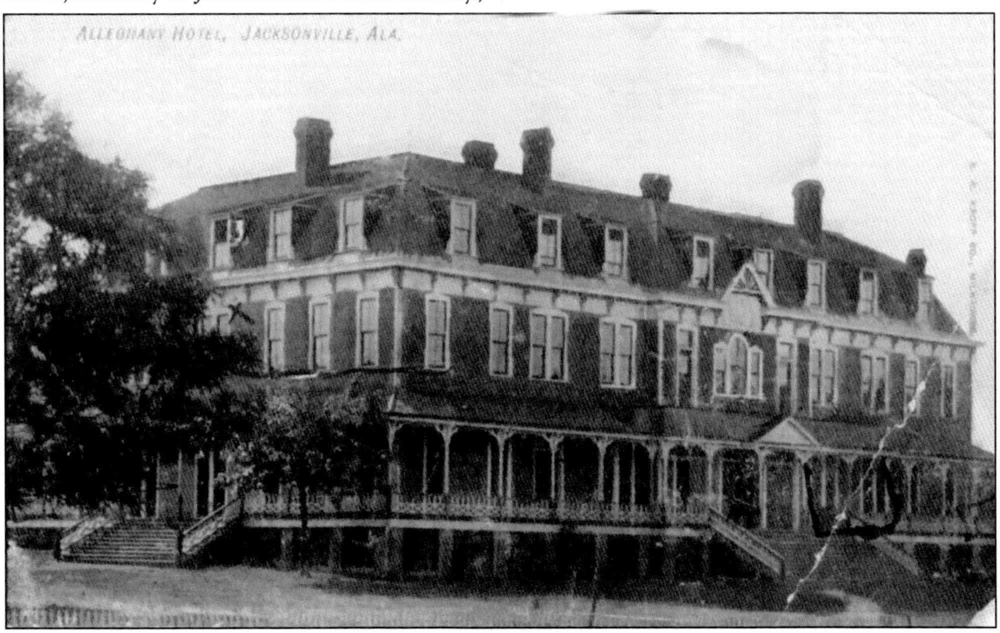

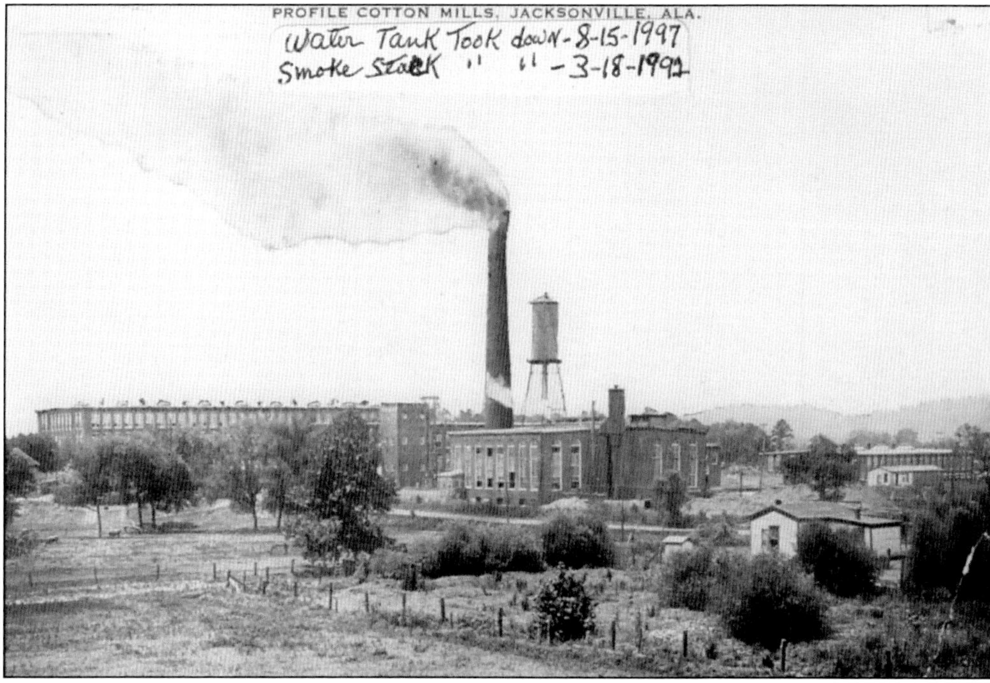

This is an early view of the Profile Cotton Mill. Based on the name on the water tower (Profile), the photograph was taken after 1911, when ownership of the mill changed and, with it, the name, from Ide Cotton Mill to Profile Cotton Mill. (Courtesy of Mrs. Homer Barnwell.)

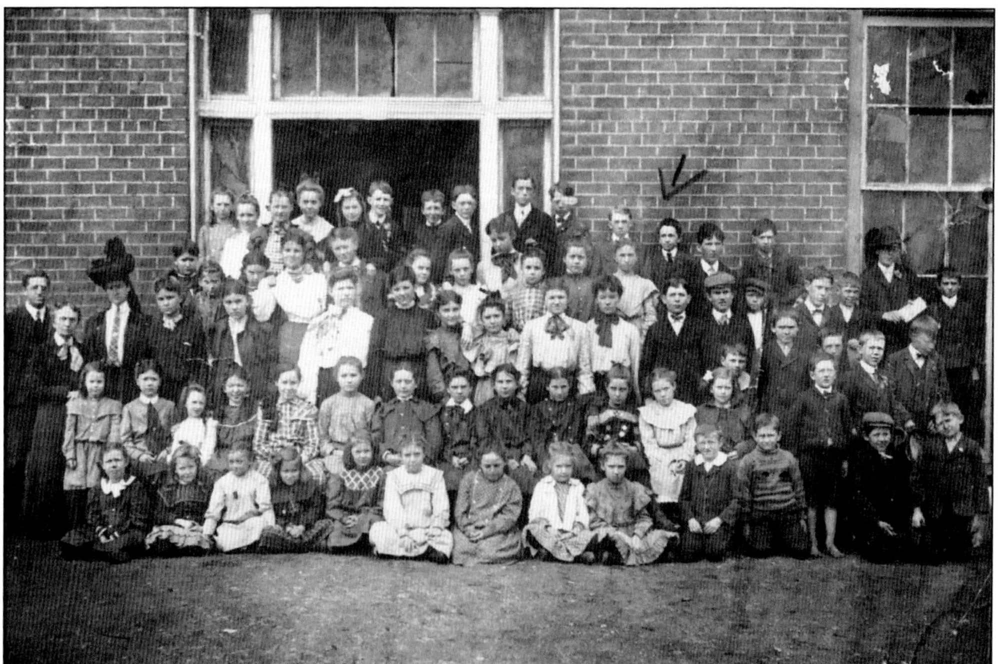

This 1902 photograph shows training (primary) school students in front of Hames Hall, which was in a state of disrepair. The arrow points to J. Thomas Martin. Also pictured is Liston Crow (first row, far right). (Nisbet family collection.)

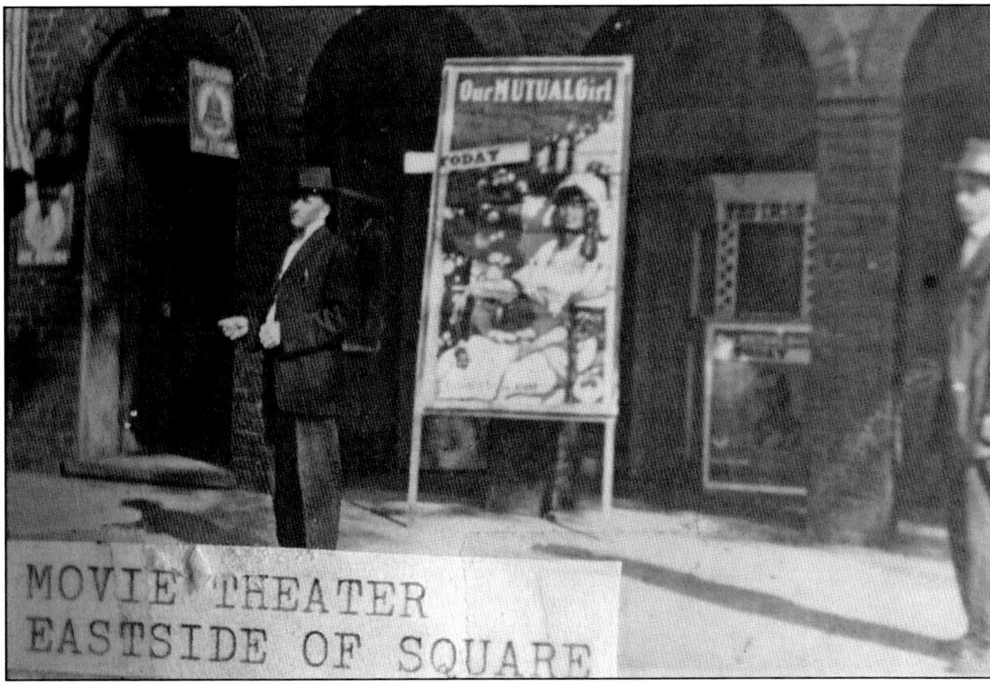

The Iris Theatre opened in 1914 on the first floor of the building seen here. The theater operated until 1922. On the first floor in the center of the building is a doorway leading to a stairway to the second floor, possibly to a balcony for black patrons to watch movies at the Iris. The Iris Theatre operated in the right side of the building. This building survived the 1883 fire.

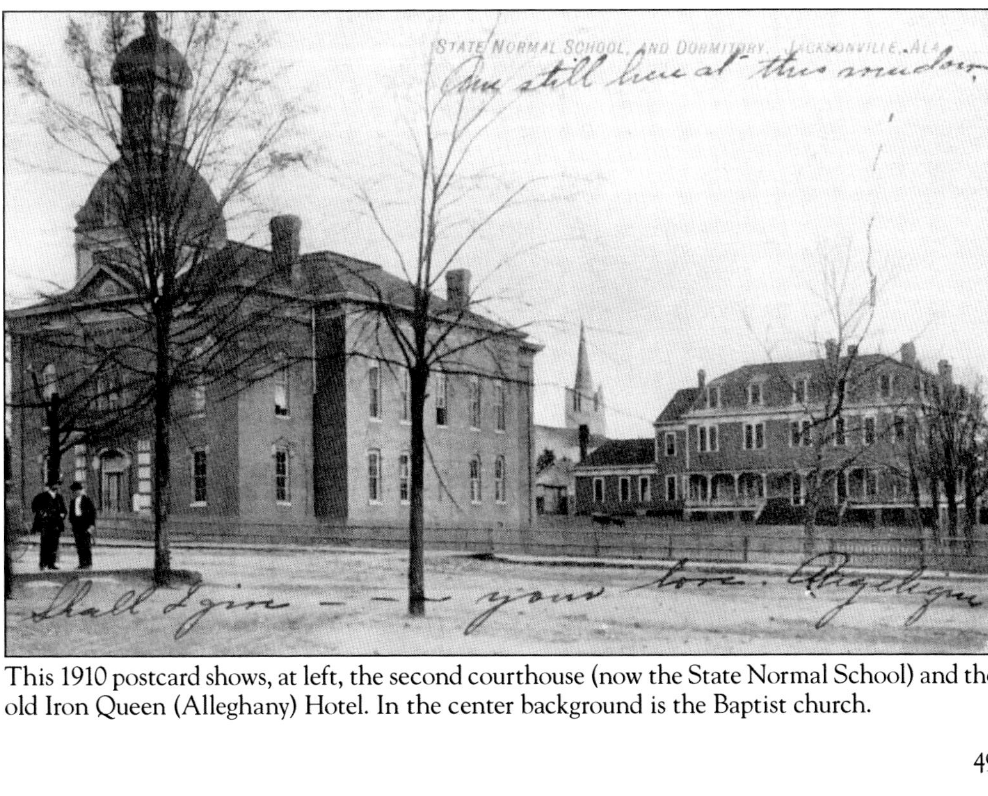

This 1910 postcard shows, at left, the second courthouse (now the State Normal School) and the old Iron Queen (Alleghany) Hotel. In the center background is the Baptist church.

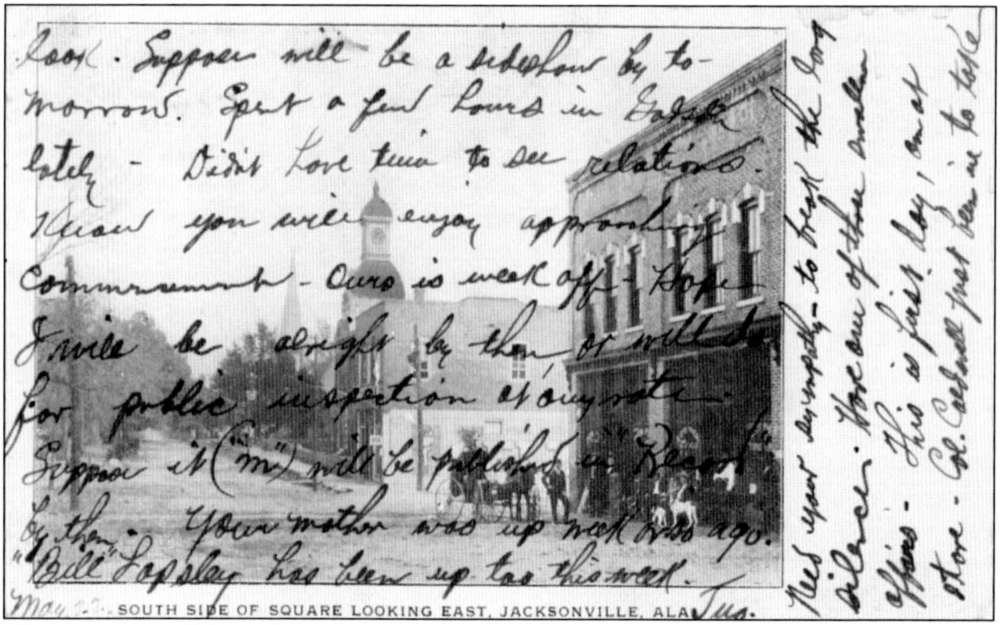

This 1908 postcard shows the south side of the square, looking east up Ladiga Street from the west side of the public square. Shown are, from left to right, the steeple of the Episcopal Church, the clock tower of the old courthouse/Ames Hall, State Normal School, a dry-goods store, Ramagnano's Opera House, and Ramagnano's Saloon. Today, the dry-goods store is The Quality Shoppe, the opera house is vacant, and the saloon is now Jacksonville Computer.

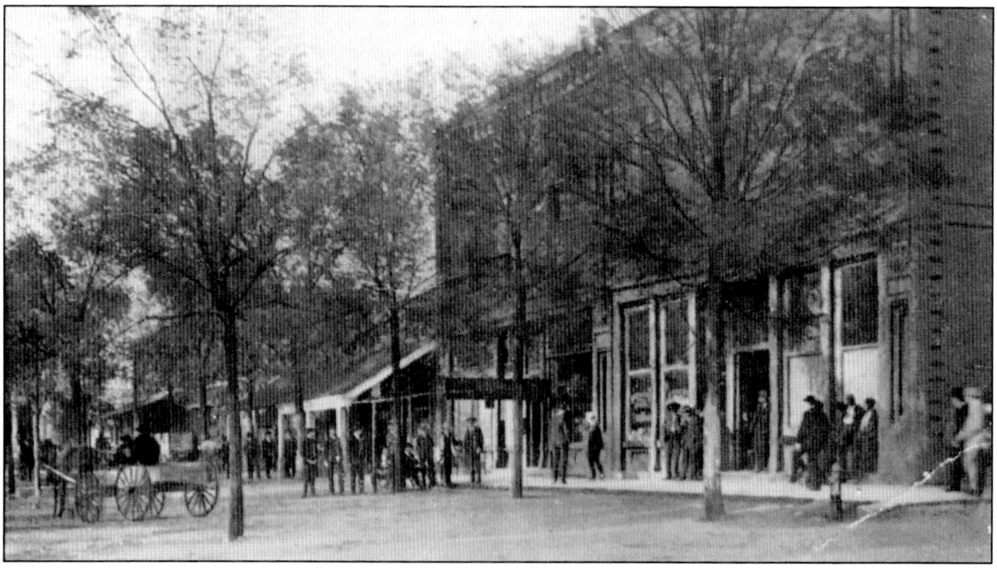

This 1908 postcard shows the east side of the square, looking north up Main Street (now Pelham Road) from the south. The buildings are, from left to right, as follows, with the 2014 occupants in parentheses: the brick tavern being operated as a general store (partially obscured by trees) (the Swank); a dry-goods and clothing store (Jillybeans); a furniture store (vacant); a drugstore (Crow Drug Store); under the awning, John B. Nisbet's Pharmacy (Crow Drug Store); and, on the corner, Rowan Dean & Co., a dry-goods, clothing, and general merchandise store. Today, the building houses Pointers Menswear and Roma's Pizza.

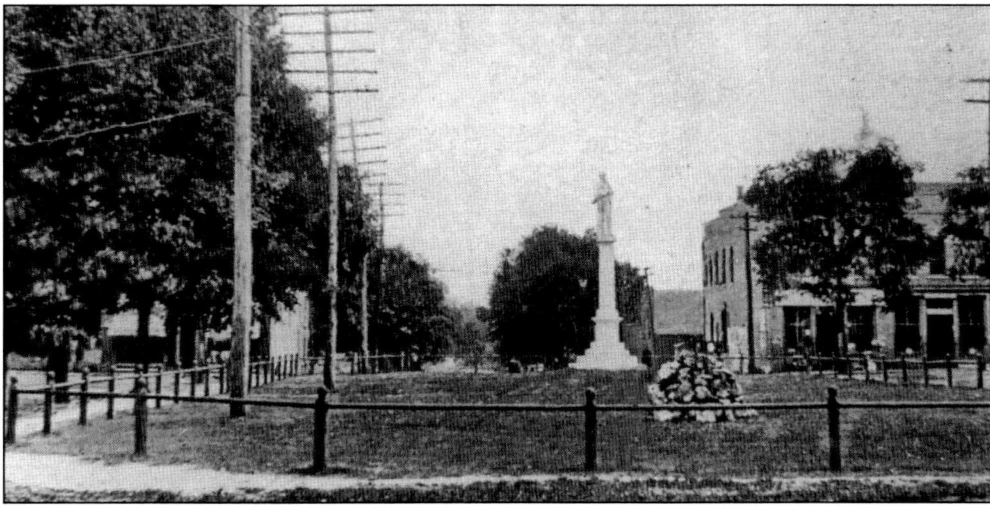

The soldier on the monument faces north, keeping a lookout for any new invasion by the Northern aggressors. It was erected in 1905 by the John H. Forney Chapter of the United Daughters of the Confederacy. The figure on the statue is not the likeness of John Pelham. Consistent with the "Lost Cause" mythology, the inscription on the monument reads, "Let none of the survivors of these men offer in their behalf the penitential plea, 'They believed they were right.' Be it ours to transmit to posterity our unequivocal confidence in the righteousness of the cause for which these men died." The large pile of rubble in the center of the photograph is the remnants of the original courthouse.

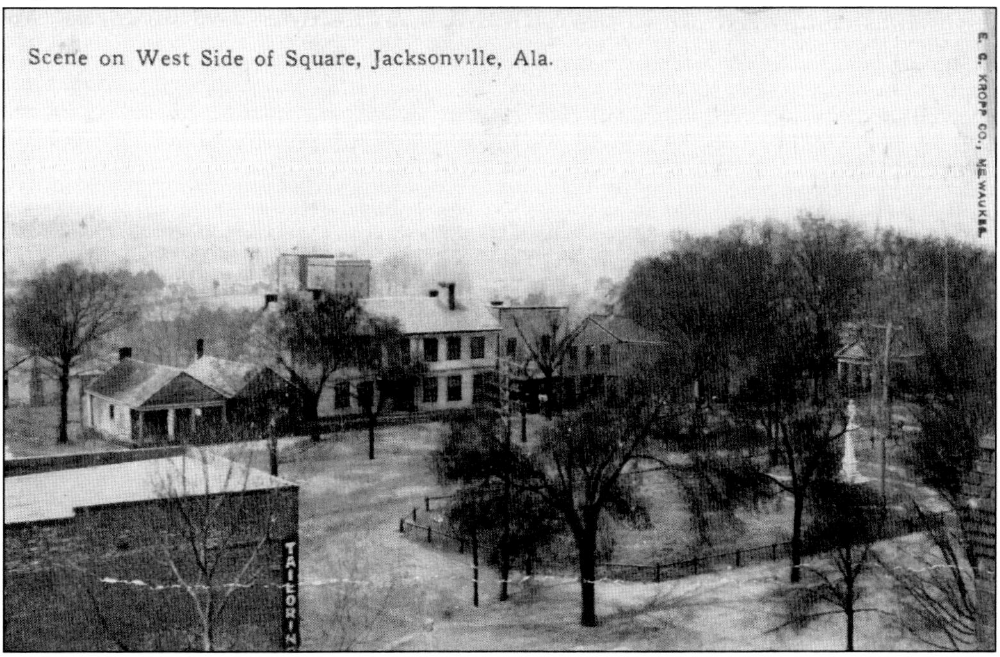

The view in this 1908 postcard is of the west side of the square, looking west. The buildings are, from left to right, C.A. Stephens Hardware Co. (foreground), two dwelling houses, the Jacksonville Hotel, a furniture store, a marble shop, and a dwelling house. The facade of Dr. Francis's office is visible at far right. In the center distance is what would later be called Hames Hall on the State Normal School campus. (Public Library of Anniston–Calhoun County Alabama Room.)

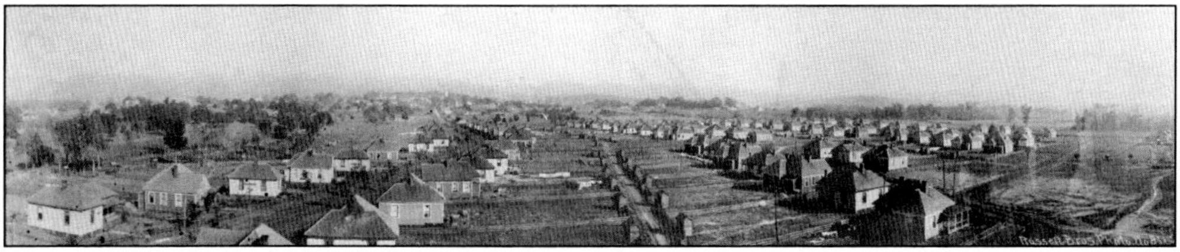

This c. 1910 photograph shows the houses constructed by the Ide Cotton Mill for its workers. The houses were rented to the workers. The Ide Cotton Mill constructed 40 "operative" houses early in 1905 and, in 1908, built an additional 90. Note the line of outhouses in the center of the photograph. Each house was designed with enough space for a family to have a garden and outbuildings. Most families kept a milk cow at home at night and grazed it in the communal pasture next to the mill during the day. (Courtesy of Mrs. Homer Barnwell.)

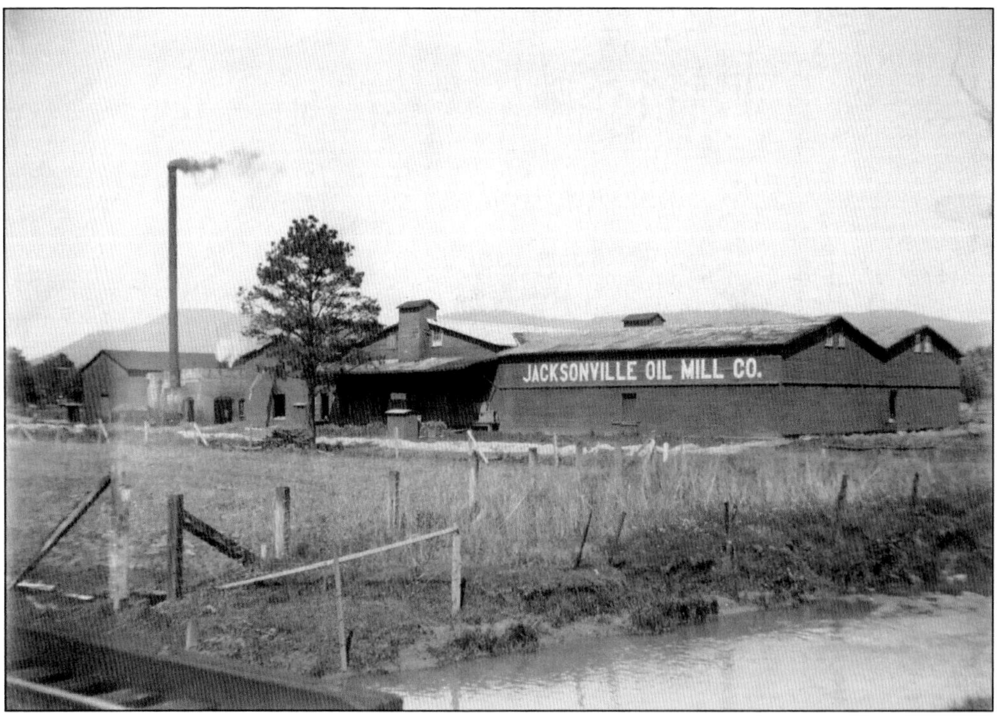

This is a photograph of the Profile Cotton Mill plant that produced cottonseed oil. This plant appeared on the 1899 Sanborn map of Jacksonville as the Jacksonville Oil Mill Company. The company sold the cottonseed oil on the square in the building that became the First National Bank. (Courtesy of Mrs. Homer Barnwell.)

This undated photograph shows the plant of the cotton gin of the Profile Cotton Mill. As indicated by the "Murray" weathervane on the vent stack, this facility used the Murray cotton gin system to produce cotton to be used in the mill next door. Built of concrete, the building is still standing and was the original home to the Jacksonville Knife Co. (today, Bear & Son Cutlery). Note the black Greenleaf water system fire hydrant in the right foreground. (Courtesy of Mrs. Homer Barnwell.)

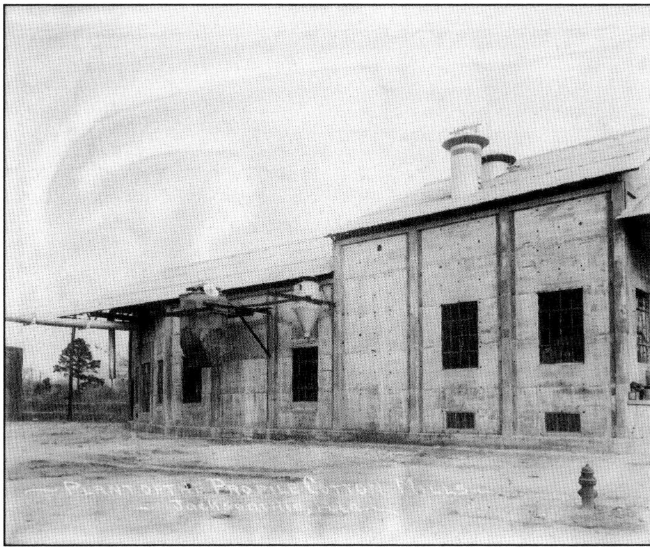

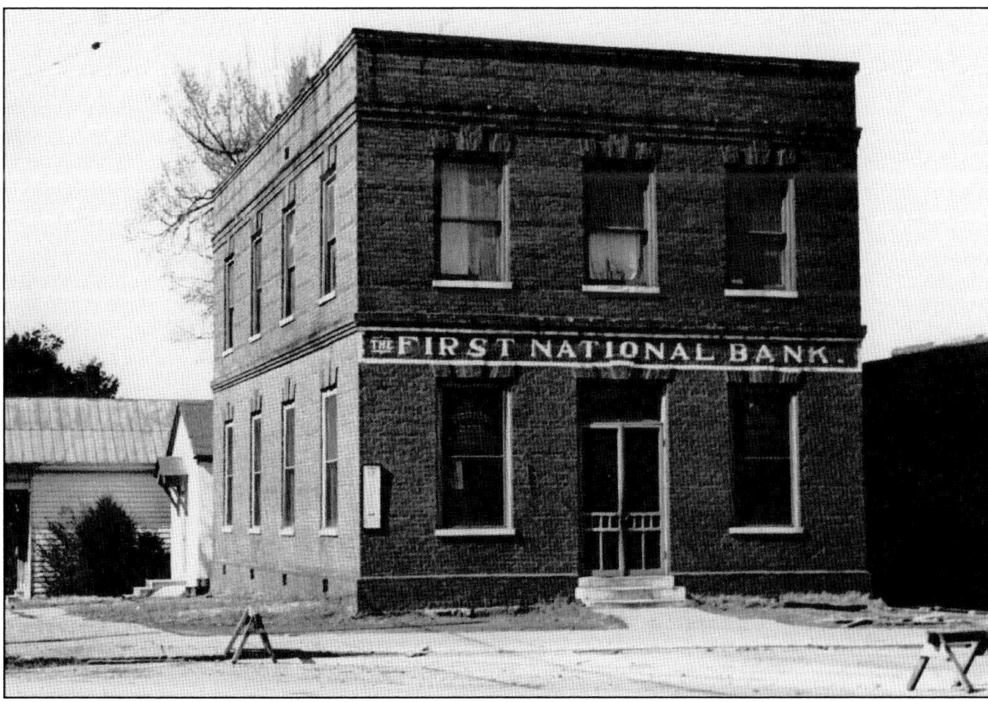

In 1902, the Tredegar National Bank moved into this building. The Jacksonville Oil Mill Co. had been located in this structure. In 1913, the Tredegar National Bank became the First National Bank of Jacksonville. The first officers were Maximillian Wellborn, Clarence Daugette, and Hubert Montgomery, cashier. The building at the far left is Dr. Francis's office. (Courtesy of Jacksonville State University.)

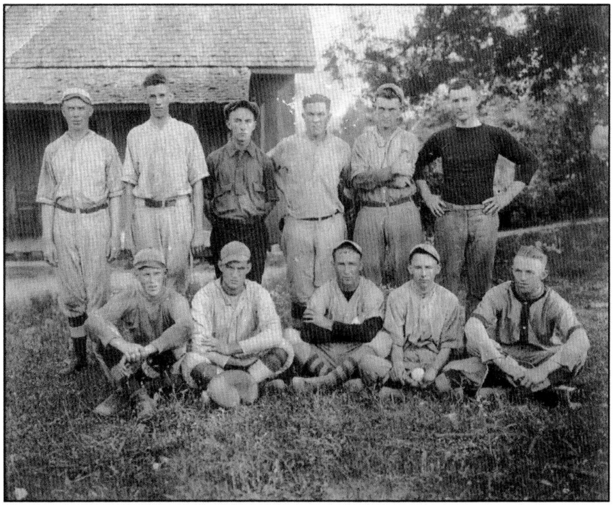

This photograph shows an early Profile Mill baseball team. Among those identified are the following: (seated) Van Hamilton and Cobb Hammett; (standing) Jud Harrelson and Coach Stevenson (far right in dark shirt).

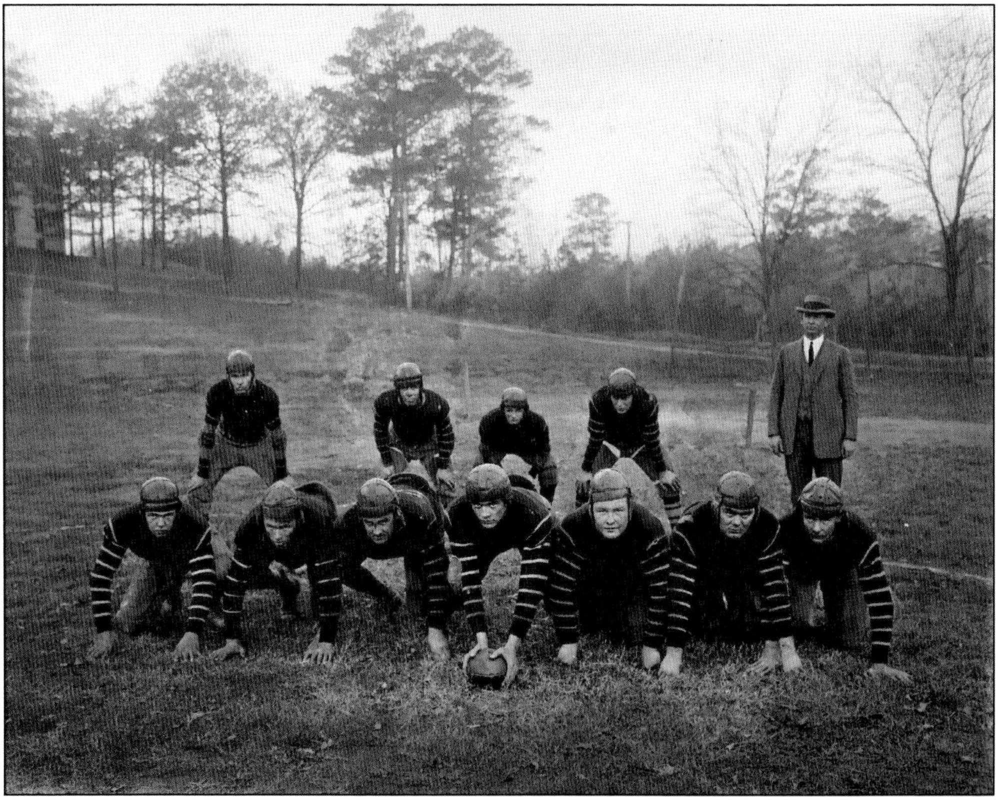

This photograph shows the 1912 football team of the State Normal School. The 1914 State Normal School yearbook, *Purple and White*, recounts the exploits of this team: "our foot ball season was all that could be desired under the circumstances, and we are looking forward to next season as being our banner year. A number of boys have signified their intentions of coming back next year. From the battle with Howard which took place early in the autumn till the curtain fell on the last contest last Thanksgiving day, a splendid record of grit, perseverance, and honor, was won by those who battled for the Purple and White—during the foot ball season." (Public Library of Anniston–Calhoun County, Russell Brothers Collection.)

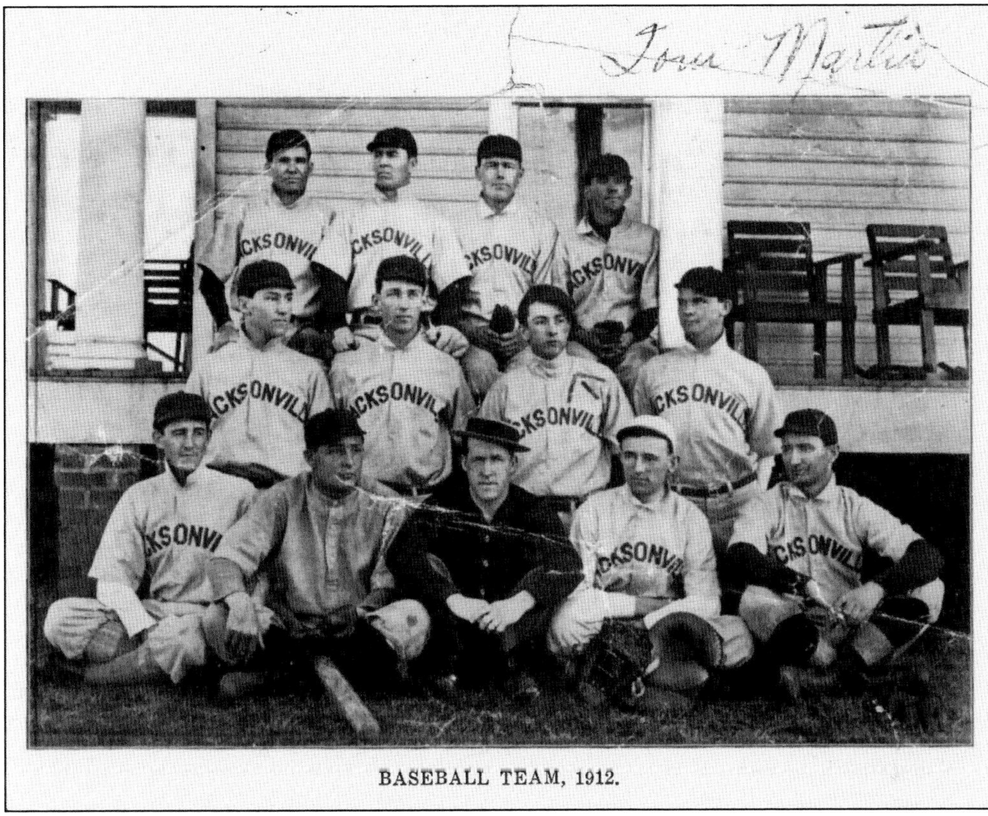

Tom Martin (noted by arrow) and other players of the 1912 State Normal School baseball team pose for a photograph. The 1912 *Purple and White* reported that "Baseball has also been very good. Early in the season bad weather held the practice back considerably, and as a result we lost several close games by reason of an error or two. The team reached the 'pink of condition' when during the last days of April they defeated Albertville two out of three and gave them a good run for the third game, it ending 4 to 3." (Nisbet family collection.)

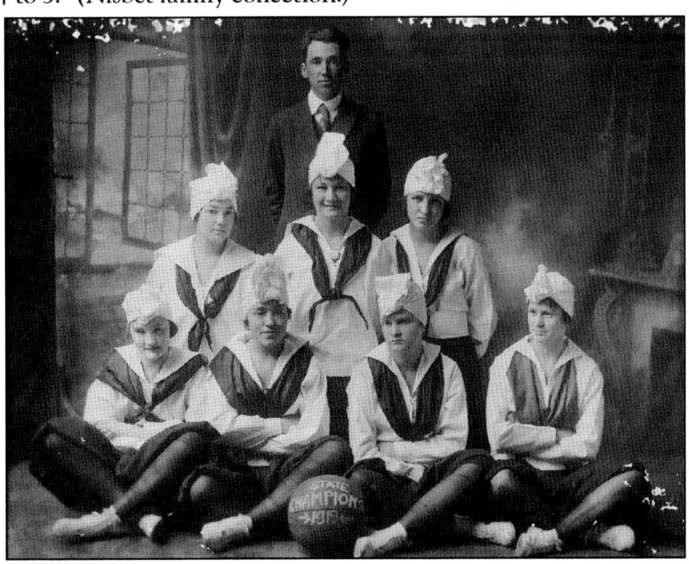

This photograph shows the 1919 State Normal School girls' basketball team. Written on the basketball is "State Champions 1919." The team also won the state championship in 1920. An early adopter of women's basketball (the first ever such game was played in 1882), the State Normal School had a girls' team by 1902. (Courtesy of Jacksonville State University.)

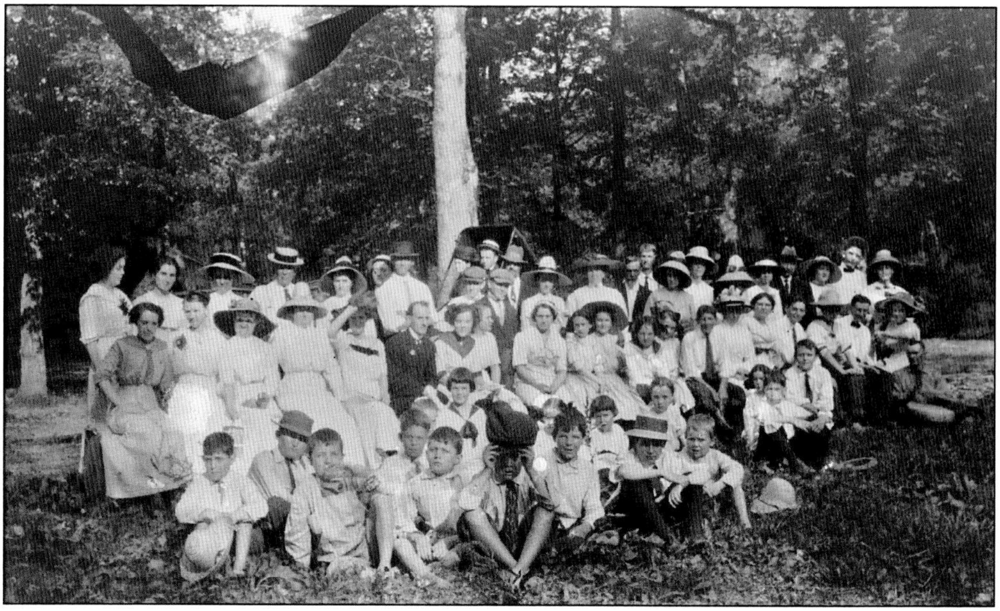

Above, members of the First Presbyterian Church enjoy an afternoon at a church family picnic at Nisbet Lake in July 1908. The 1900s postcard below shows the main building, dam, and lake at Nisbet Lake and Club House. (Above, Nisbet family collection; below, courtesy of Jacksonville Public Library.)

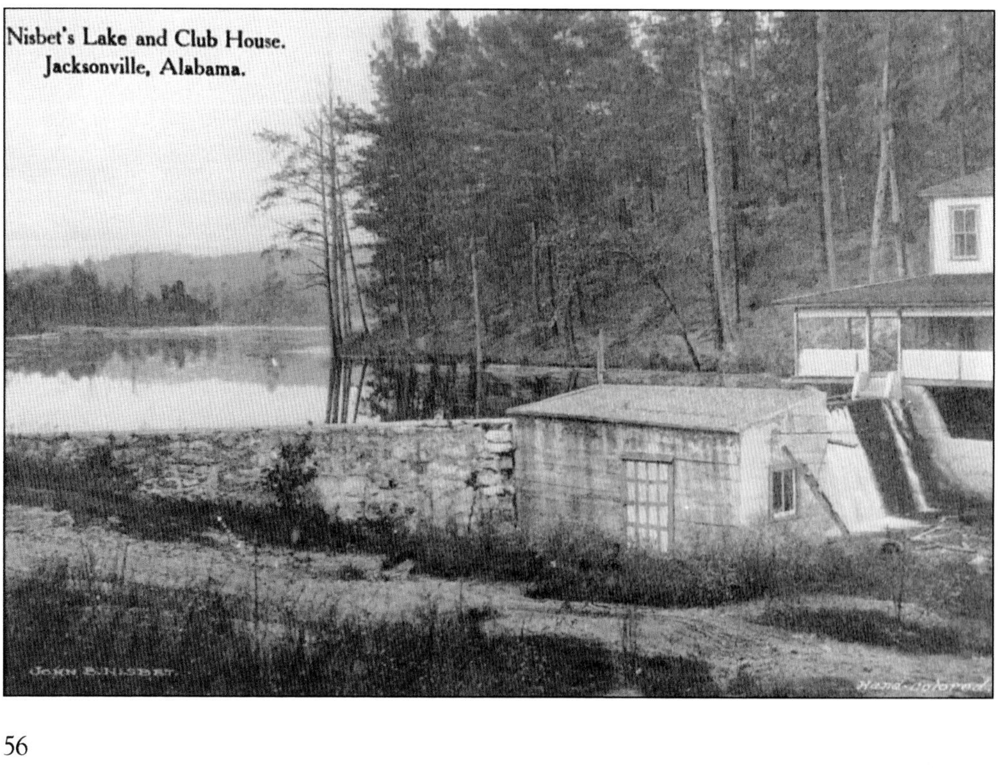

Organized in 1899 as a second literary society at the State Normal School, the Morgan Literary Society's motto was "train each one." A quotation from the 1926 yearbook, *Teacola*, reads that "this society stands strictly on the religion of our forefathers and prohibits profanity and unmanly conduct at all times." John Morgan had lived in Jacksonville early in his life before moving to Selma. He went on to become a general in the Confederate army, a six-term US senator from the state of Alabama after the war, and a grand dragon of the Ku Klux Klan.

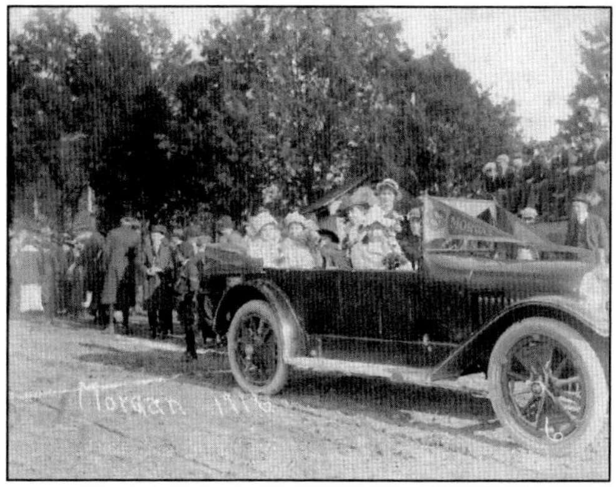

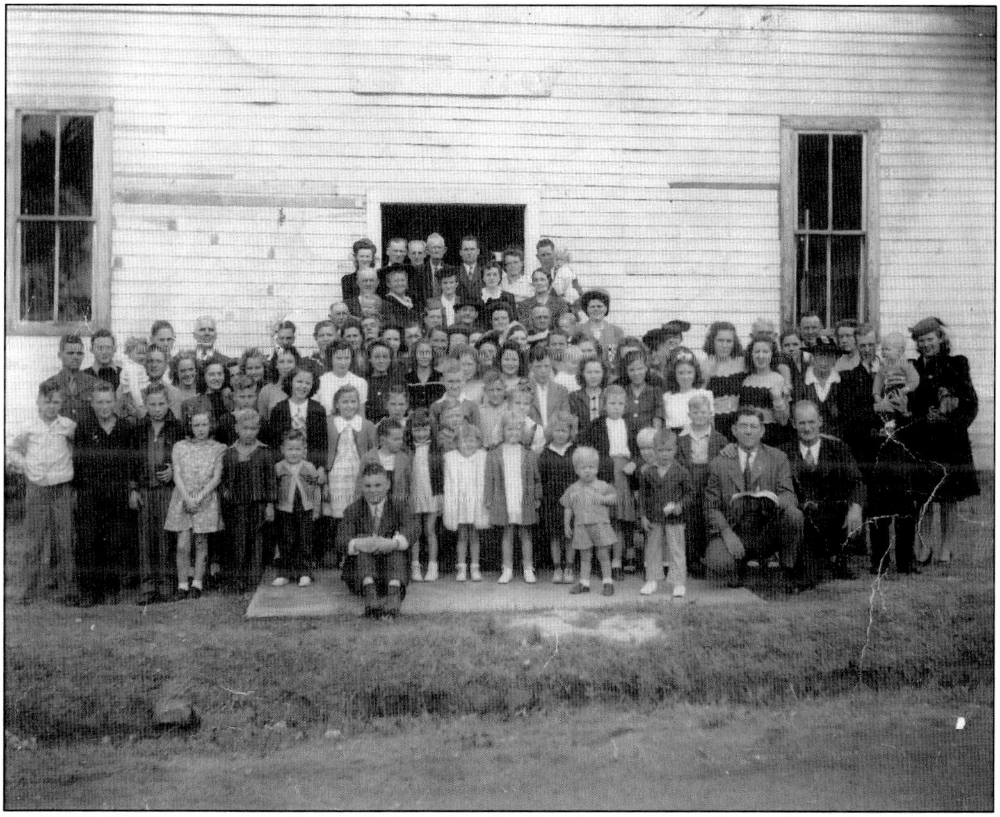

In 1910, J.B. Ellis, an evangelist with the Church of God, came to Jacksonville and started a tent revival across from the congregation's current location on West Francis Street. The congregation dedicated a wooden frame building in 1916; the church was bricked in the 1970s. Included in this 1940s photograph (in no particular order) are Oscar Daniels, Ruth Daniels, Dave Johnson, Edna Johnson, Alex Shealy, Imogene Shealy, Juline Willingham, Clarence Parris, Mary Parris, David Daniels Sr., Henry Morris, Grandpa Roberson, Edna Willingham, Maggie Turner, Jay McGinnis, Mrs. G. Bennefield, John Cobb, G.C. McGinnis, Odis McGinnis, Edna Ford, Harry Homesley, Sarah Martin, Lucille Fordson, Herman Willingham, Maude Allen, Fannie Willingham, Dora Ford, Lowell Shealy, James Ford, Betty Ann McCullum, Betty Ruth Forsyth, Eddie Bell Ford, Craig Ford, Ida McGinnis, H.E. Ebb Ford, Hattie Ford, Bevlah Morris, Mary Etta Cobb Parris, and Jackie Cobb. (Courtesy of Rev. David Daniels.)

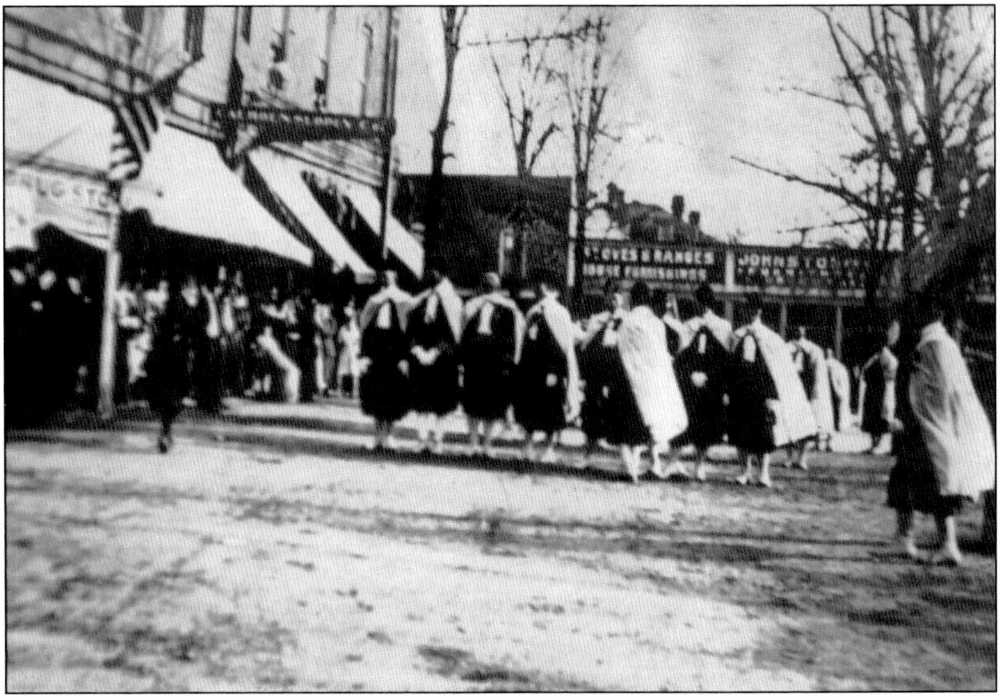

The above photograph shows the east side of the square during a temperance election. Below, a temperance group marches around the square to protest the sale of alcoholic beverages in Jacksonville. The group disembarked from the train at the depot and walked to College Street, beside the Methodist Church. The movement was so successful in Jacksonville that John Ramagnano had to close his saloon in 1917. No alcoholic drink, other than beer, was legally sold in Jacksonville until 1989 or 1990. (Above, courtesy of Jacksonville Public Library; below, Nisbet family collection.)

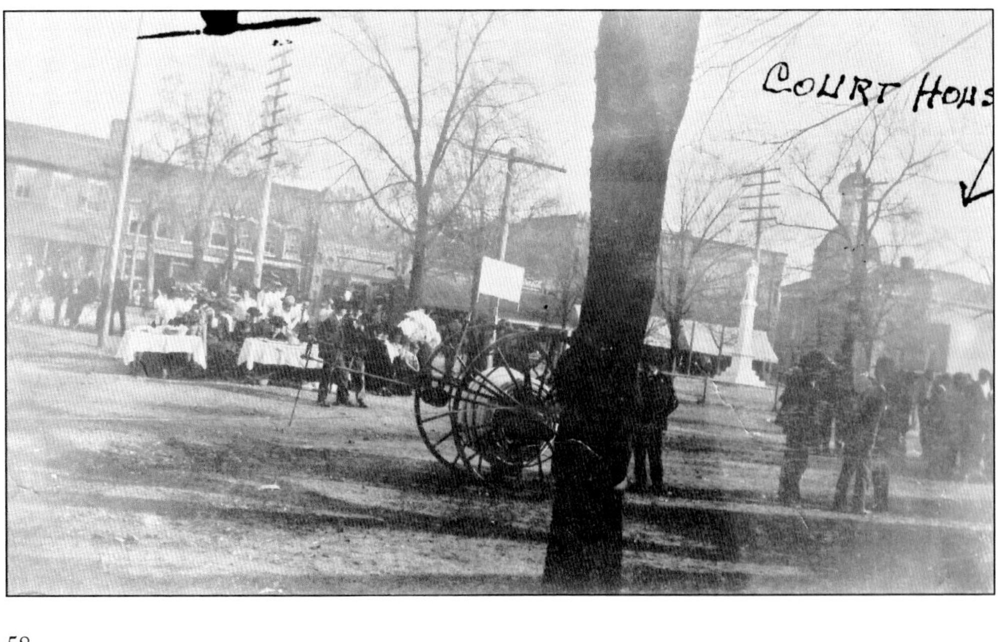

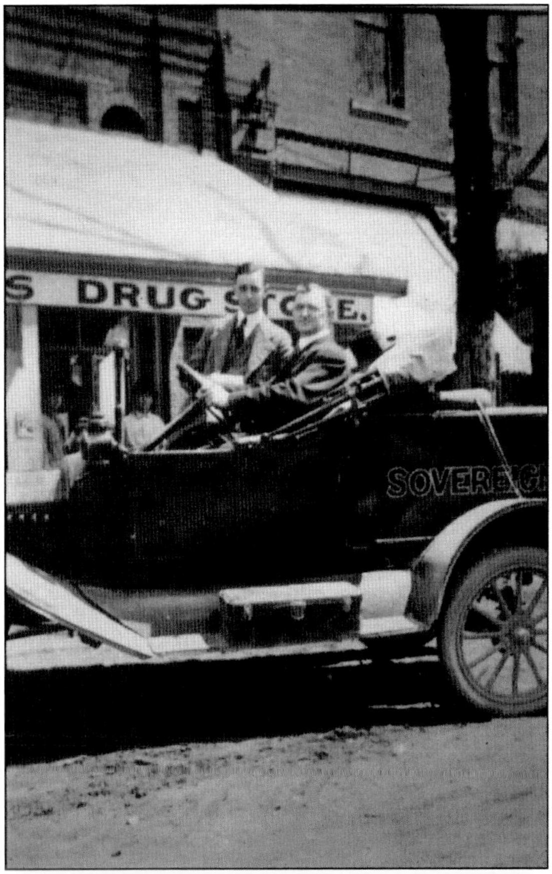

An early, and large, automobile (right) is parked in front of John B. Nisbet's pharmacy. Inside the pharmacy (below), John B. Nisbet (in hat) stands at the soda fountain. The other men are not identified.

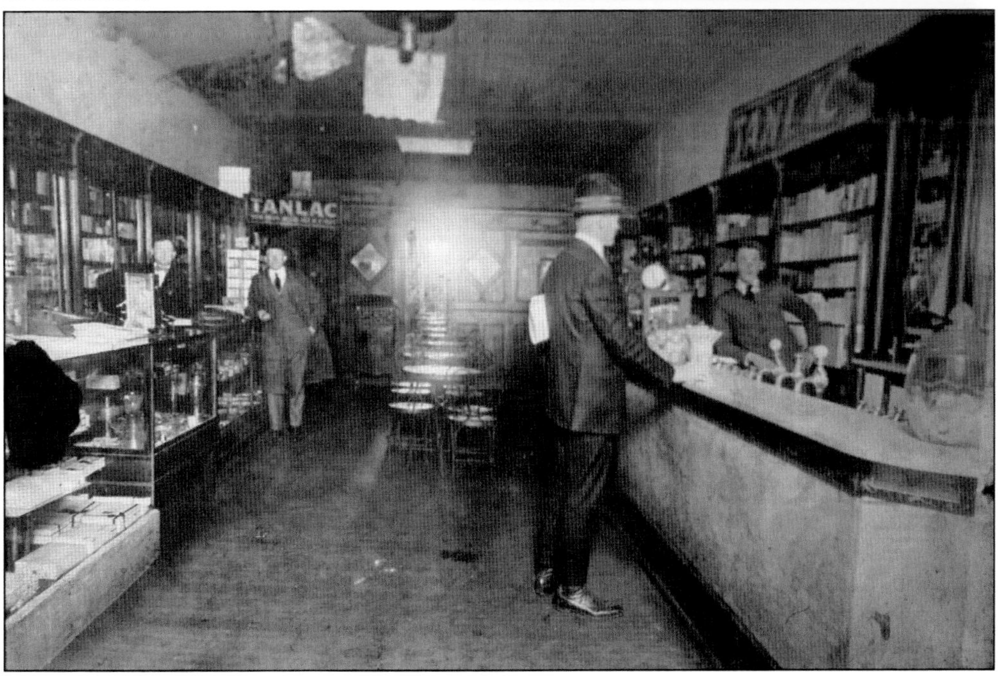

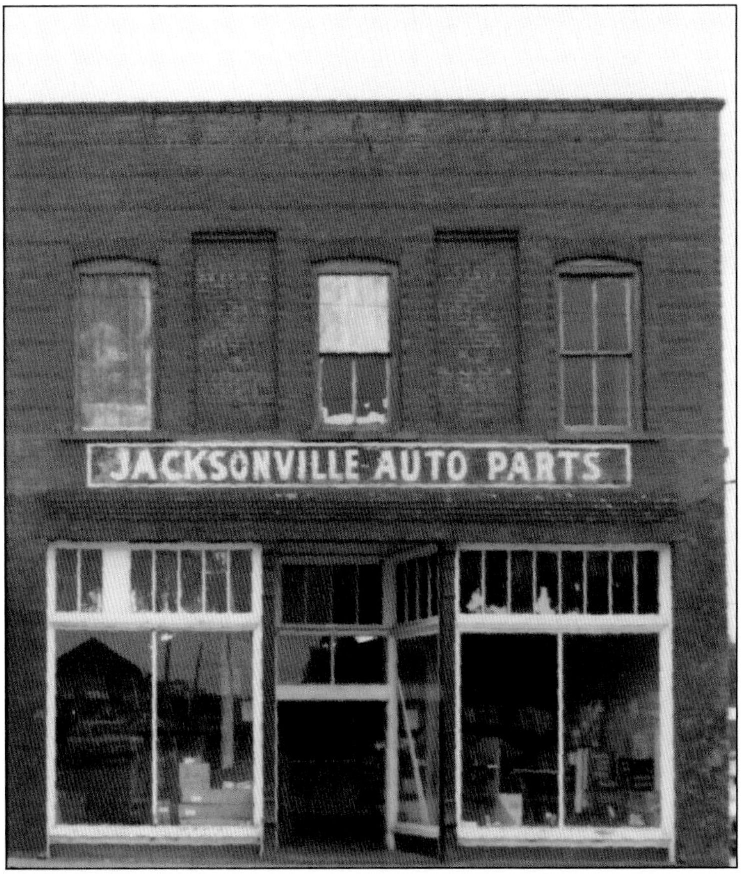

The building shown to the left in a 1970 photograph was constructed around 1905. At the time, it was the largest building on the square. In 2012, it was completely remodeled, and the Quality Shoppe moved in. The Quality Shoppe is the longest continuously operating business on the square in Jacksonville, tracing its operation to 1935. The bottom photograph, taken in the 1920s, shows the interior of the C.A. Stephens Hardware Co. Pictured below are, from left to right, John Odus Pyron, George Williams, and Charles Alexander Stephens.

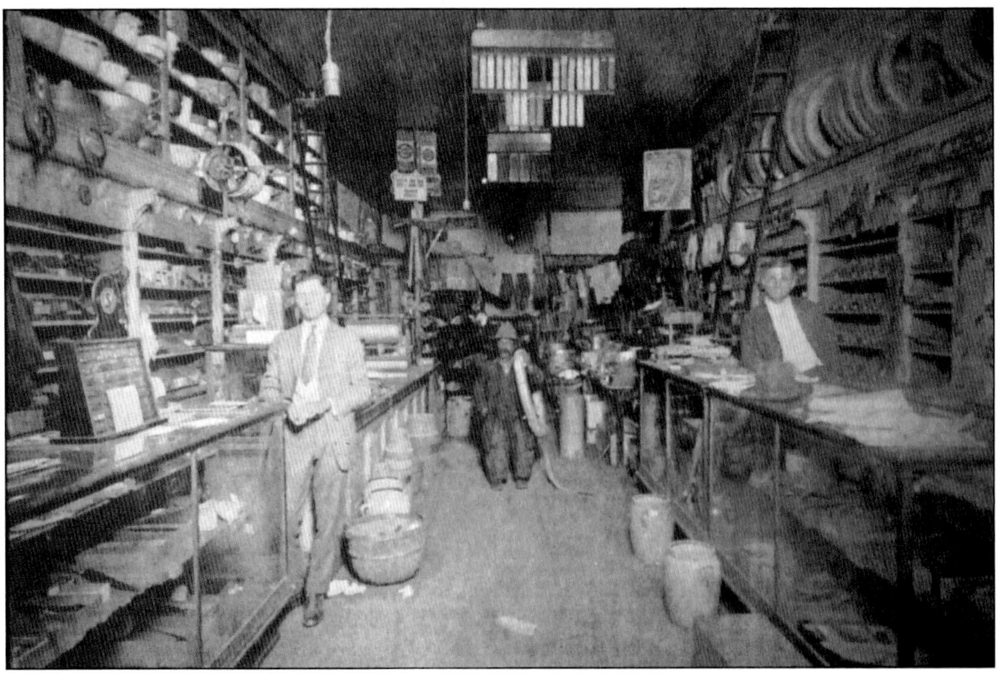

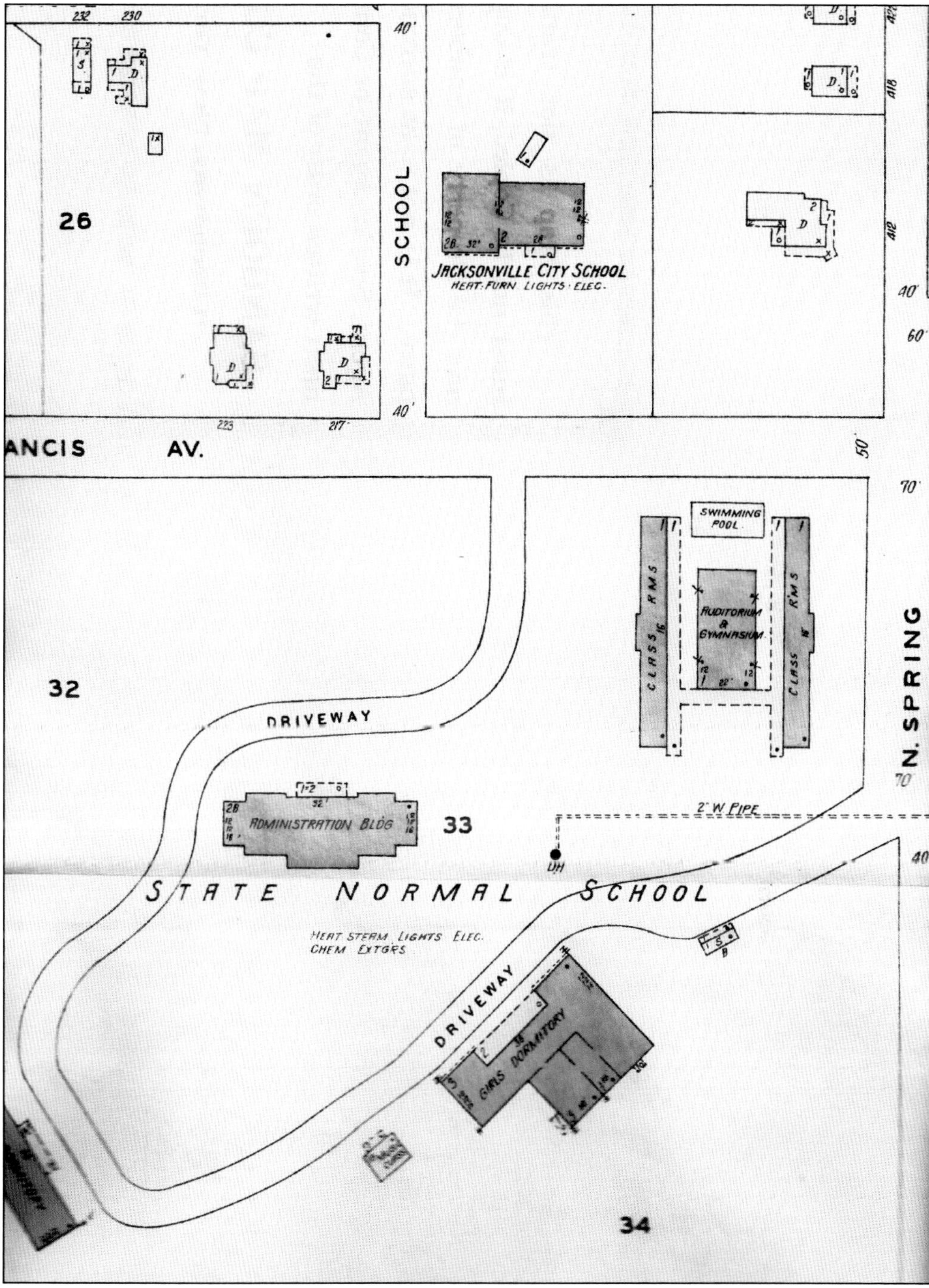

This 1928 Sanborn map shows the State Normal School campus, located at the corner of Francis Avenue and Spring Street. College Street (just off the right side of the map) runs into the school's driveway at Spring Street. The building at top is Jacksonville City School. At right are classrooms with gymnasium/auditorium and swimming pool (Kirby Hall). The girls' dormitory (Weatherly Hall) is at bottom, and the boys' dormitory (Forney Hall) is at lower left. In the center of the normal school campus is the administration building (Hames Hall).

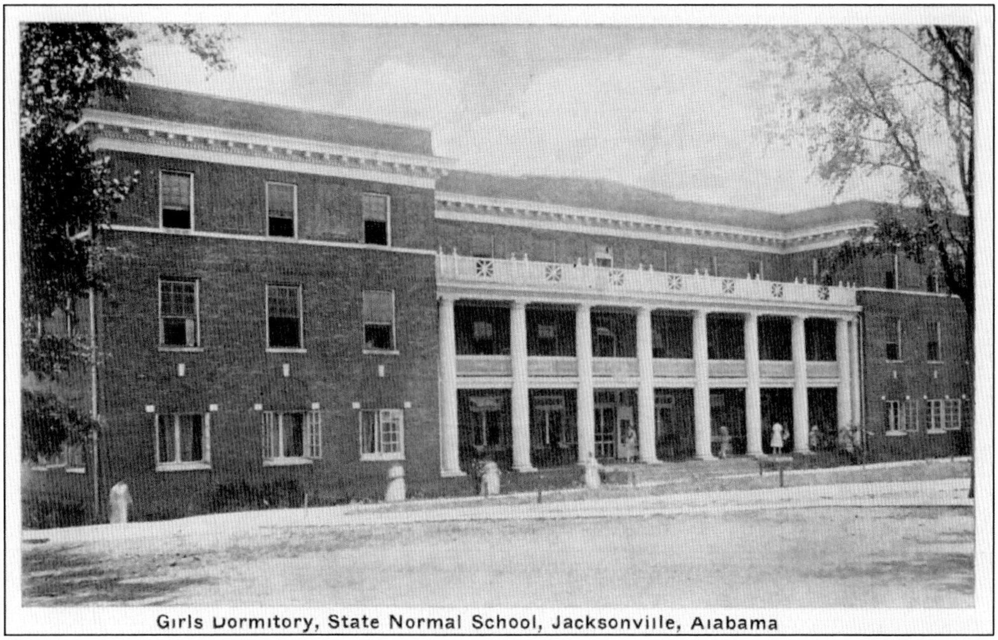

The first girls' dormitory burned down in 1916, just prior to being occupied by the State Normal School. The girls' dormitory pictured here was rebuilt in 1917 and was eventually named Weatherly Hall in honor of Florence Weatherly, a teacher and secretary at the school.

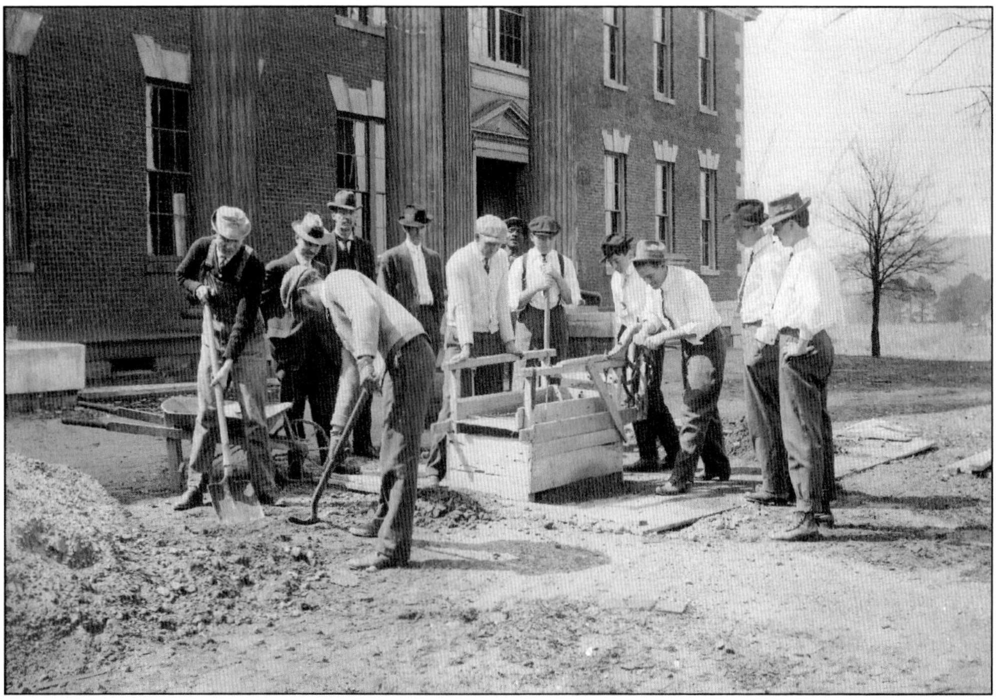

Furthering its purpose to prepare teachers for one-room schools, the normal school held classes in farming techniques, concrete work, cooking, sewing, and woodworking, among other skills. Most of these classes were coeducational. Here, boys learn how to pour concrete. (Courtesy of Jacksonville State University.)

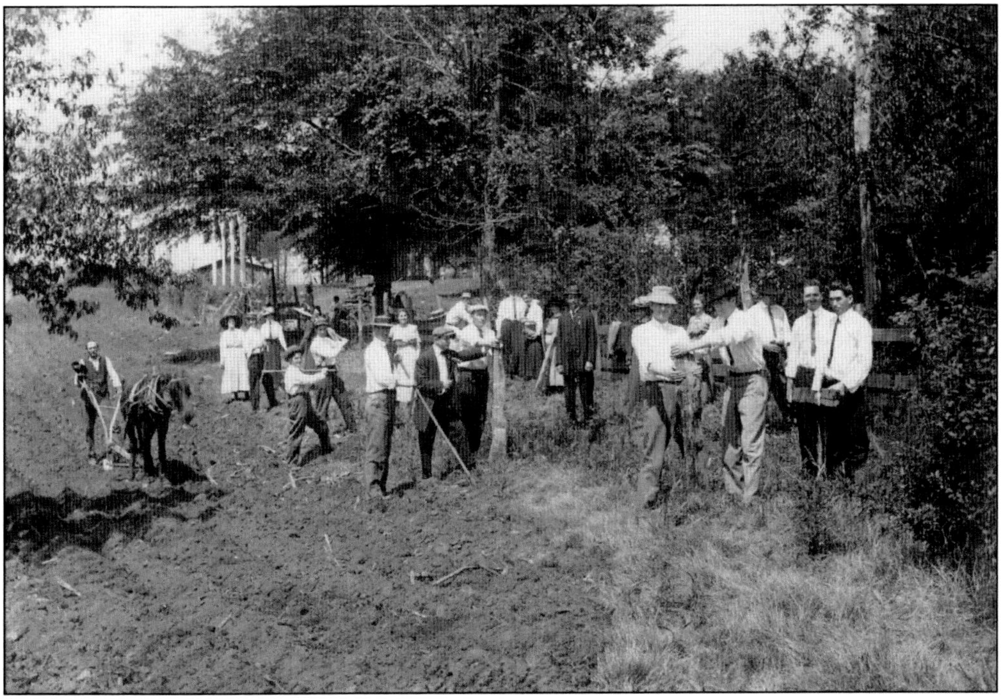

This 1913 photograph shows future teachers learning how to farm. (Courtesy of Jacksonville State University.)

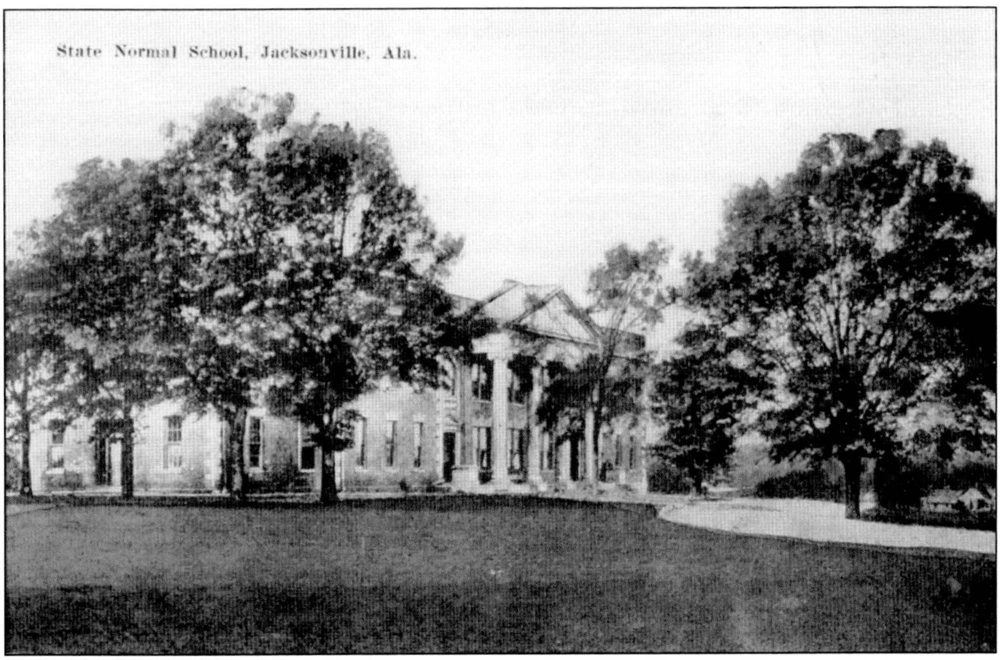

This is the administration building of the State Normal School, named Hames Hall in honor of William M. Hames, who was the president of the board of directors. In 1925, the State Normal School started a boarding high school and held classes in this building.

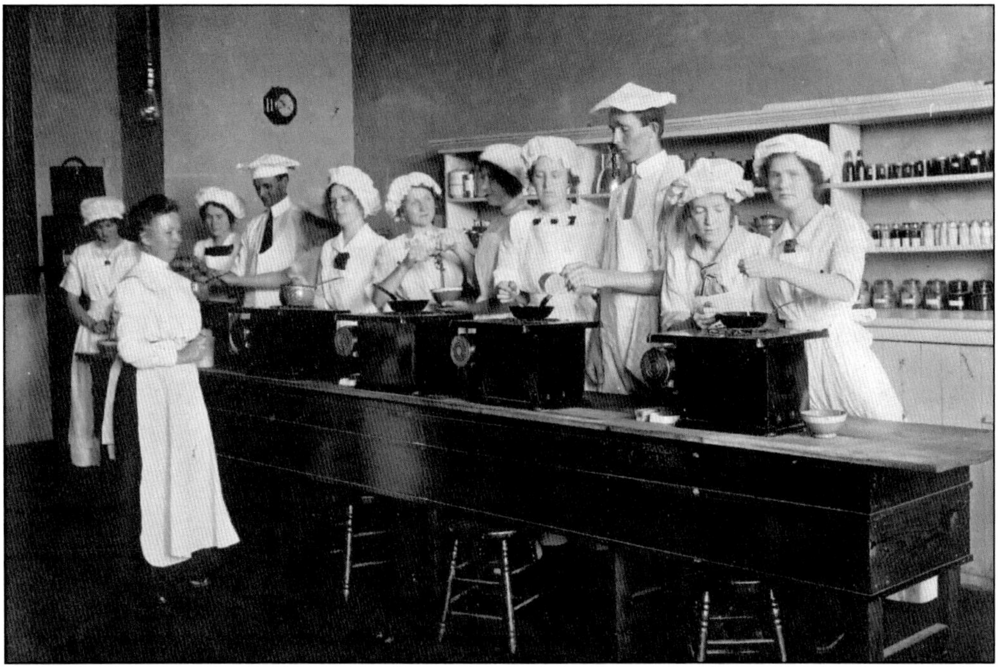

This is a photograph of a 1913 coeducational cooking class at the State Normal School. The students are wearing proper attire and hats. (Courtesy of Jacksonville State University.)

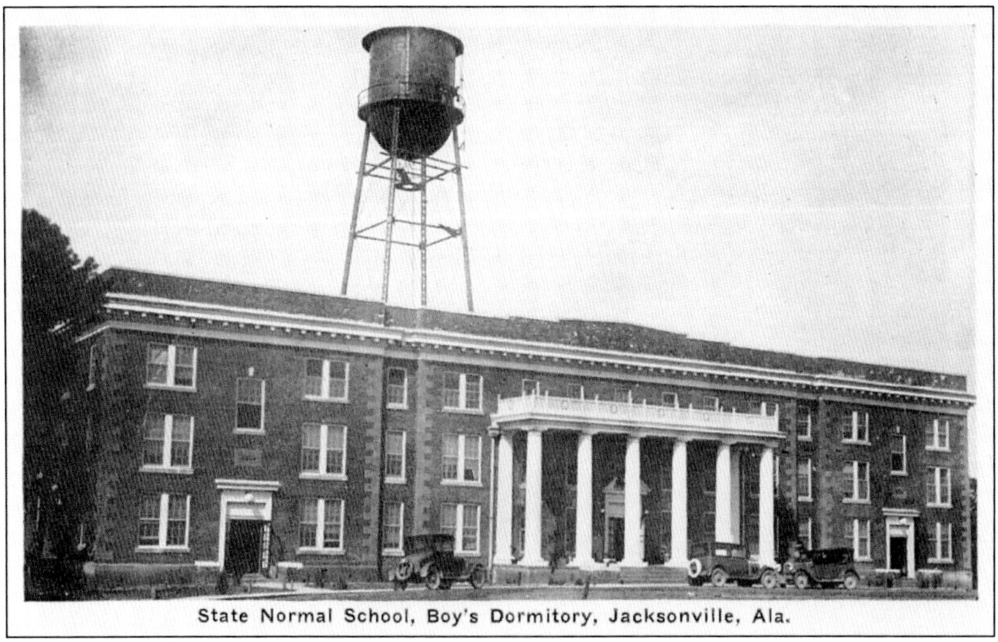

This postcard shows the boys' dormitory, later named Forney Hall. The dormitory was built in 1927 with private funds, at a cost of $75,000. The Forney family had a long history with the State Normal School. Jacob Forney IV graduated from the school in 1886 and then returned to be its president from 1893 to 1899. Mary C. Forney taught at the school for 40 years. John H. Forney, Jacob Forney IV, and Mary C. Forney's father donated the property for the second courthouse, which the State Normal School occupied for a number of years.

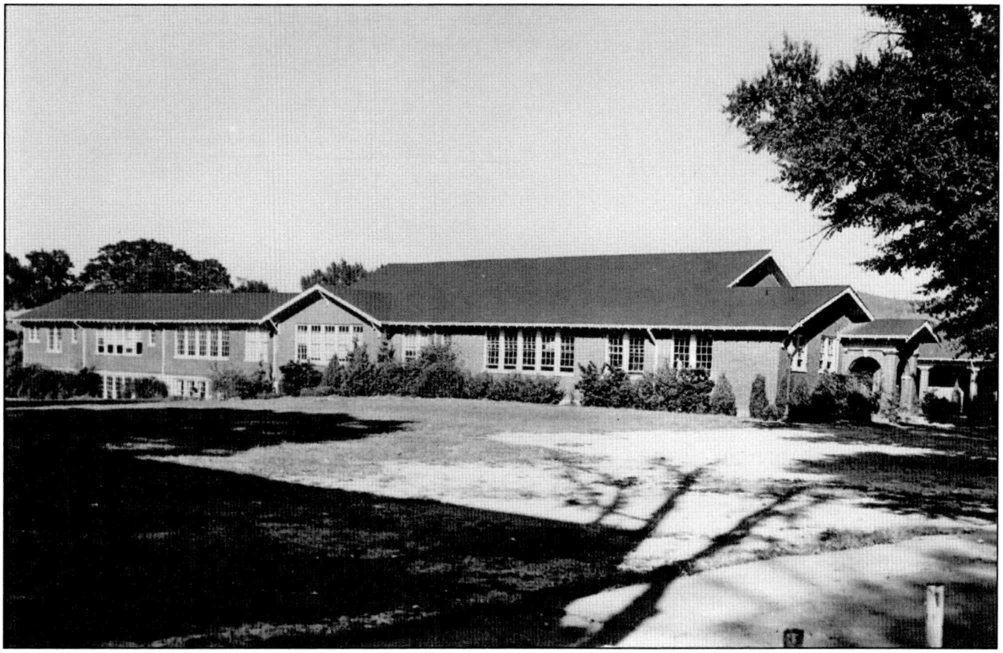

Built in 1921 and named for Gov. Thomas E. Kilby, the structure shown above housed the "training school" of the State Normal School. The 1930 *Illustrated Bulletin for the State Teachers College* stated that the training school "is the heart of the Teachers College, because it is the laboratory for methods of teaching." Shown below is Jacksonville's first "public" pool. In the 1940s, one had to take summer-school classes in order to use the pool. (Above, courtesy of Jacksonville State University; below, courtesy of Jacksonville State University.)

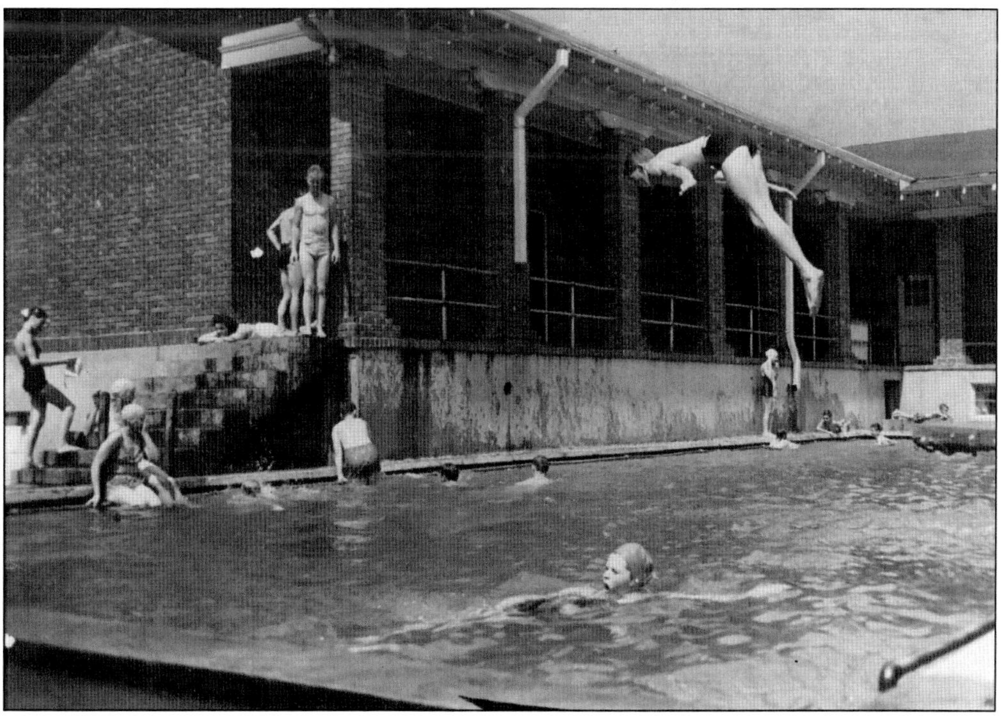

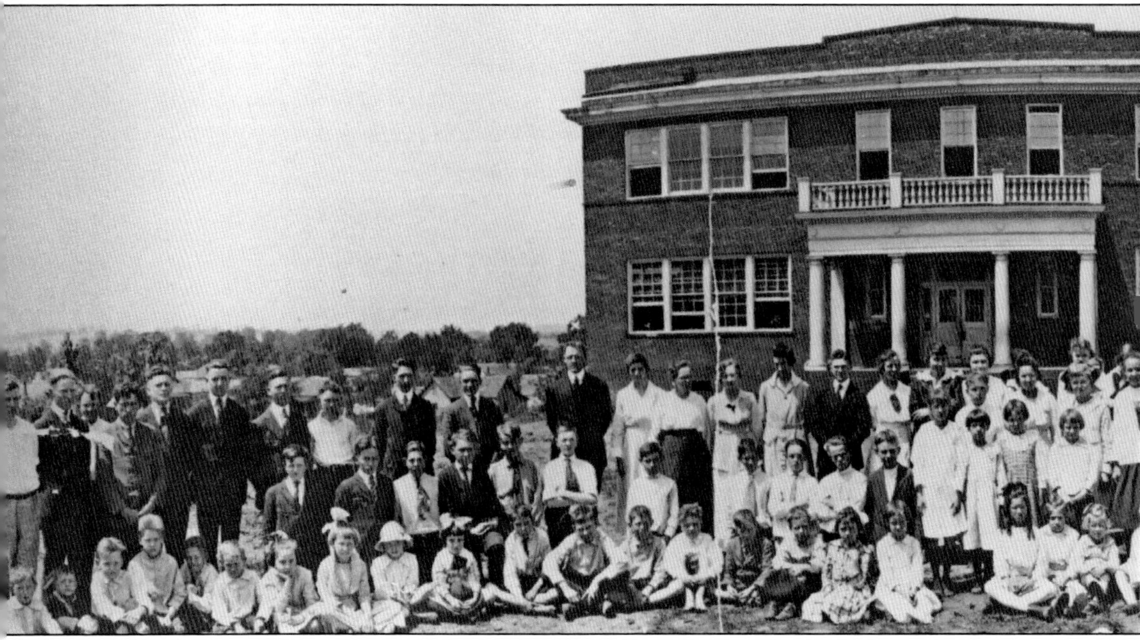

This 1919 photograph shows all the teachers and students of the Jacksonville training school, including the high school. Knox Ide and his graduating class of four are on the left side of the

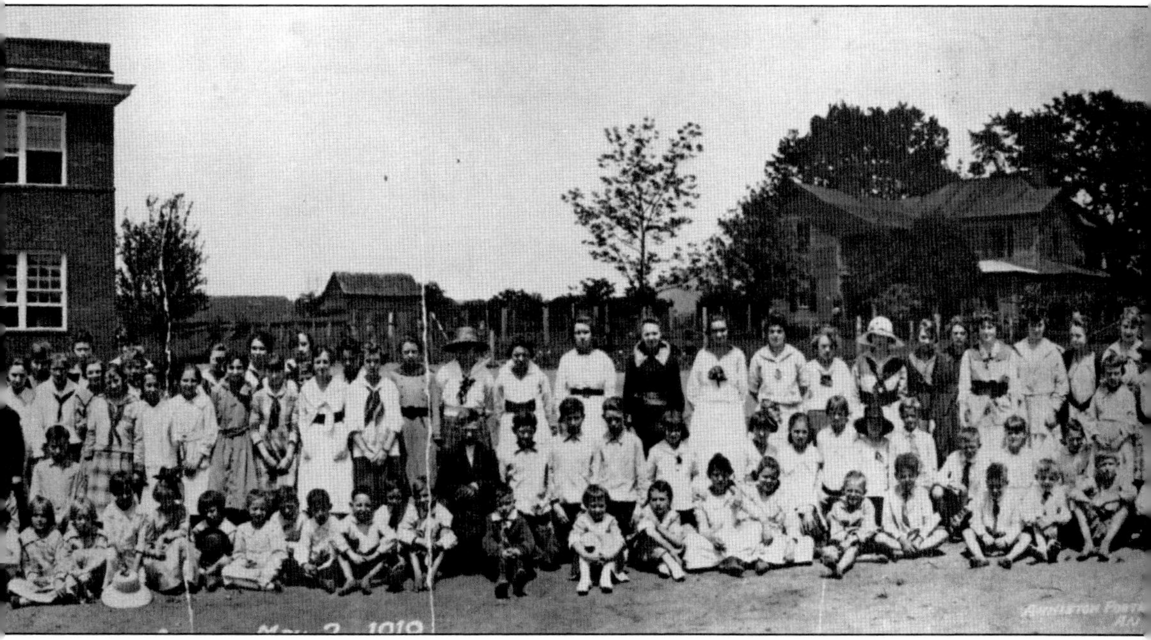

photograph. This building appears on the 1899 Sanborn map as "Jacksonville City School." (Courtesy of the Public Library of Anniston–Calhoun County, Russell Brothers Collection.)

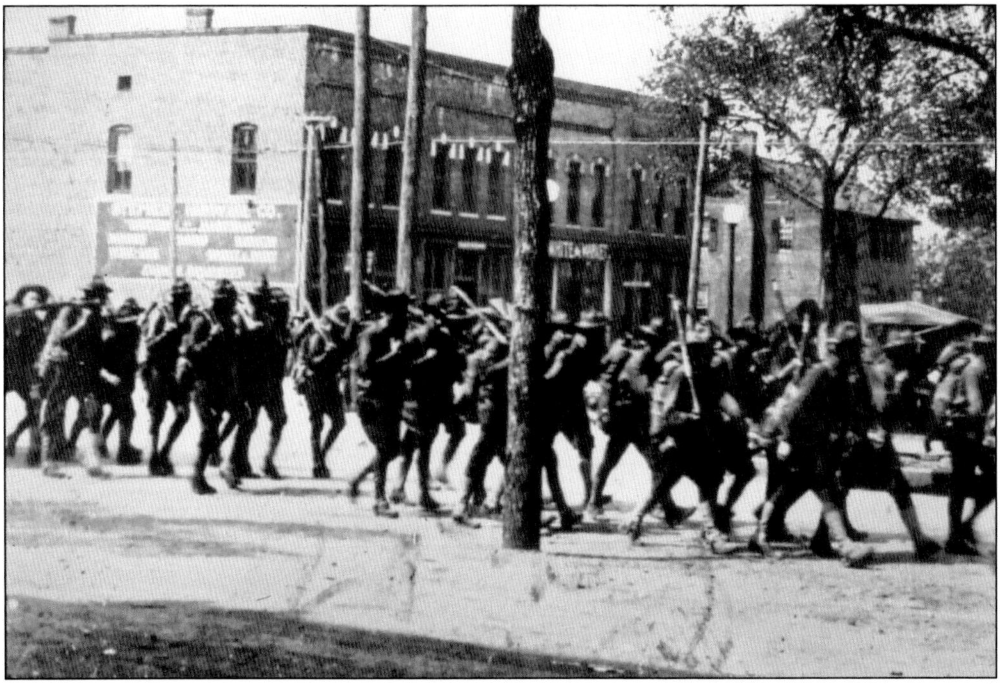

With the Stephenson Hardware Co. sign in the background, these World War I soldiers march north around the square. These soldiers were probably from Camp McClellan.

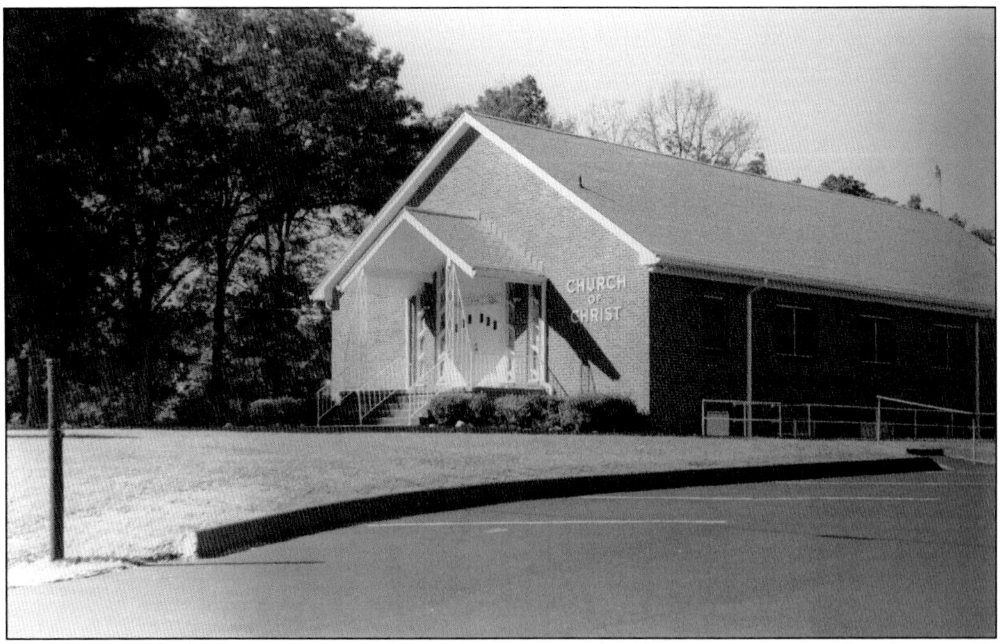

The Church of Christ congregation began meeting in a building with a tin roof and tin walls on Alexandria Road, near the mill. The members met there until 1925, when they moved into a building on Madison Street. In December 1960, the congregation moved into a much larger building (pictured here) on Nisbet Street. The congregation still worships here.

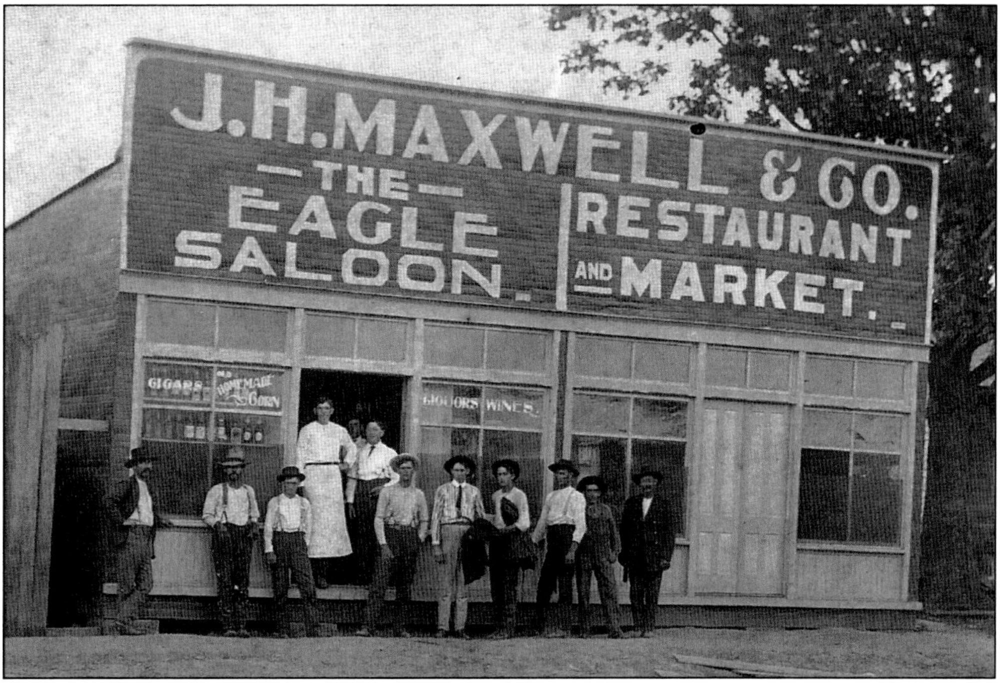

Shown below in a 1960s photograph, West Side Baptist Church began in 1919, when 100 percent of the members of Walnut Springs Baptist Church organized the new congregation, which met on the first and third Sundays. Services were held at an empty storefront in the building pictured above. The saloon was located on the west side of Mountain Street, just east of the Chief Ladiga Trail. The name was changed in 1921 to Jacksonville West Baptist Church and then, in the 1940s, to West Side Baptist Church. (Above, courtesy of Mrs. Homer Barnwell; below, courtesy of Jacksonville Public Library.)

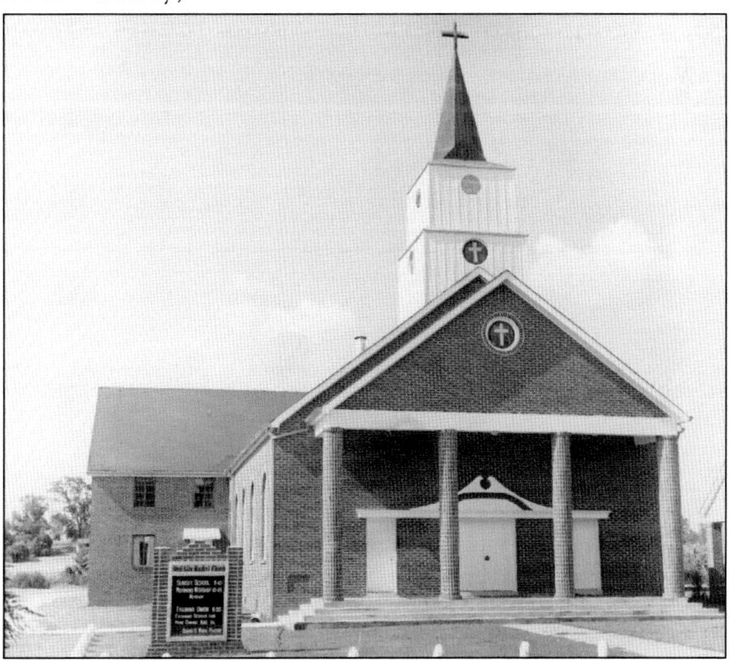

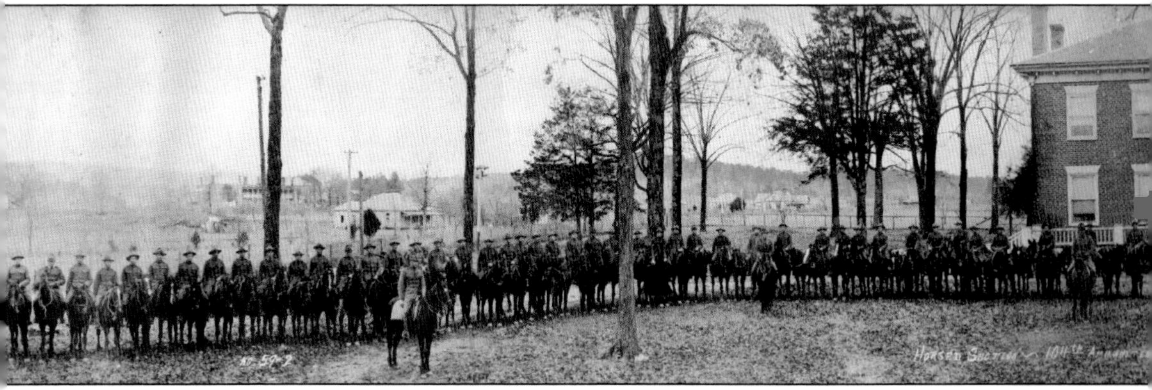

The photograph shows the horse section of the 104th Ammunition Train mounted in front of William I. Greenleaf's home on February 14, 1918. The unit was part of the Richmond Light Infantry Blues (1st Squadron, Cavalry), 29th Division (nicknamed the "Blue and Grey") that

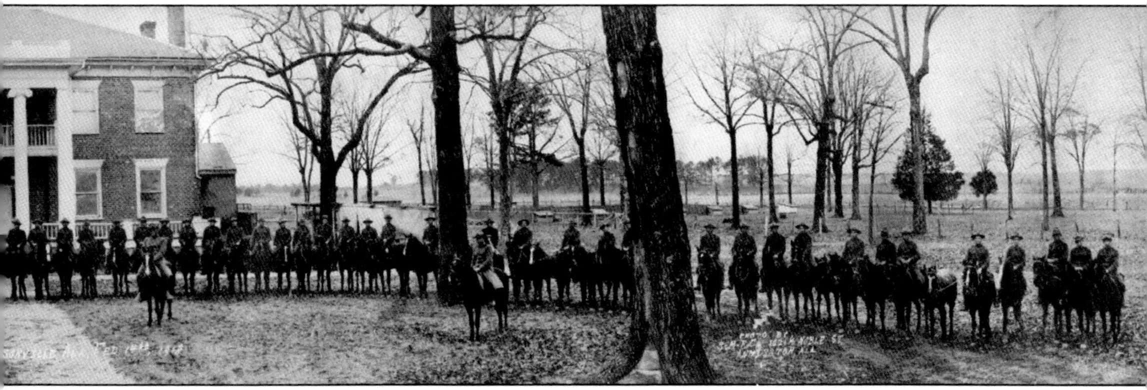

trained at Camp McClellan. The unit went to London on the ship *Medic* in June 1918 and then to Saint-Denis, France, in July 1918 and was moving to the front when the armistice was signed. Today, CVS Pharmacy and Hampton Inn are located where Greenleaf's home stood.

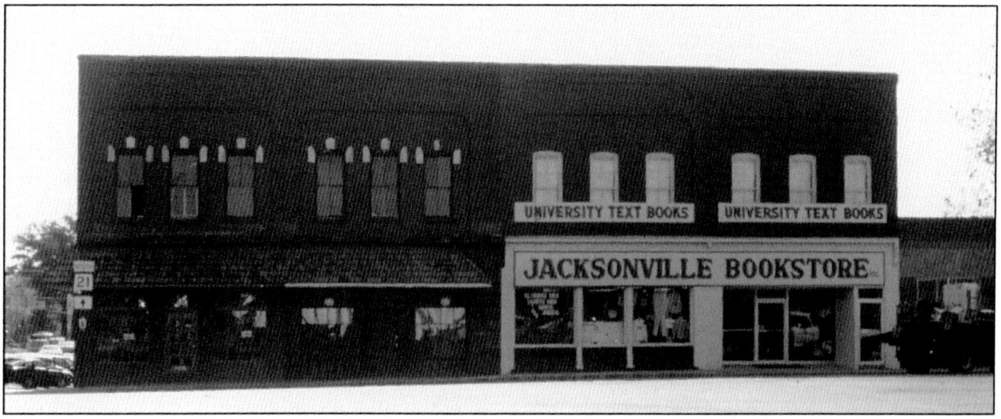

The building on the left in the above photograph is often referred to as Ramagnano's Corner. Built in 1875, it was a combination general merchandise store and warehouse. The first floor is separated into identical halves, and the second floor is an open room. John Ramagnano converted the upper floor in 1895 to an opera house with a seating capacity of about 200. Ramagnano initially rented the building, but he purchased it in 1897. The first moving picture shown, *Cinderella*, appeared in 1910. The building on the right, with the Jacksonville Bookstore sign, was erected in 1892. James H. Fryar operated a general store in the building. John Ramagnano, and later his son-in-law, Lee Burton, operated a saloon and pool hall in the east side of the building. The poolroom (below) operated from 1892 to 1917. The saloon operated from 1892 until the temperance movement successfully outlawed the sale of alcoholic beverages in 1917. The saloon had a back door accessible from the "Christians' Alley," a secluded walkway that led to the street behind the building.

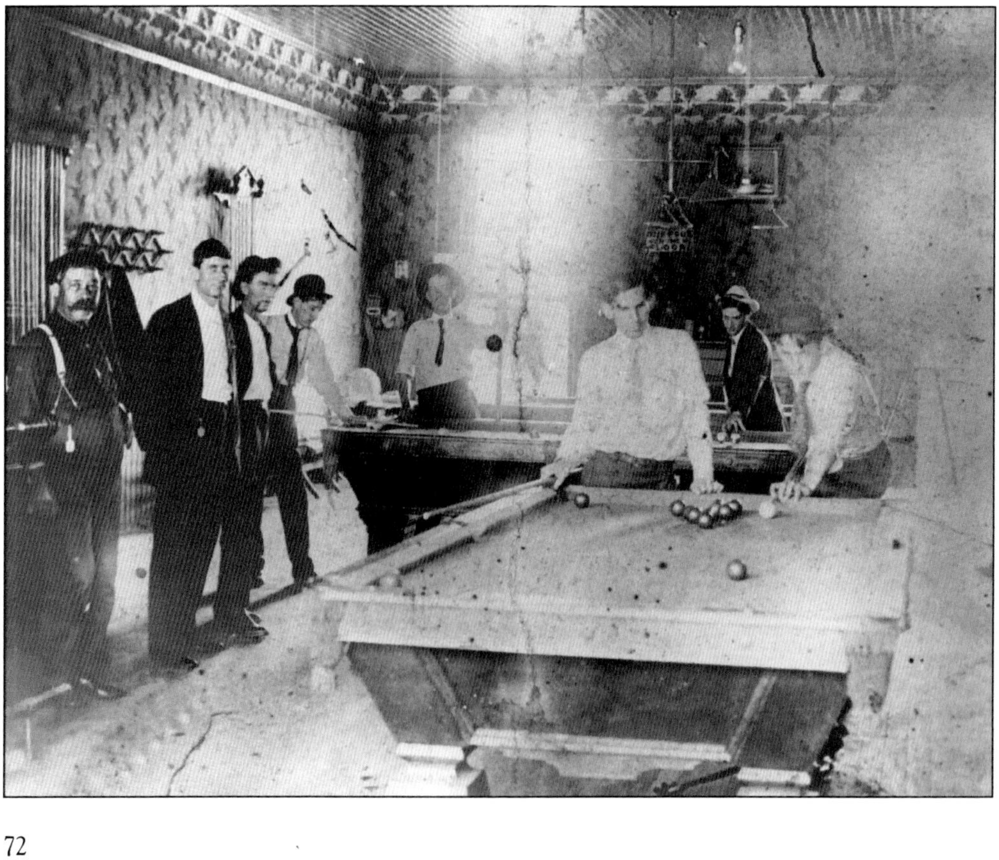

Four

1920 TO 1950

In 1933, Pres. Franklin D. Roosevelt signed legislation that created a minimum wage of $12 a week; Profile workers at the time made $7. In response to the new wage law, William I. Greenleaf, president of Profile Yarn Mills, offered the workers a raise of 25¢ per week. On August 2, 1933, the mill workers went on strike, and Greenleaf closed the facility. It was one of the only times in the history of the labor movement in the United States that management closed a mill in response to a strike. After a long and difficult strike, as Rick Bragg says, "By the winter of '33, the workers had all they could stand and went back to work." In a dispute with the major stockholders of the Profile Yarn Mills, William Greenleaf resigned as company president in April 1934, six months after the end of the strike.

As with other small towns across the country, the Depression and World War II created hardships in Jacksonville, including the mill issuing its own currency. Fortunately, enrollment at the college continued, and the college was able to erect a few new buildings.

As the troops returned home, Jacksonville began to grow. Churches built additions or erected completely new buildings. Businesses expanded, and enrollment at the college exploded. Enrollment expanded so quickly that the college had to put up surplus Army barracks from Fort McClellan as temporary dormitory buildings all over the Spring Street campus.

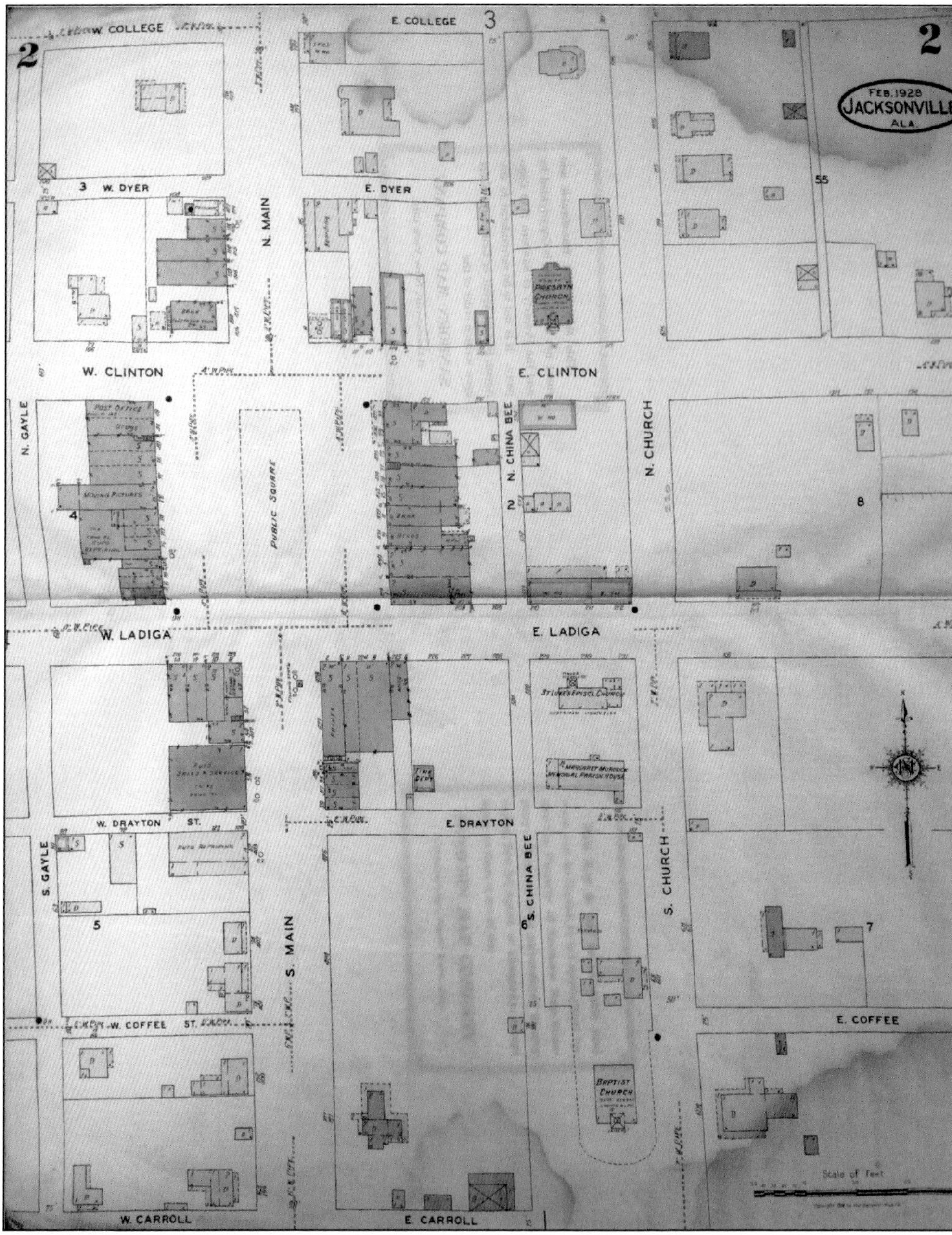

This 1928 Sanborn map shows Depression-era Jacksonville. Although there are no building lots on the east and west sides of the square, several building lots are vacant just off the square. The Iron Queen Hotel is gone from the map, as is the second courthouse.

The 1921 summer school attendees gather at the State Normal School. The girls' dormitory (Weatherly Hall) is directly behind the group, and Hames Hall is at right. (Courtesy of Jacksonville State University.)

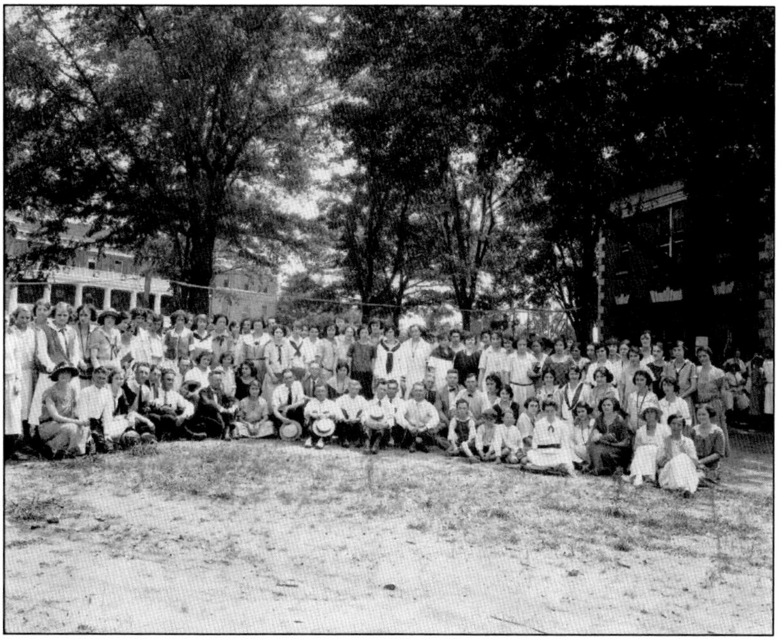

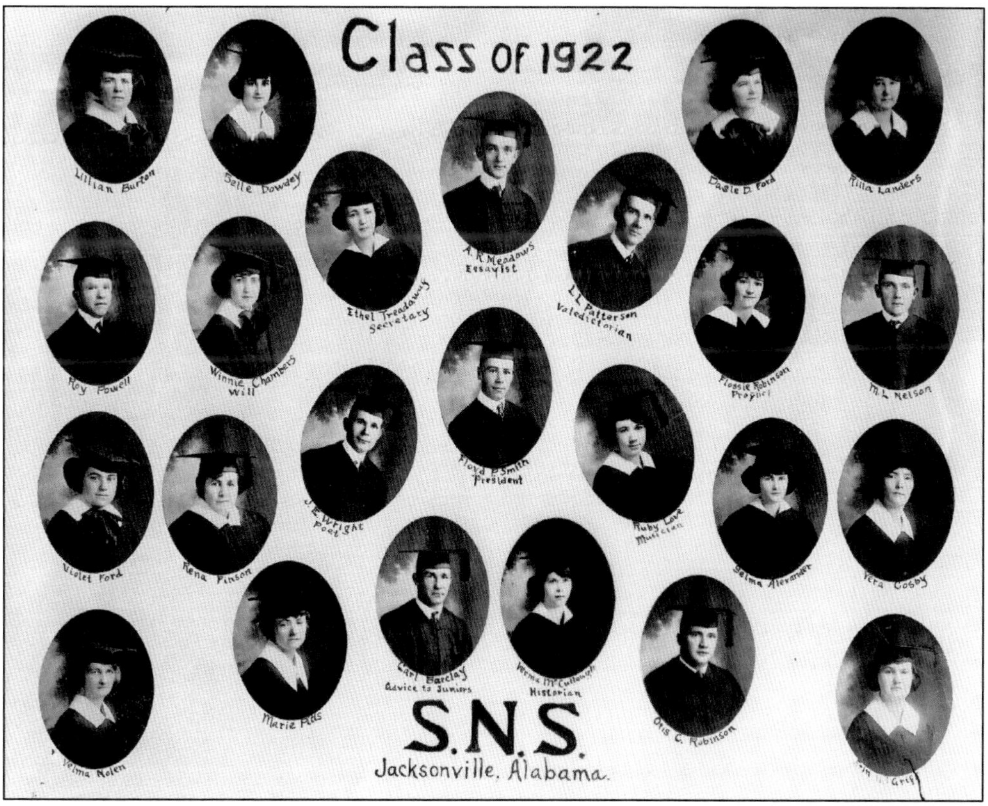

This composite photograph depicts the 1922 graduating class of the State Normal School. Most of these graduates went into the world to teach. (Public Library of Anniston–Calhoun County Alabama Room.)

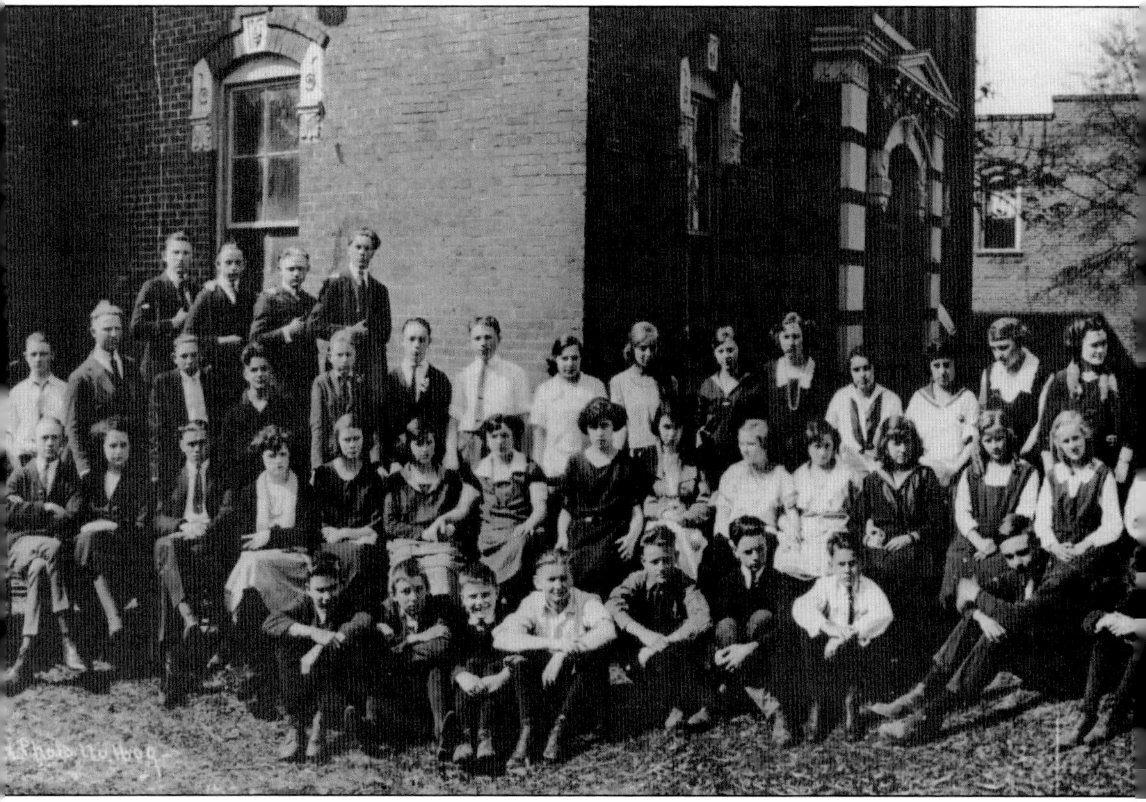

This 1922 photograph shows all the teachers and students of Jacksonville training school, including the high school, standing in front of the old courthouse. The school bounced back and forth between serving as the Jacksonville City School building and as the old courthouse for a number

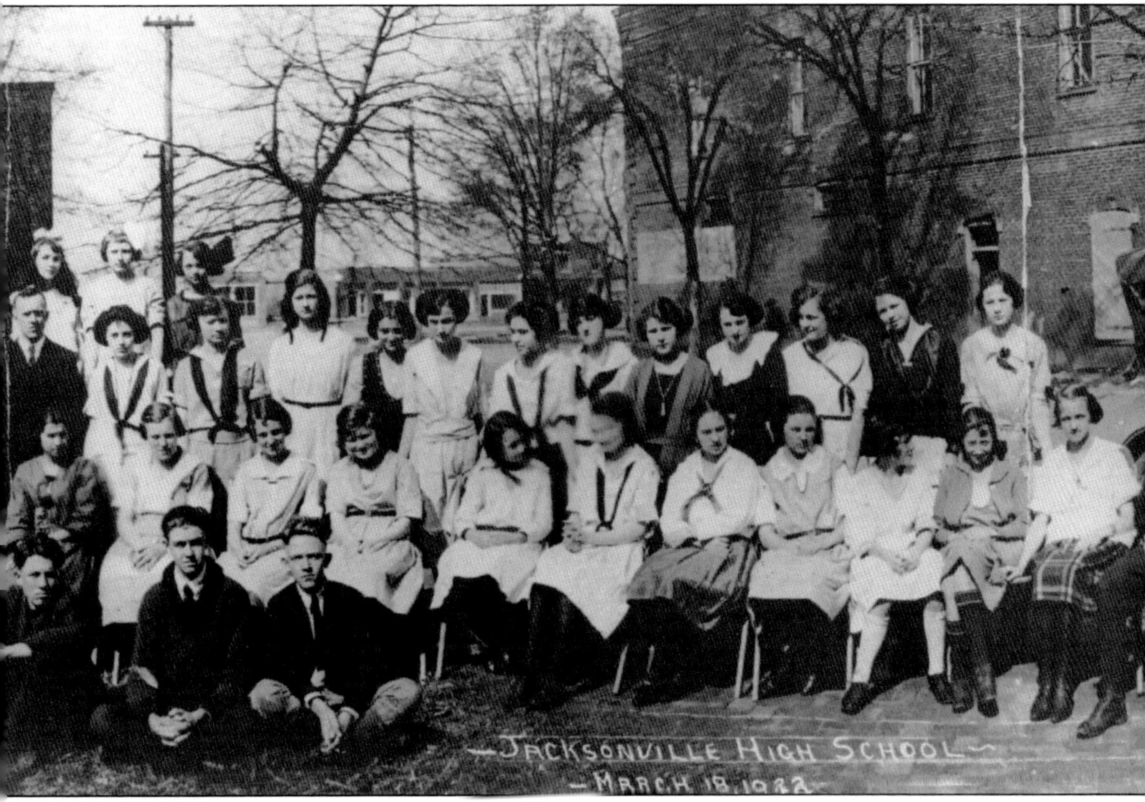

of years, until Kirby Hall was constructed. (Public Library of Anniston–Calhoun County, Russell Brothers Collection.)

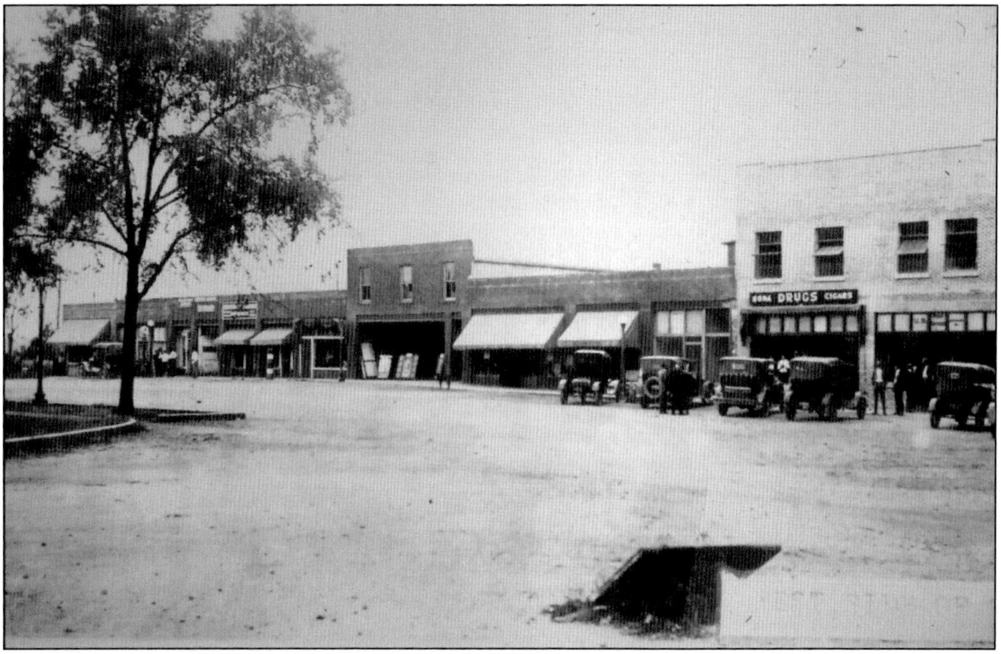

The above photograph shows the west side of the square in the 1920s. West Side Drug Store is on the far right of the photograph. The Princess Theatre is the two-story facade left of center. The four buildings on the right side of the photograph (to the right of the Princess Theatre) were built in 1923 by William I. Greenleaf. The below photograph shows the interior of West Side Drug Store. Posing for the photographer are, from left to right, Pike Carpenter, Hubert Lester, an unidentified man (rear, left), Hoke Rowan (in a suit, standing in front), an unidentified man, Lucille Rowan, R.T. Knight (wearing cap), Mrs. William I. Greenleaf, and Steve Greenleaf. In 2014, Cardio Zone is located at the site of West Side Drug Store, and Nails and Spa is in the former post office space. (Above, courtesy of Jacksonville Public Library; below, courtesy of Mrs. Homer Barnwell.)

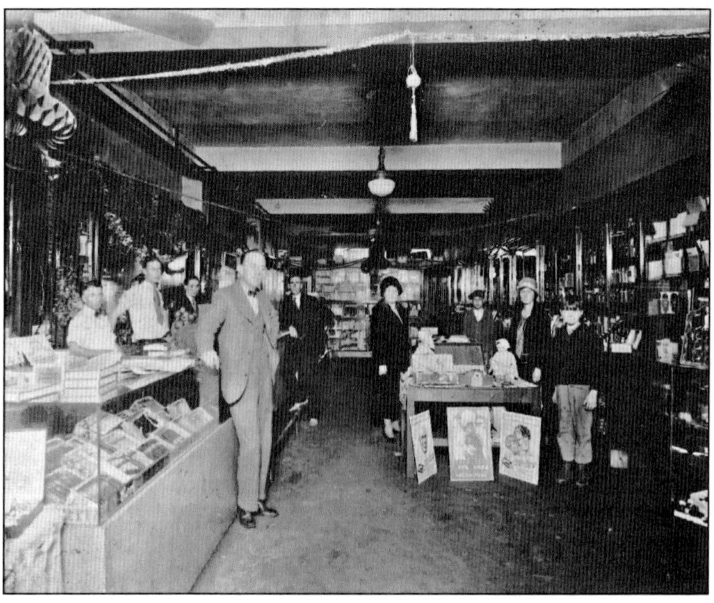

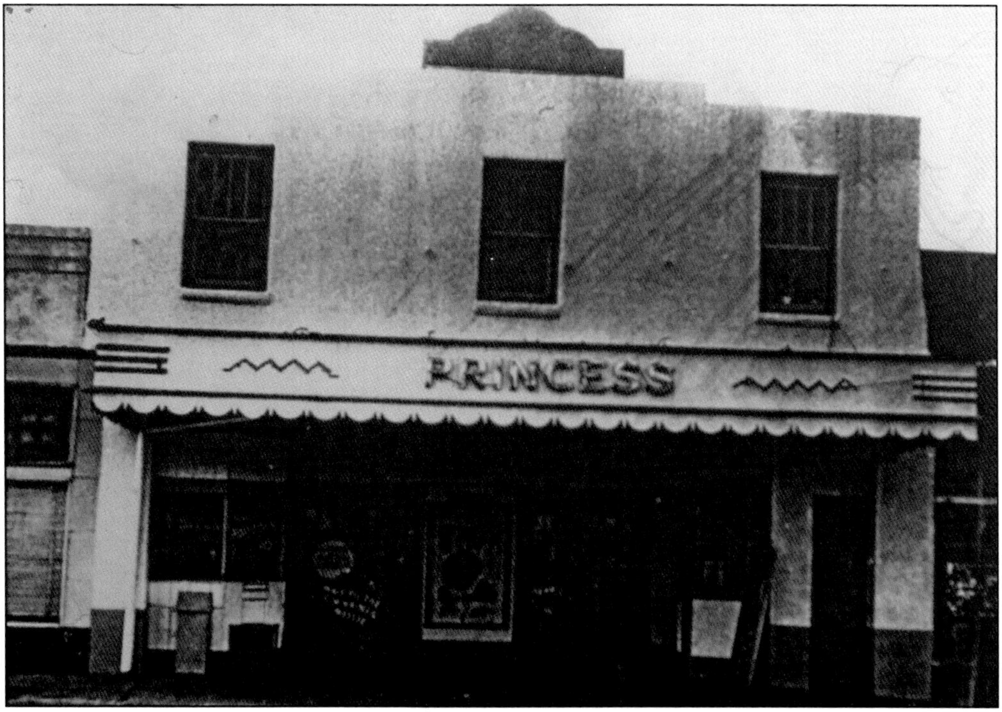

The Princess Theatre was in a two-story building in the middle of the west side of the square. The small door on the left of the photograph led to the segregated balcony. The building was erected in 1922 specifically for the Princess. The venue closed in the 1950s.

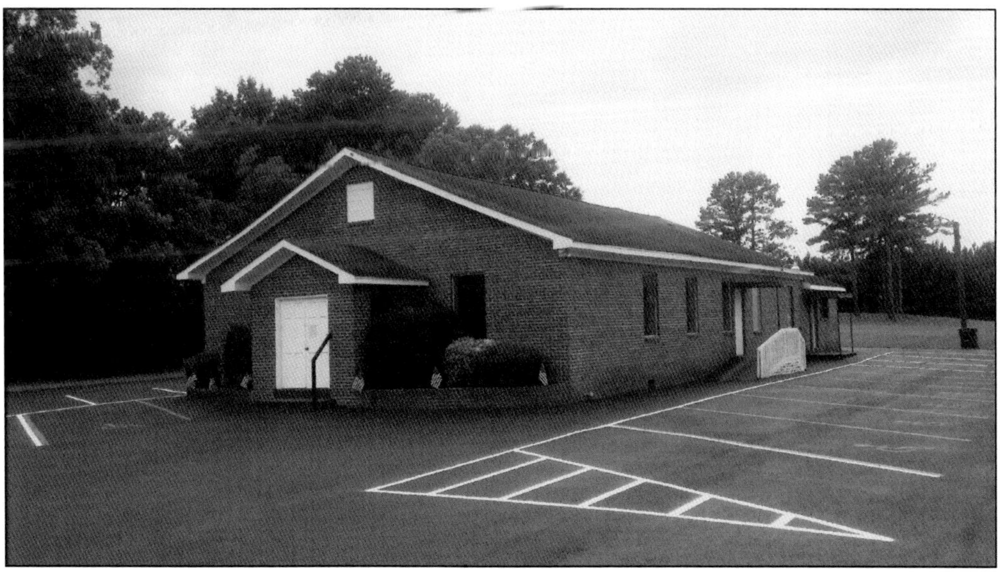

This congregation began in the 1920s after a "brush arbor" meeting with Rev. D. Little. In 1927, the church became organized and erected a building in 1928. The church burned down in 1932. The current structure was built in 1938, and a brick veneer was added in 1959. The nickname for the church in the mill village was the "hog pen church," because of the communal hog pen at the end of the street next to the church. The hogs could come up the creek right beside the church. (Nisbet family collection.)

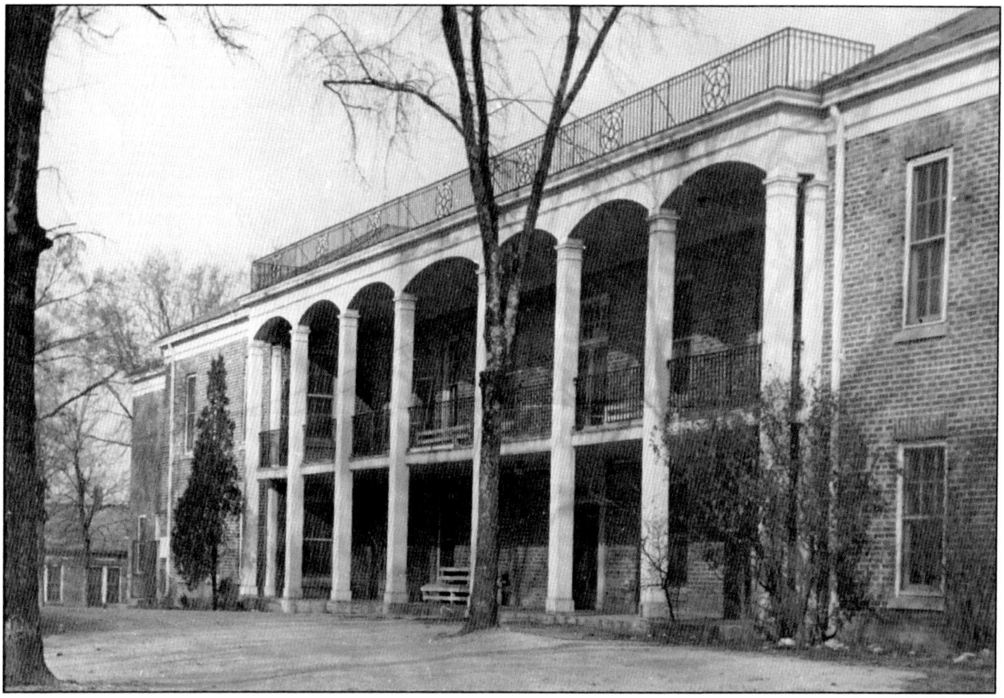

The undated photograph above shows the poor folks' home at the intersection of South Church Street and White's Gap Road. Used in this capacity during the Depression, the buildings have, since the 1940s, served as a trade school. The carpenter shop is shown below. (Both, courtesy of Mrs. Homer Barnwell.)

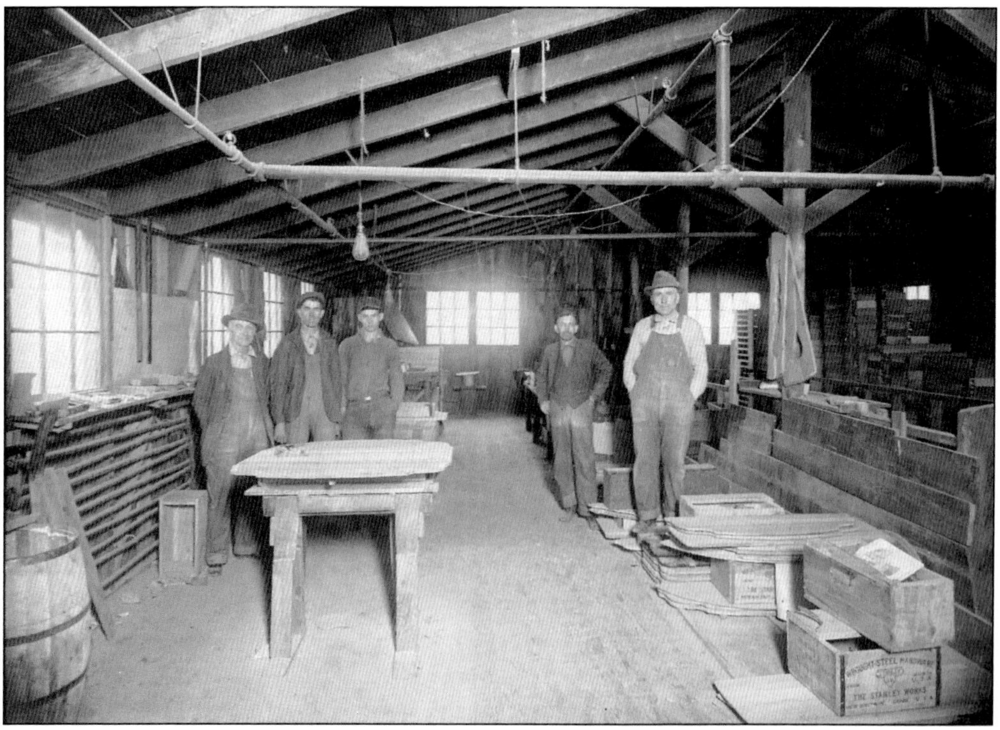

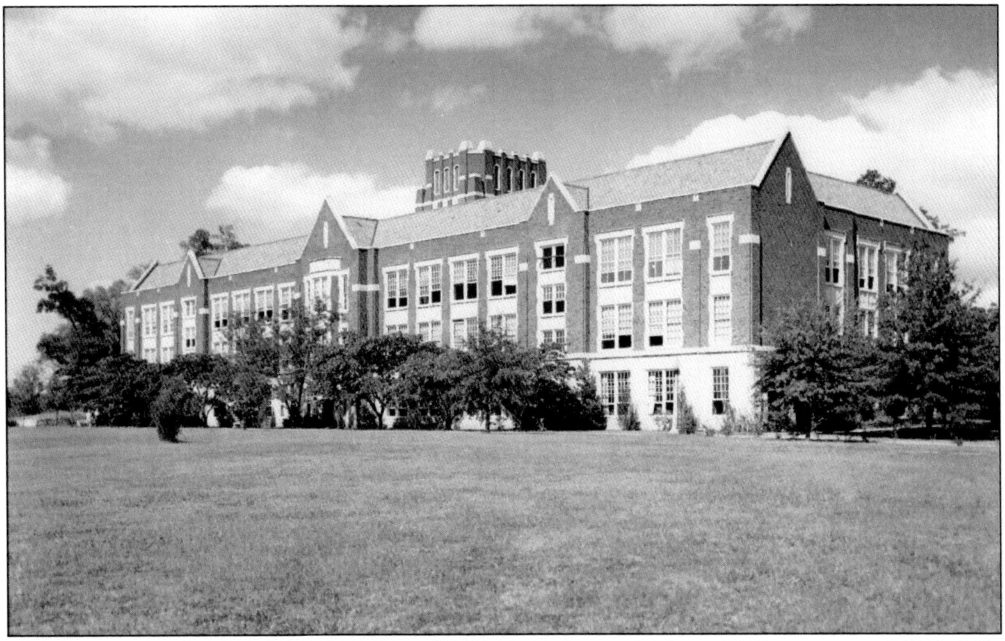

Bibb Graves Hall, named for Gov. David Bibb Graves, was built in 1930 at a cost of $300,000. The building originally housed classrooms, administrative offices, and, on the third floor over the main entrance, a library. (Courtesy of Jacksonville State University.)

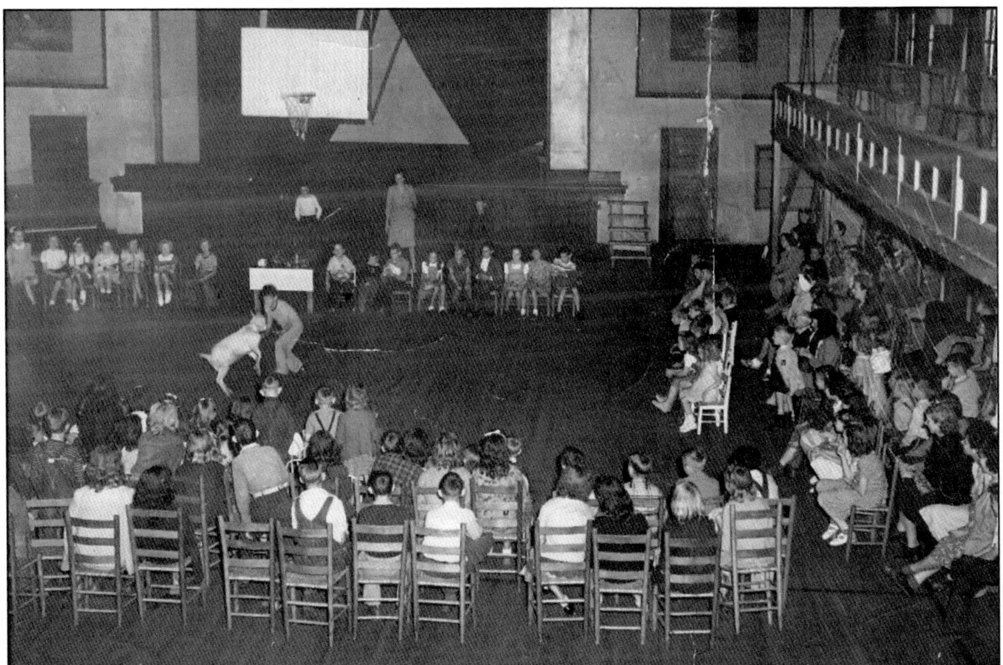

Apparently, goats came to school in Jacksonville. This 1940s photograph shows an assembly in the Kirby Hall gym. Weekly assemblies occurred in the auditorium into the 1970s. During assemblies, a class would put on a custom play to entertain all of the school's students, who processed into the gym by class, carrying their chairs. (Courtesy of Mrs. Homer Barnwell.)

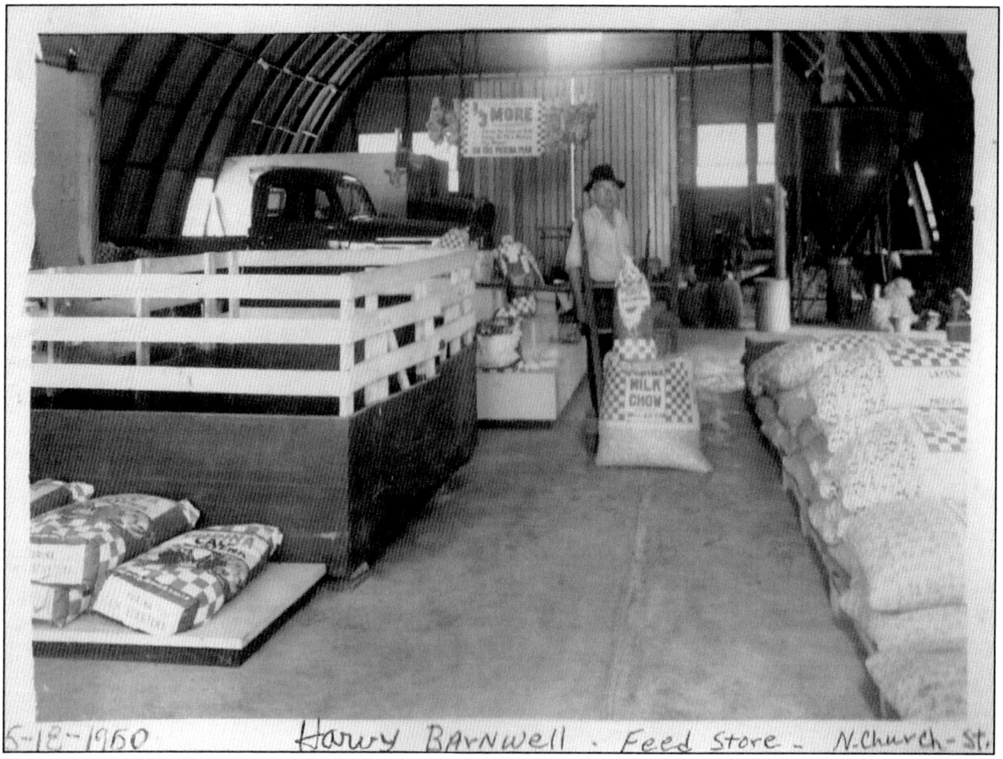

Harry Barnwell is hard at work at the feed store on North Church Street on May 18, 1950. The feed store was in a Quonset hut on the west side of Church Street, just south of East Francis Avenue. (Courtesy of Mrs. Homer Barnwell.)

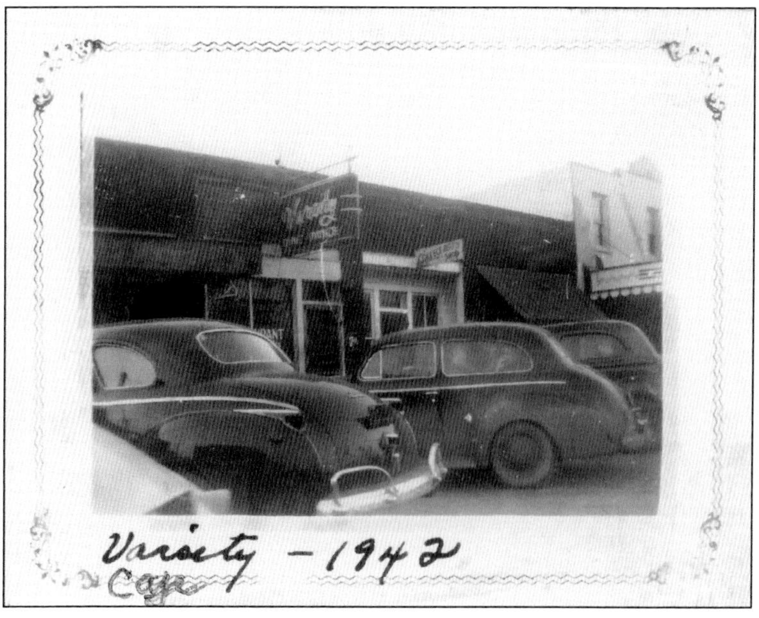

This 1942 photograph shows the Varsity Café, adjacent to the Princess Theatre on the west side of the square. (Courtesy of Mrs. Homer Barnwell.)

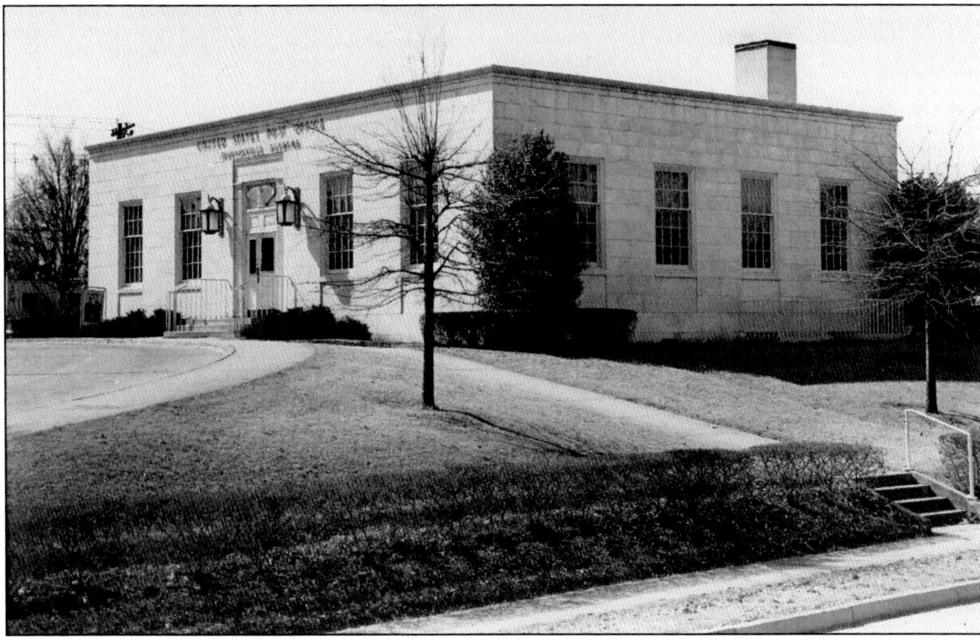

Built by the Work Projects Administration, this Alabama marble building was completed in May 1941. J. Thomas Martin was the first postmaster. Jacksonville has had a post office since 1835, when John Lawson was the postmaster. In 1984, the Mildred Johnson Memorial Library moved into this building and was renamed the Jacksonville Public Library.

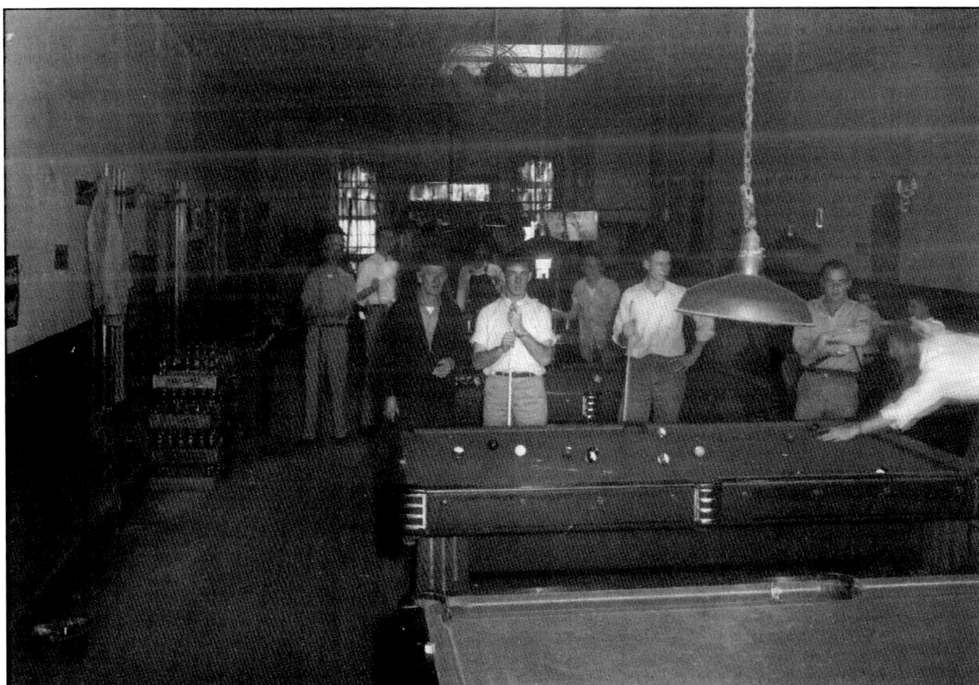

Shown here in 1946, Austin's pool hall was a popular place. Homer Barnwell is second from right with the pool rack under his arm. Louis Snider is on the far right. (Courtesy of Mrs. Homer Barnwell.)

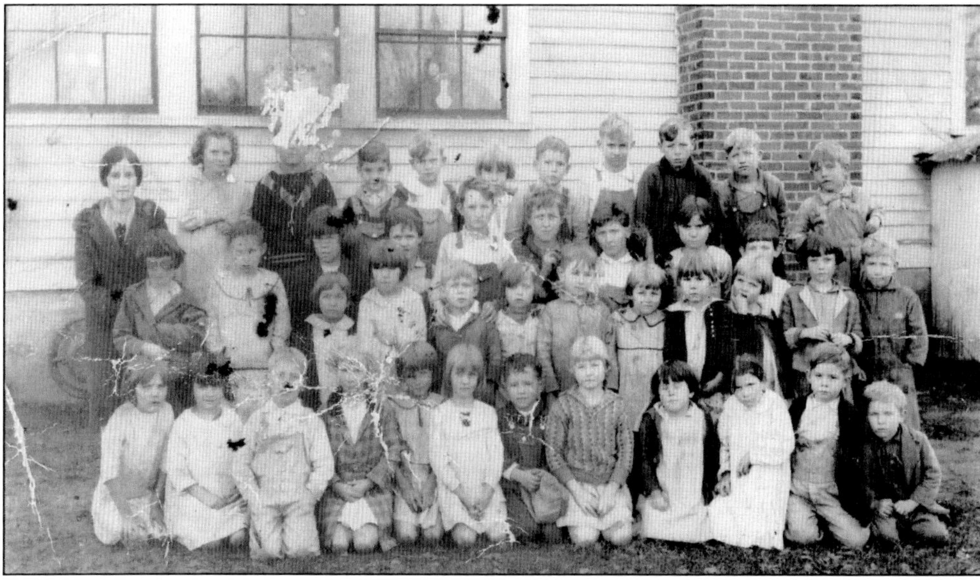

The above photograph shows Miss Heathcock's 1929–1930 class at Profile Mill Village School. Posing for the photographer are, from left to right, the following: (first row) Maudie Webb, Fannie Mae Bragg, Jessie Jenkins, Collette ?, unidentified, Ruth Wilkerson, J.D. Murray, Kathryn Homesley, Cora Turner, Mammie Ledbetter, John Edward Hammett, and Paul Smith; (second row) Dempie Drake, unidentified, Edna Scott, three unidentified students, Joe Edward Hays, Johnnie Homesley, Evelyn Barnwell, unidentified, Juline Ford, and Lewis Smith; (third row) Annie Turner, Charles Snider, Early Bragg, Ramsey Huggins, Carl Ledbetter, Pauline Wilkerson, and unidentified; (third row) Lois Heathcock (teacher), two unidentified students, Gene Hammett, unidentified, Vinnie Wilkerson, unidentified, Cleve Hammett, unidentified, Harry Homesley, and Lamar Goodwin. According to the annual report filed by Ethel W. Posey for the school year 1932–1933 (below), the Profile school was a four-teacher elementary school with 147 children in six grades. (Above, courtesy of Mrs. Homer Barnwell; below, Nisbet family collection.)

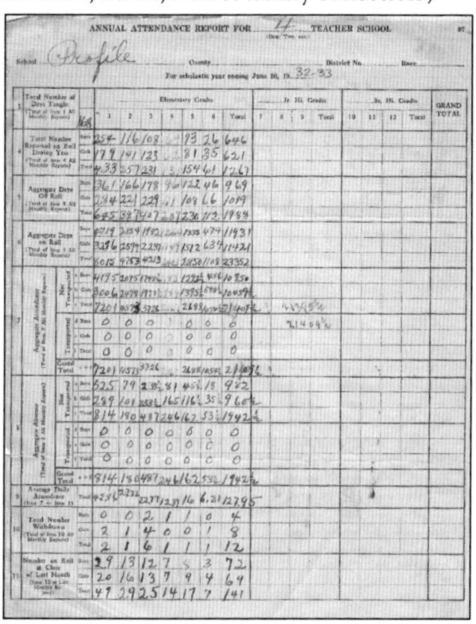

ANNUAL ATTENDANCE REPORT FOR 4 TEACHER SCHOOL

School Profile County District No. Race

For scholastic year ending June 30, 19 32-33

Item		1	2	3	4	5	6	Elementary Total	Jr. Hi. 7	8	9	Total	Sr. Hi. 10	11	12	Total	GRAND TOTAL
1 Total Number of Days Taught	168																
4 Total Number Reported on Roll During Year	Boys	254	116	108	[illegible]	93	26	646									
	Girls	179	141	123	[illegible]	81	35	621									
	Total	433	257	231	[illegible]	154	61	1267									
5 Aggregate Days Off Roll	Boys	361	166	178	96	122	46	969									
	Girls	284	221	229	[illegible]	108	66	1019									
	Total	645	387	407	207	230	112	1988									
6 Aggregate Days on Roll	Boys	2719	2154	1982	[illegible]	1333	474	11931									
	Girls	3296	2599	2231	[illegible]	1572	634	11421									
	Total	6015	4753	4213	[illegible]	2850	1108	23352									
7 Aggregate Attendance, Not Transported	Boys	4195	2075	[illegible]	[illegible]	[illegible]	[illegible]	10950									
	Girls	3006	2498	[illegible]	[illegible]	1395½	[illegible]	10459½									
	Total	7201	4573	3726	[illegible]	2688	[illegible]	21409½									
Transported	Boys	0	0	0	[illegible]	0	0	0		21409½							
	Girls	0	0	0	[illegible]	0	0	0									
	Total	0	0	0	[illegible]	0	0	0									
Grand Total		7201	4573	3726	[illegible]	2688	1059½	21409½									
8 Aggregate Absence, Not Transported	Boys	525	79	233½	81	45½	18	982									
	Girls	289	101	253½	165	116½	35½	960½									
	Total	814	180	487	246	162	53½	1942½									
Transported	Boys	0	0	0	0	0	0	0									
	Girls	0	0	0	0	0	0	0									
	Total	0	0	0	0	0	0	0									
Grand Total		814	180	487	246	162	53½	1942½									
9 Average Daily Attendance	Total	42.86	27.22	22.37	12.39	16	6.21	127.95									
10 Total Number Withdrawn	Boys	0	0	2	1	1	0	4									
	Girls	2	1	4	0	0	1	8									
	Total	2	1	6	1	1	1	12									
11 Number on Roll at Close of Last Month	Boys	29	13	12	7	8	3	72									
	Girls	20	16	13	7	9	4	64									
	Total	49	29	25	14	17	7	141									

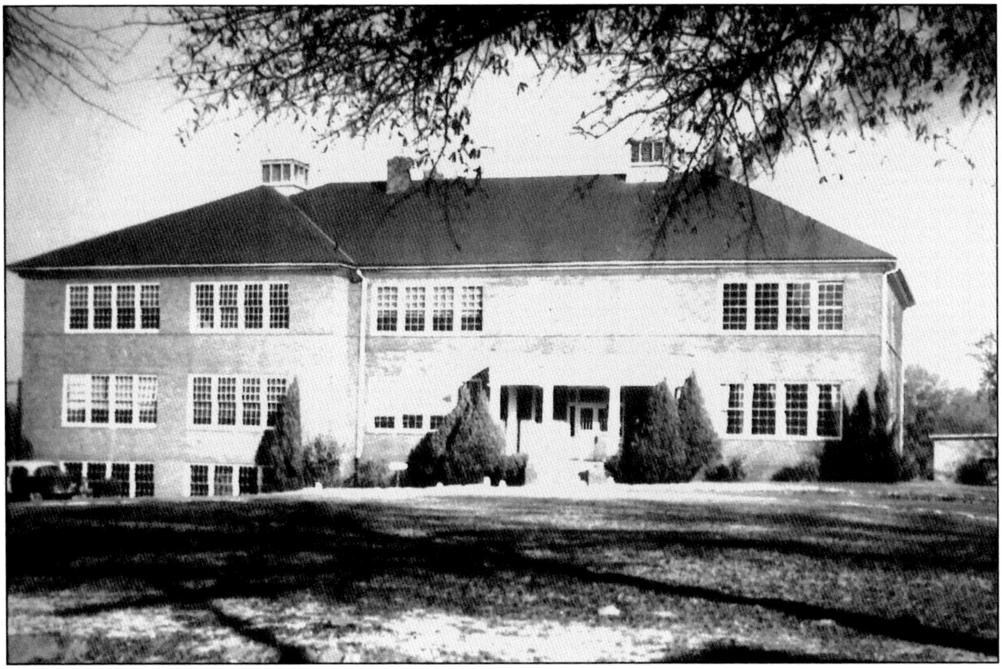

This 1950s photograph shows Jacksonville High School. The building was used by the State Normal School and its successor, State Teachers College/Jacksonville State College, from 1915 to 1948. Between 1919 and 1928, the west wing was added to the left side of the building pictured.

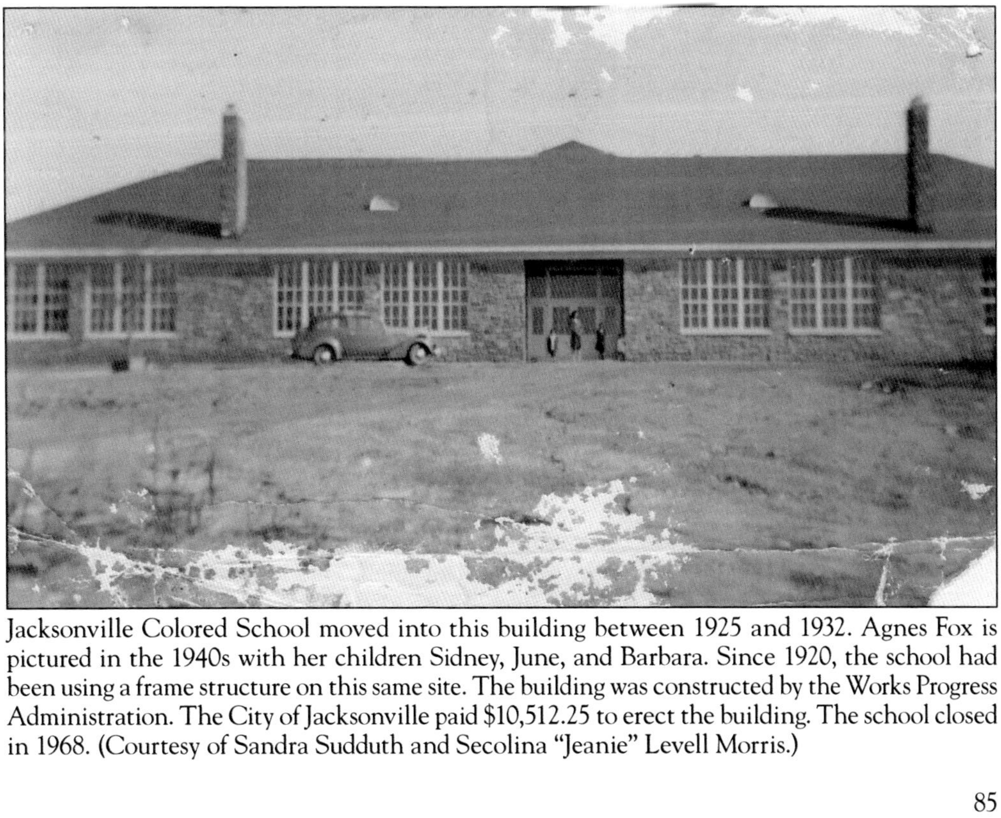

Jacksonville Colored School moved into this building between 1925 and 1932. Agnes Fox is pictured in the 1940s with her children Sidney, June, and Barbara. Since 1920, the school had been using a frame structure on this same site. The building was constructed by the Works Progress Administration. The City of Jacksonville paid $10,512.25 to erect the building. The school closed in 1968. (Courtesy of Sandra Sudduth and Secolina "Jeanie" Levell Morris.)

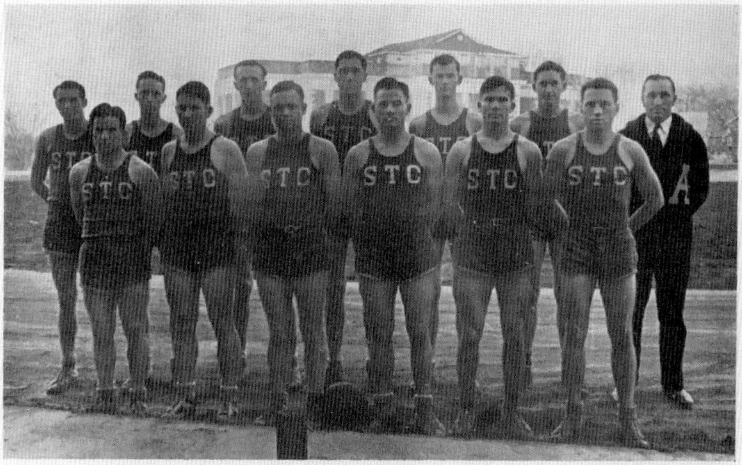

MEN'S BASKETBALL TEAM.

These photographs show the 1930 men's and women's basketball teams. The 1930 STC *Illustrated Bulletin* states that "we have each season splendid basketball teams for both boys and girls. Both teams have a record of victories over some of the best teams of the State this season. The boys won the Junior College Championship and the girls won the Junior and Senior College championships of Alabama for 1928 and 1929 [and 1919 and 1920]." (Both, courtesy of Jacksonville State University.)

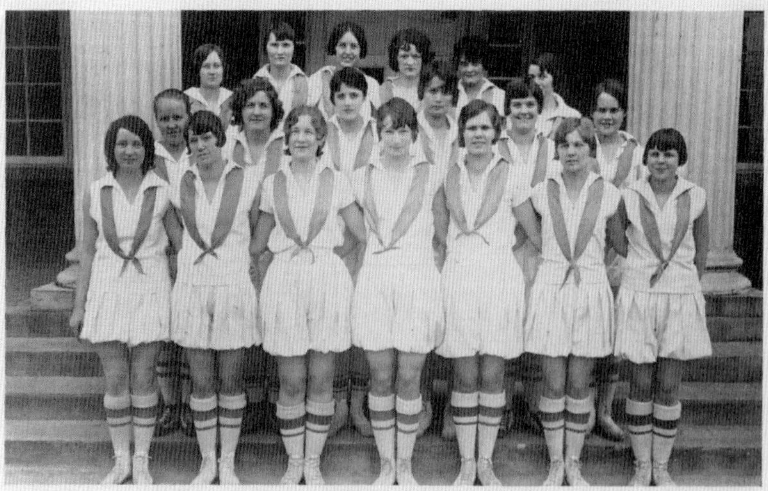

GIRLS' BASKETBALL TEAM—STATE CHAMPIONS OF ALABAMA 1929-1930.

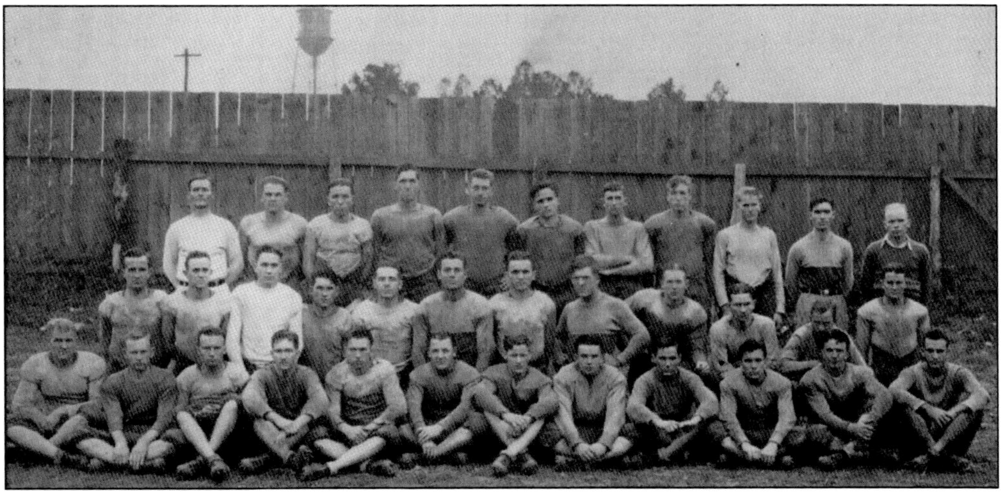

The 1931 State Teachers College football team poses for a photograph. The 1930 STC *Illustrated Bulletin* gives these superlative facts about the team: "No Junior College in the state has a better record of long standing than Jacksonville Normal had. Our team plays every year a very attractive schedule including some of the best Junior and Senior Colleges throughout this section. Prospects seem much better since we have gone on to a four-year basis." (Courtesy of Jacksonville State University.)

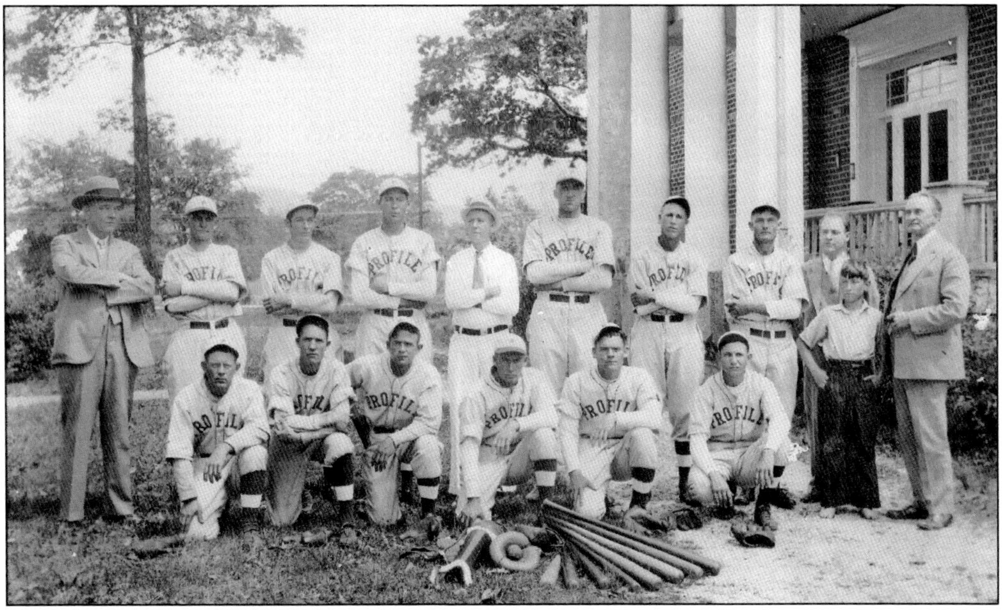

The Profile Mill workers were paid every other Saturday. The baseball games in the mill village, sometimes doubleheaders, took place on "Blank Saturday," the Saturday when the mill workers did not get paid. On these "blank" Saturday afternoons, after working a morning shift, the men played baseball. Large crowds often came to the games. Rick Bragg devotes an entire chapter about this team in *The Most They Ever Had*. Pictured here in 1932, standing on the front lawn of the Greenleaf home, are, from left to right, (first row) Van Hamilton, Jud Harrelson, Elk Hamilton, Clay Hammett, Leonard Little, and Homer Wilkerson; (second row) mill superintendent George Few, Bailey McClellan, Albert Slaught, Otto Burrows, manager Neal Lane, Bartow "Dago" Hughes, Sam Hill, Guy "Boss" Hammett, unidentified, Ivan Greenleaf, and W.I. Greenleaf.

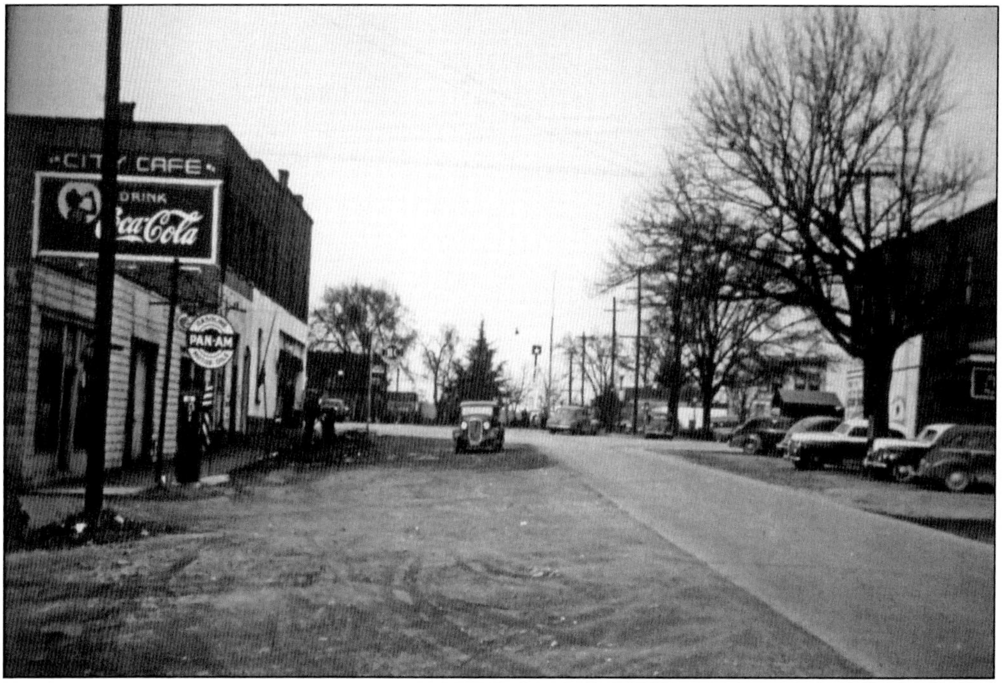

At left in the above photograph is an advertisement for the City Café. The profile of the woman drinking the bottle of Coca-Cola dates this photograph to the 1940s. The café is directly across Pelham Road from this sign. The below photograph shows the exterior of Curtis Powell's City Café taxi stand. Also in this photograph is Reid's Shoe Shop (far right). Although the City Café started in the taxi stand space, by the time the photograph was taken, Powell had moved the café to the south end of the building, on the other side of the shoe shop. (Above, courtesy of Jacksonville Public Library; below, courtesy of John Curtis Powell.)

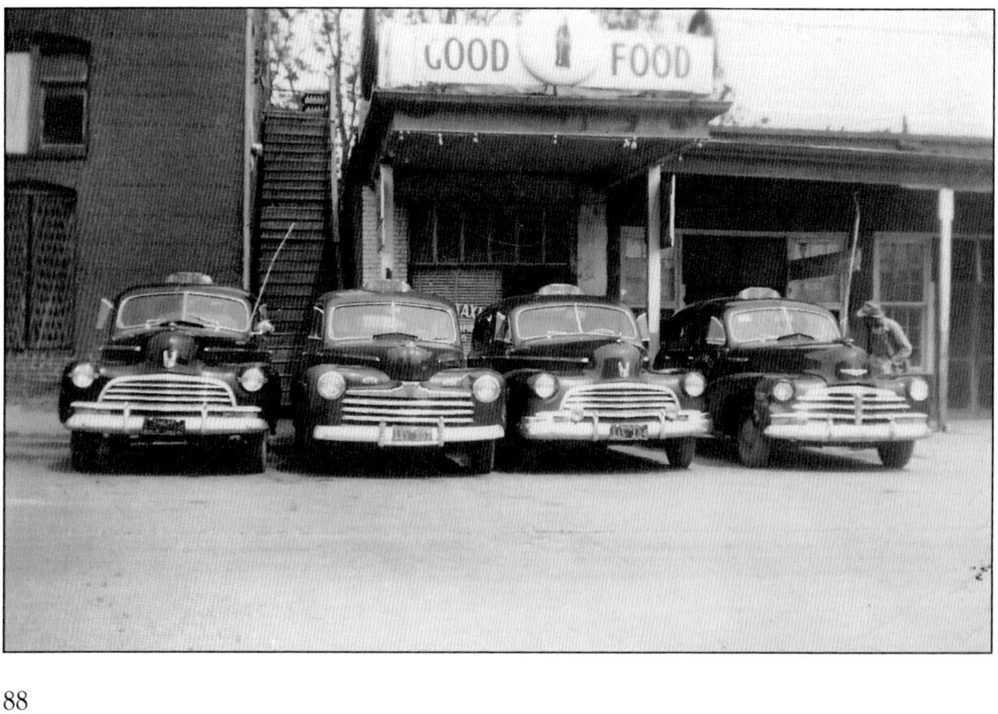

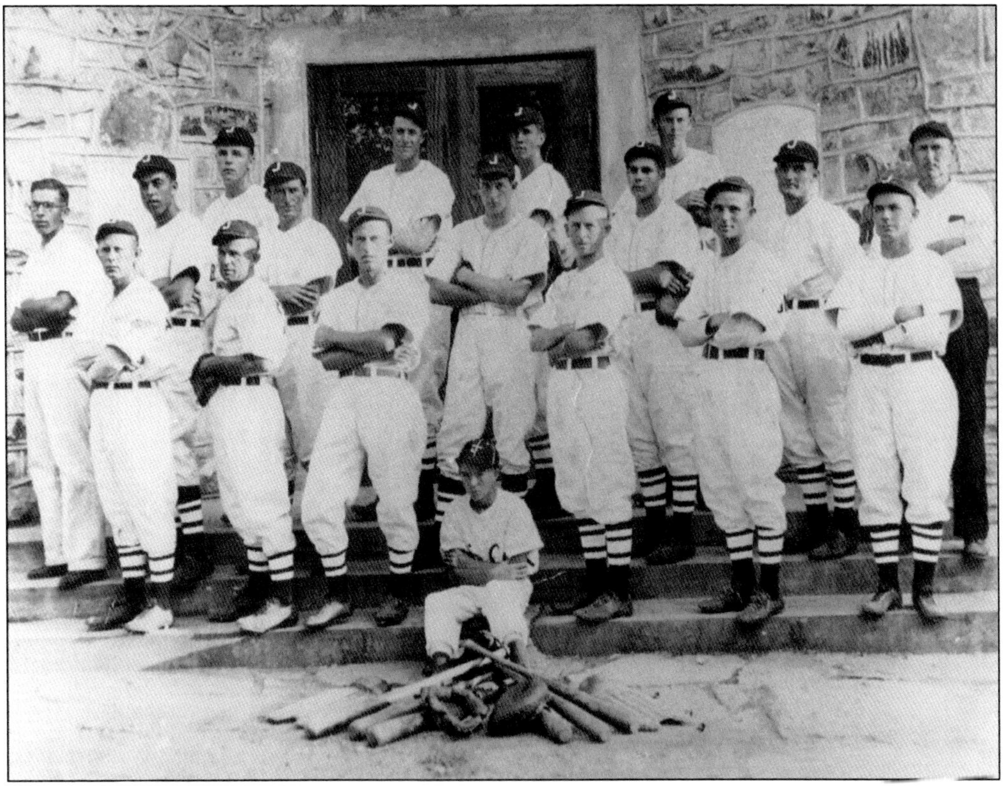

Members of the 1935 Profile baseball team stand on the steps of the newly completed City Hall. Shown here are, from left to right, the following: (first row) Van Hamilton, Elk Hamilton, Guy Key, Vallis Davis, John Medley, and Joe Martin; (second row) Edward Deason, Carl Rochester, Jim Champion, Woodrow Coheely, Johney Mac Ponder, Guy Boss Hammett, and Dascum Davis; (third row) Tal Porter, Arthur Snider, Bill Deason, and Troy Snider. The bat boy is James Edward Johnston. He was featured in a September 22, 1993, episode of the television series *Unsolved Mysteries*. In that episode, Bruce Kelly claims that he is the reincarnation of James Johnston, who died on the USS *Shark* in the Makassar Strait in Indonesia on February 11, 1942. The show concluded that Bruce Kelly "is almost certain that he is the reincarnated Johnston." (Courtesy of Mrs. Homer Barnwell.)

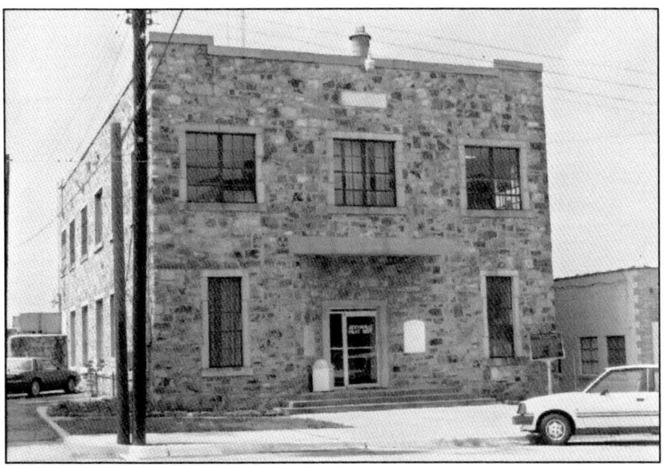

Completed in 1935 with Works Progress Administration labor, this building replaced the courthouse, which had burned down. This structure served as City Hall until the mid-1970s. Jail cells were built upstairs. In 2014, the police department occupies this building.

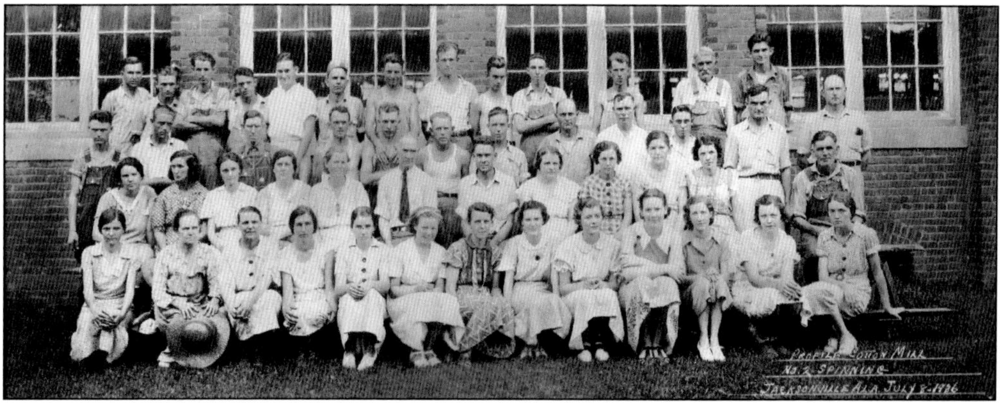

In July 1936, Profile Cotton Mill had photographs made of several shifts of its employees. This photograph, taken on July 8, 1936, is of No. 2 spinning shift. (Courtesy of Mrs. Homer Barnwell.)

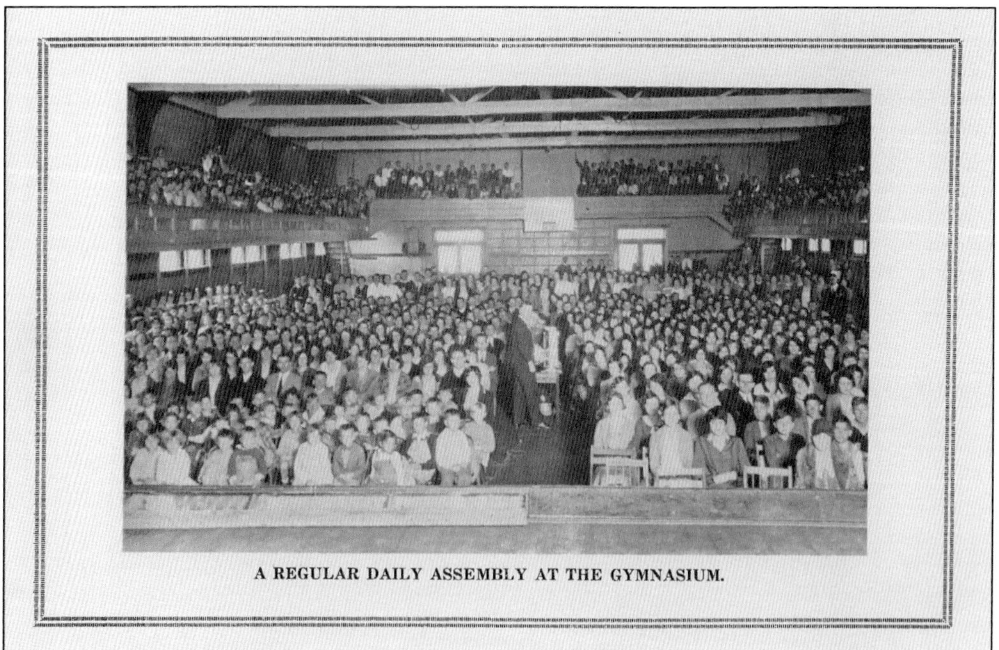

A REGULAR DAILY ASSEMBLY AT THE GYMNASIUM.

This 1930 photograph shows the interior of the gymnasium at Kilby Hall during a daily assembly of the State Teachers College and demonstration school. In 2014, the gymnasium is still in occasional use. The balcony has since been removed. (Courtesy of Jacksonville State University.)

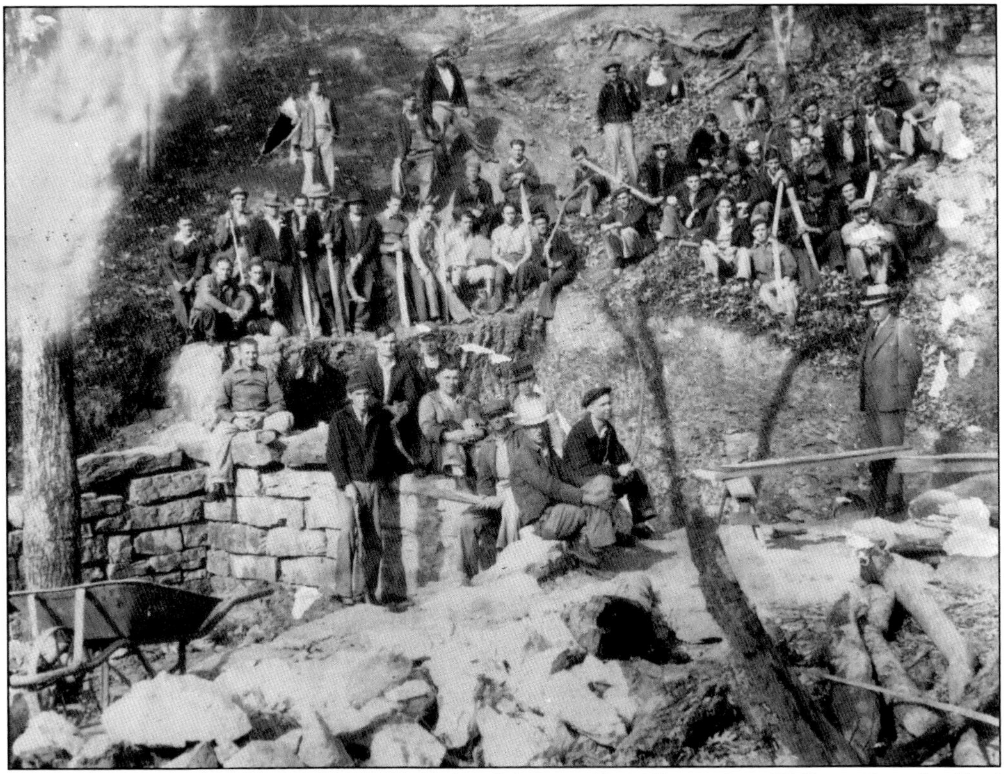

At some point in 1934 or 1935, a rumor circulated that Profile Mill president William Greenleaf had threatened to shut off the water supply to the mill village houses. This group of men confronted Jacksonville mayor Charles Stephens (at right in suit, tie, and hat) at the big springs. Note that all the men have some sort of ax handle except Guy W. Key, who has a noose (at left center with his left hand on his hip and a noose in his right hand on his right thigh). The men hanged Greenleaf in effigy at this event. Shown here holding wooden axe handles are, in no particular order, as follows: Columbus McColloum, Jack Harris, Guy "Boss" Hammett, Wence Snider, Roy Watts, ? Hudgens, Viles Davis, ? Hudgens, Joe Marin, John Medley, Matthew Turner, Luke Key, Eli Huidgens, Ardell White, Kermit Evans, Milas Davis, Bill Murray, John Garmon, Wilton Bedwell, Earl Hendrix, Forney Davis, Early Poole, Doug Smith, Buster Webb, Dewey Garmon, I.G. Morgan, Sam Patterson, Carl Ford, Bryce Harris, O.R. Deason, J.P. McCurry, George Robinson Jr., J.D. Murray, Rudolph Ponder, William Barnwell, Horace Holbrook, Irby Harp, Carl Ledbetter, John Goodwin, Huse Erwin, John Davis, and Jess Crook. (Courtesy of Mrs. Homer Barnwell.)

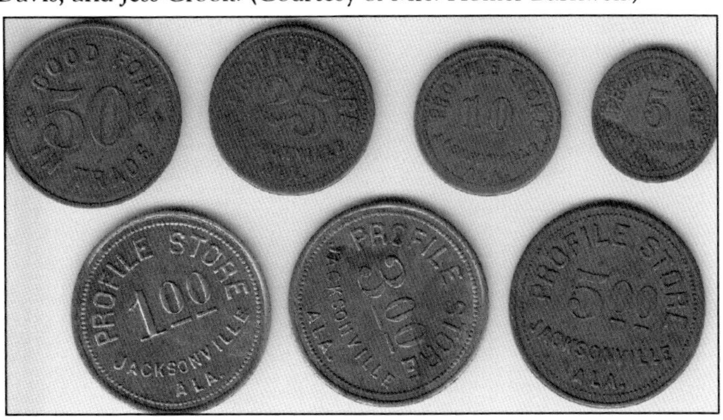

During the Great Depression, the Profile Mill paid its workers with these coins, nicknamed "clinkers." They could only be used at the company store. (John Henricks private collection.)

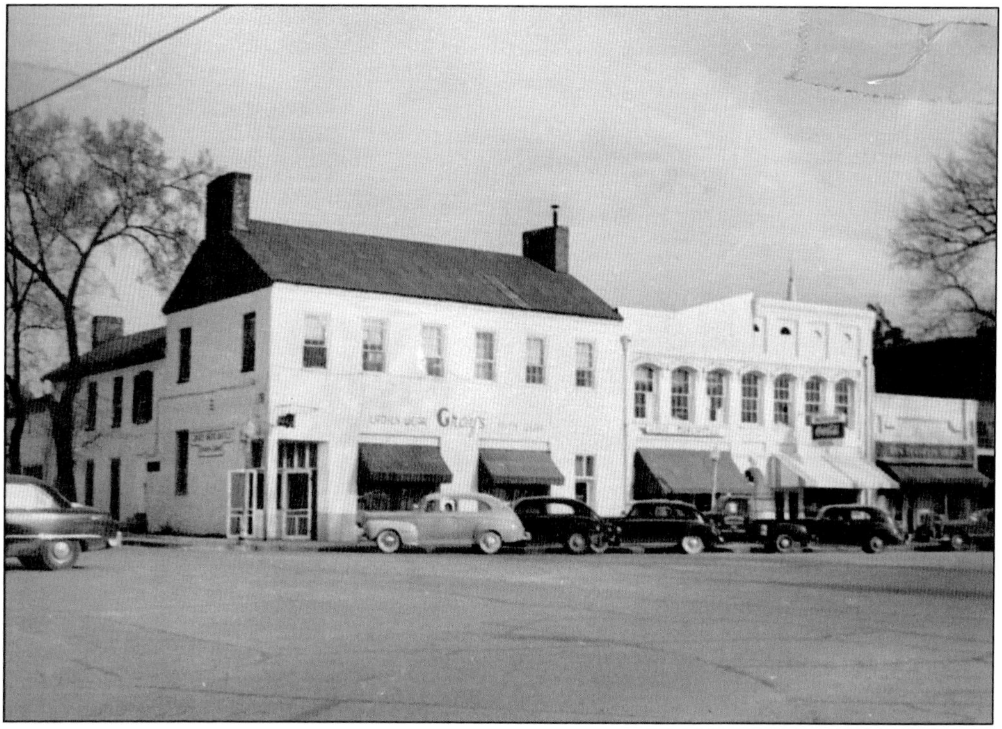

Located in the old brick tavern building, Grey's Store (above) operated from the 1930s to the 1960s. Posing in the below photograph, taken inside of Grey's, are, from left to right, unidentified, Mom Fillingham, Willie Seibert, and Grover Currier. (Above, courtesy of Jacksonville Public Library; below, courtesy of Mrs. Homer Barnwell.)

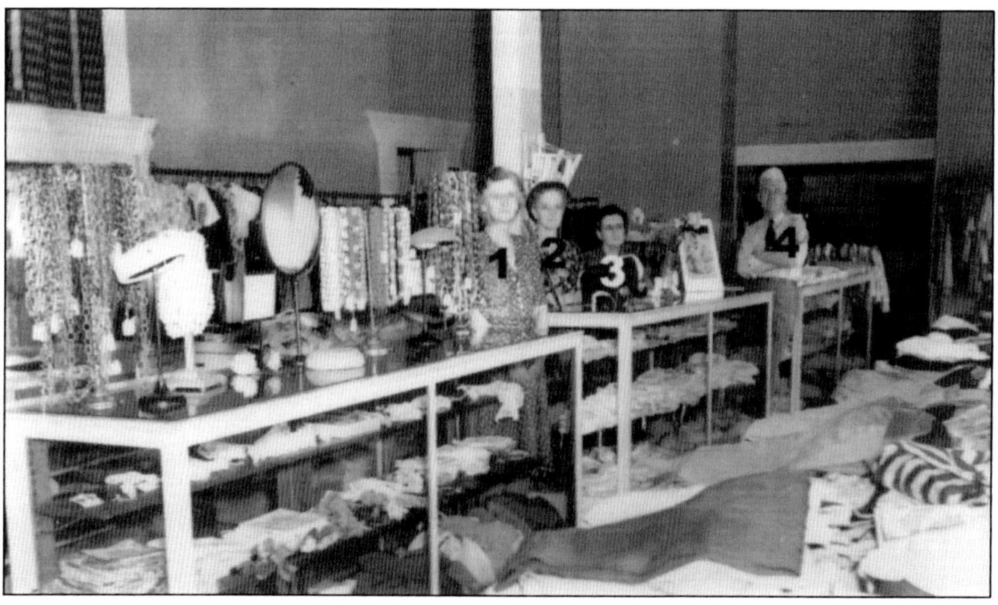

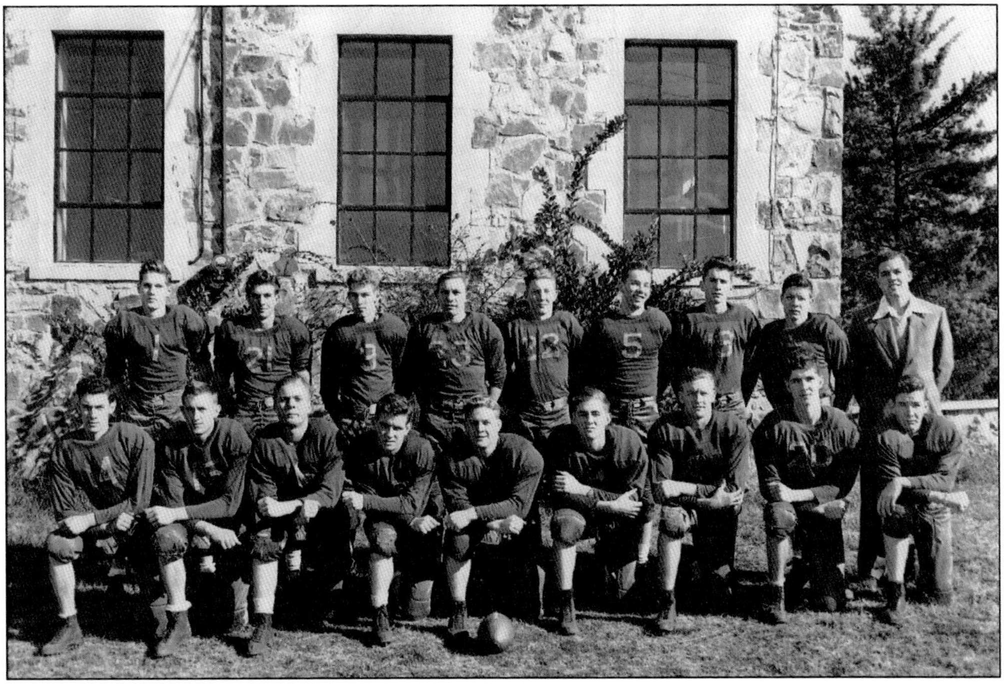

This is the 1946 Jacksonville High School varsity football team. Fort John Forney is in the background. According to the program from the October 25, 1946, game versus Piedmont, the team included the following players: James Heathcock, Benny Hilley, John Coppock, Ray Brittan, Wynsol Collier, Billy Jernigan, Tommy Boozer, J.C. Allsup, Dobbie Williams (captain), Jug Dryer, Talmadge Johnson, Ted Logan (captain), John Nisbet, Tommie Weaver, Steve Tyron, Tommy Ward, Jimmy Casey, Charles Hammet, Gordon Sides, Bobbie Dillion, Buddy Rogers, and Hebert Williamson. The Jacksonville High principal wrote in the game program, "Jacksonville is happy to visit with you this week. We are neighbors, and while we are both trying to win, we are first FRIENDS." The program suggests that "it would be a mighty fine spirit of cooperation if the students who attend the games would stay in their section and help the cheer leaders root for their team. By all means don't run up and down the sidelines during the game." (Nisbet family collection., image by Lance Johnson Studio used with permission.)

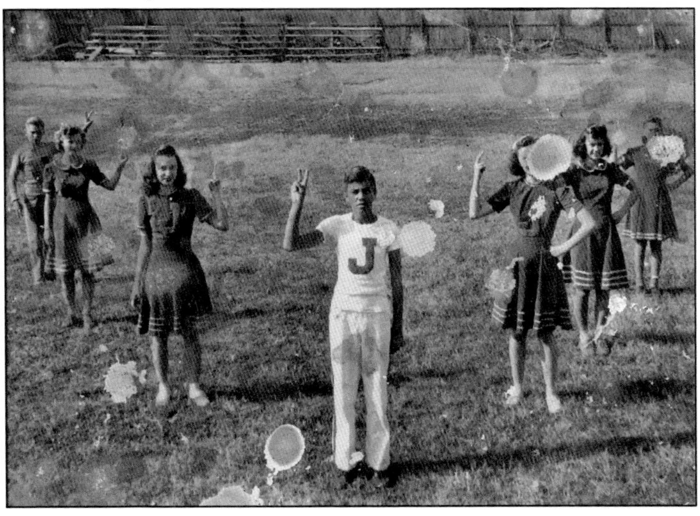

The 1947 Jacksonville High School varsity cheerleaders pose for a photograph. They appear to be on the field at Paul Snow Stadium. Pictured here are, from left to right, Jane Self, Barbara Cagley, Roy Osborn, Jean Kilgore, and Dottie Sewell. (Nisbet family collection.)

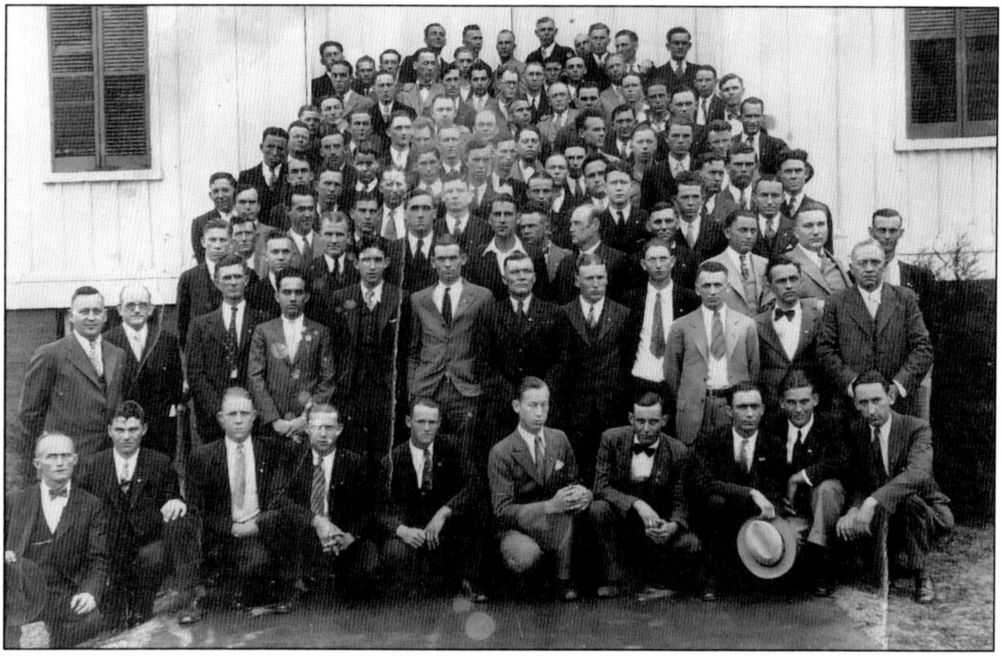

This is the First Baptist Church men's Sunday school class. Among those shown here are the following: Walt Weeks, Roy Watts, Monroe Bragg, Clifford Gore, William Veneable, Roy Webb, Paul Stewart, John Clark, Henry Burnham, Alton Boozer, Roy Bragg, Abey Cagle, ? Williams, James Bragg, Pike Carpenter, Roland Boozer, Larkin Rochester, Elkin Hamilton, Bascum Davis, Henry Baird, Paul Arnold, Olen Deason, John Medley, Elbert Ford, Lynn Boozer, Ferdie Marble, Bert Bragg, Carl Deason, Curt Powell, Eugene Peek, Johnny Ford, Henry Windy Lester, Gray Harrelson, Harvey Barnwell, Earl Allen, Floyd Gidley, Hurbert Jinkins, W.A. Fugua, Neal Lane, Macon Snider, Carl Dreyer, Charlie Martin, Malis Davis, Columbus McCollum, Cooper Parker, Floyd Owens, Ira Bragg, and Bailey McClellan. (Courtesy of Mrs. Homer Barnwell.)

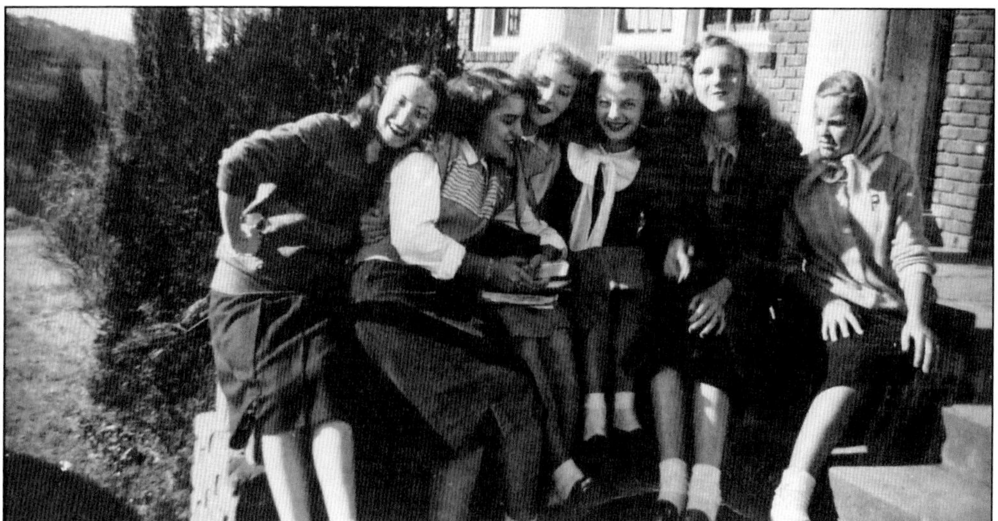

These girls are sitting on the front steps of the old Jacksonville High School building in 1946 or 1947. Among those shown here, in no particular order, are Jean Boozer, Wanda Mintz, and Betty Longshore. (Nisbet family collection.)

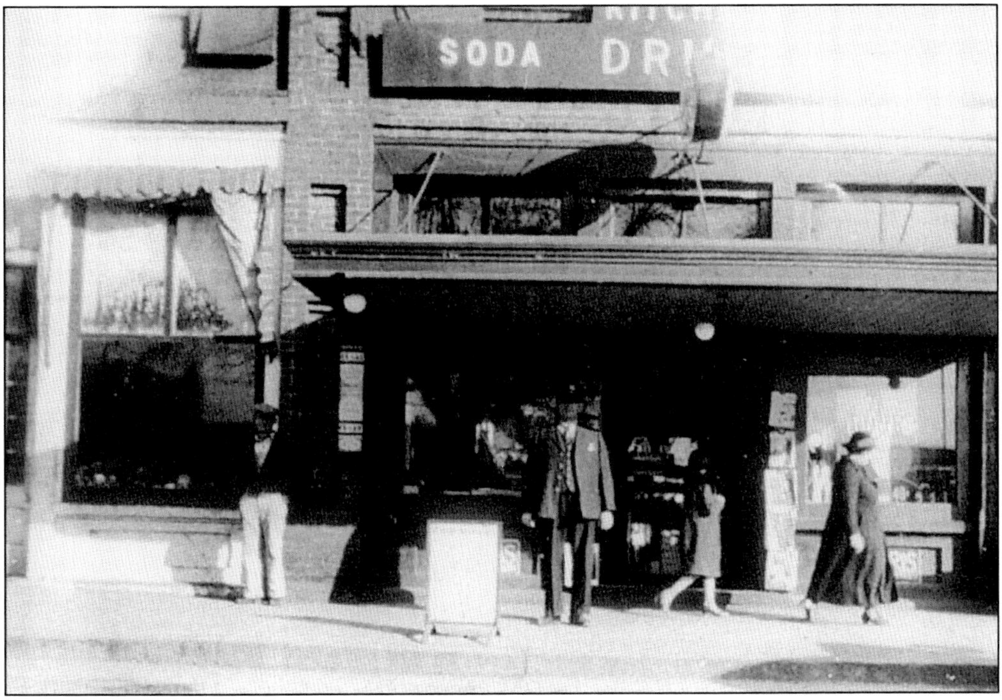

These 1930s photographs show Kitchen's drugstore. Above, a proud policeman stands in front of the building. Below are the display counters and a ready staff. Mr. Kitchen bought the drugstore from John B. Nisbet around 1922. John Nisbet's drugstore occupied the same space that William Milo Nisbet's drugstore had occupied after the east side of the square was rebuilt after the fire.

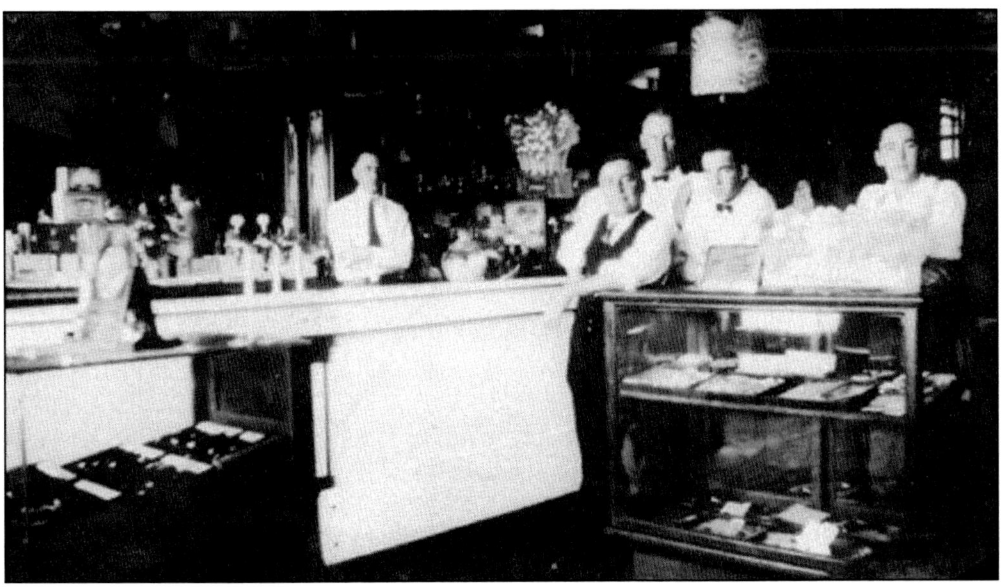

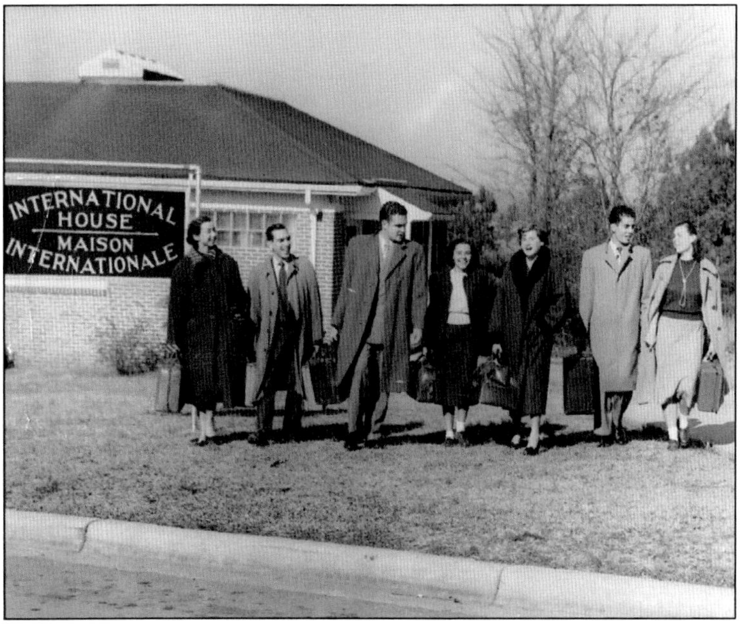

Students in the International House program head out into the world in the late 1940s. In early 1946, Dr. James H. Jones got permission to open an international house for French students, and four French exchange students (and a French chef) arrived in the fall of 1946. Only French was spoken in the International House's classrooms and dining hall. (Courtesy of Jacksonville State University.)

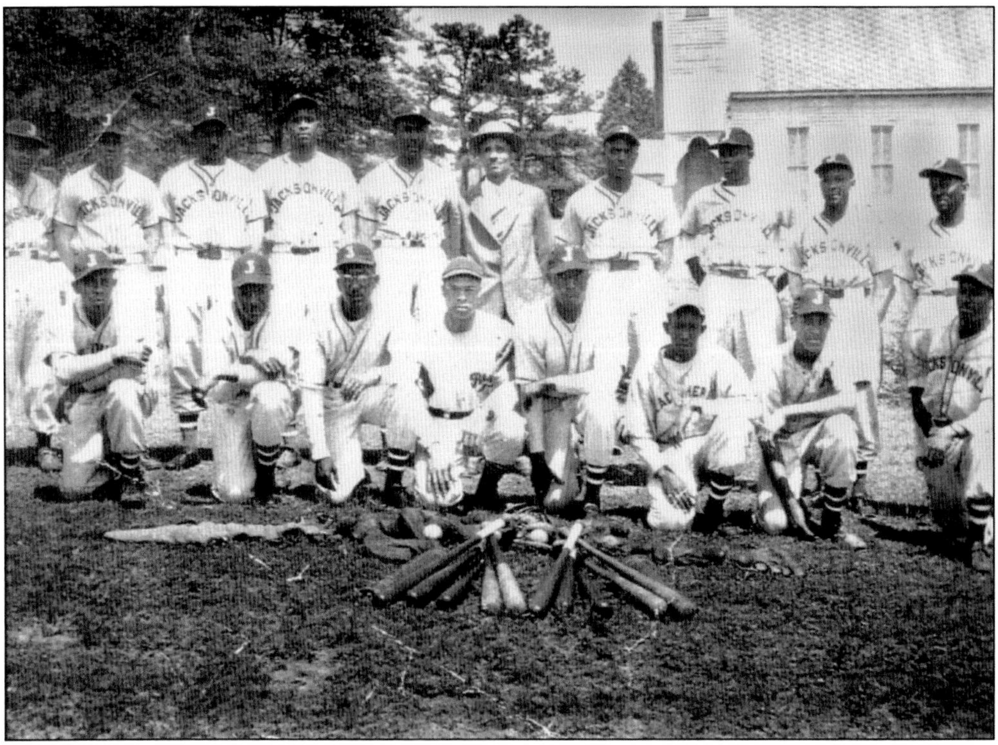

This 1940s photograph shows the Jacksonville Colored High School Browns in their finest. St. Paul's CME Church is in the background. Posing here are, from left to right: (first row) James Cannon, Clarence Williams, Whit Boozer, Sam Woodruff, Aaron Nixon Sr., Horse Weaver, Charles Evehart, and Barnell Caldwell; (second row) Robert Veasley, Rock Johnson, Charlie Harrell, Clarence Wilson, Jack Wilson, Sam Woods, Clarence Snow, Jessie Williams, Pink Woods, Leroy Monroe, and Charlie Caldwell. (Courtesy of Jennifer Snow Sims.)

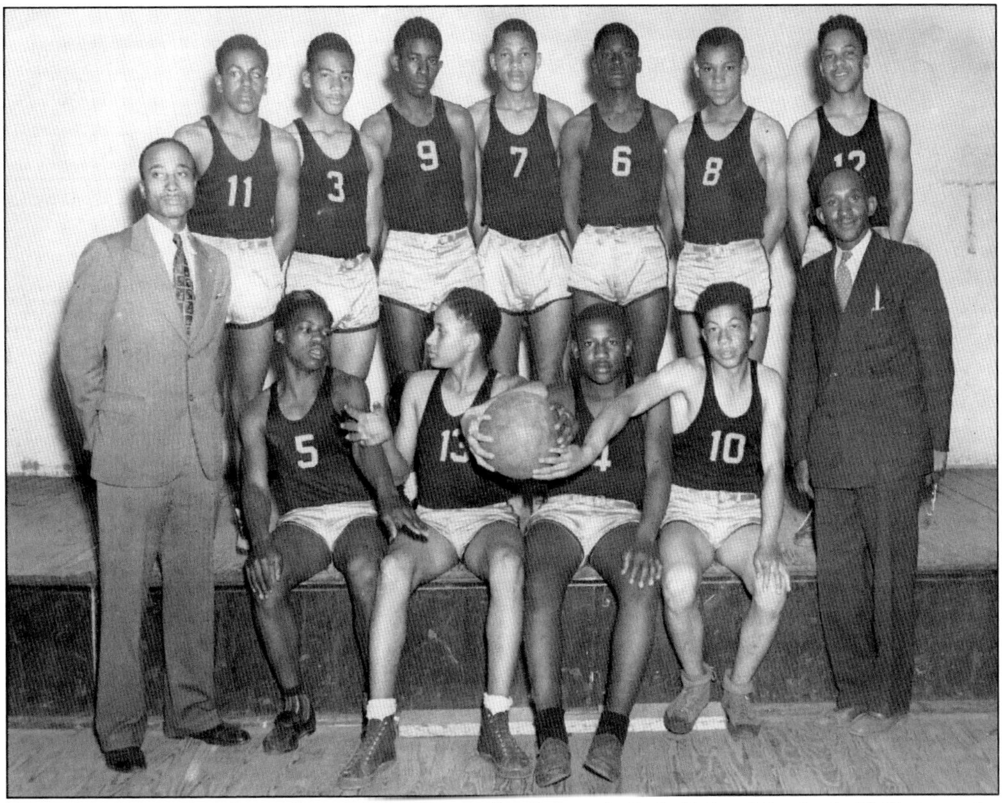

These photographs show the 1947 Jacksonville Colored High School basketball Trojans. In the photograph of the boys team are, from left to right, (first row) Johnny Brown (coach), Billy Nixon, David Levell, Ben Johnson, John Frank Williams, and S.W. Moore (principal); (second row) Edward Levell, Clarence Morgan, Horace Weaver, Charles Eberhardt, Edward Caldwell, Billy Woodruff, and Harrlson Oden. Shown in the photograph of the girls are, from left to right, (first row) Agnes Eberhardt, Maggie Williams, Sally Oden, and Johnny Brown (coach); (second row) Mary Caldwell, Cora Patterson, Doris Levell, Nettie Caldwell, and Eloise Morris; (third row) Lucille Eberhardt, Annie Blackwell, Emma Moore, Margaret Weaver, Ernestine Caldwell, Sydney Foxx, and Seclonia Levell. The girls' uniforms were bought second hand. Seclonia Levell graduated as valedictorian of her class of eight in 1952. Among the boys pictured, four went to college, and three went into the armed services. Among the girls' players, 11 went to college. The Jacksonville Colored High School had the only indoor basketball court in their district. (Courtesy of Secolina "Jeanie" Levell Morris.)

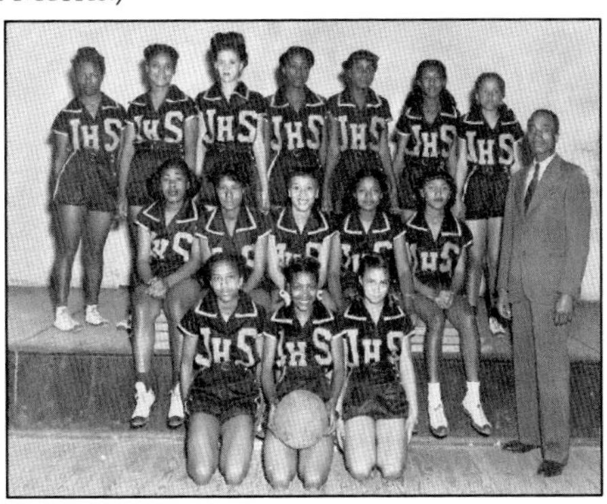

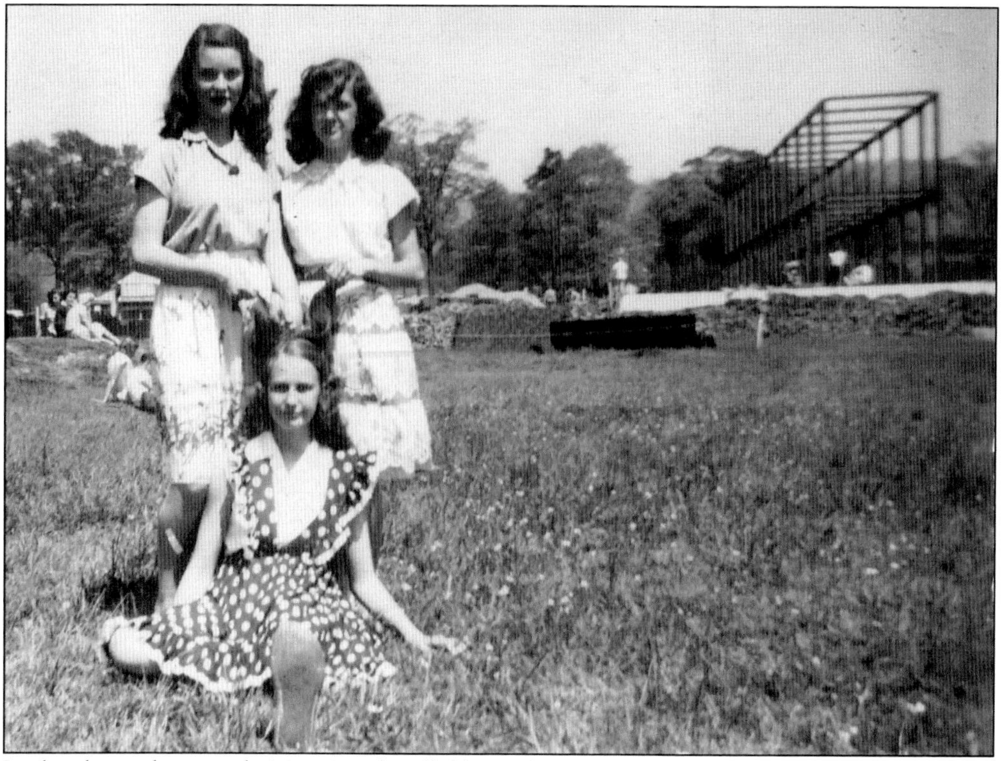

In the above photograph, Mary Landers (left), Marlene Boozer (center), and an unidentified girl pose in front of Jacksonville High School, under construction on North Pelham Road. Directly behind the girls, across Pelham Road, is the Magnolias. An outbuilding can just be seen in the lower left. These girls are facing Stevenson gym ("the old gym"), where the seventh and eighth grades met in the late 1940s. The "new" high school (below), complete with a lunchroom, was built in 1947. The students carried all the furniture and books from the old high school on Francis Street to the new building. The class of 1949 graduated from this high school building. (Above, courtesy of Nibet family collection; below, courtesy of Jacksonville Public Library.)

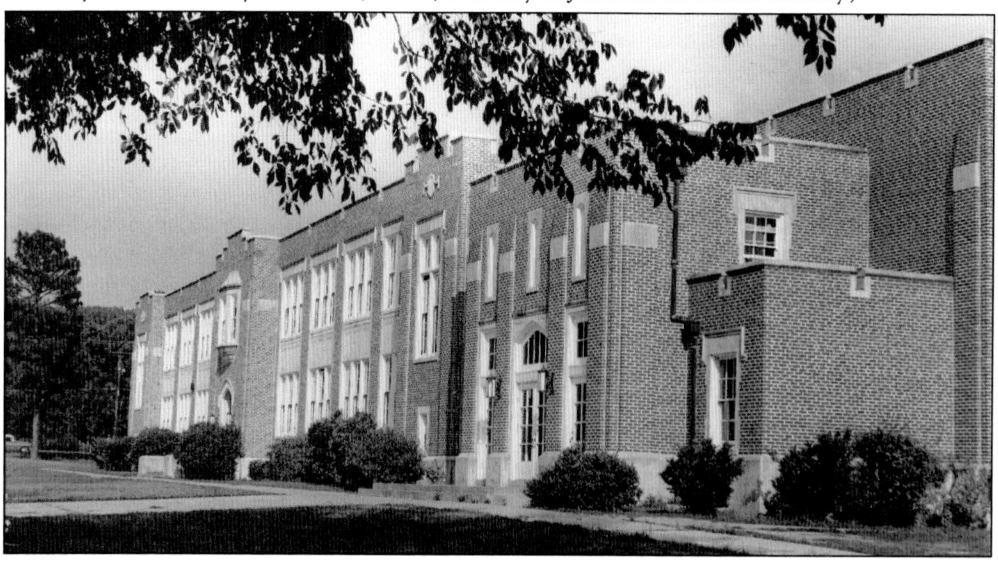

Five

1950 to 1980

In 1955, the Profile mill closed, and it remained closed until it was purchased by Union Underwear in 1956. In 1967, the Alabama Legislature renamed Jacksonville Teachers College, Jacksonville State University. The last group of Northerners to come south were the folks from Flint, Michigan (Federal Mogul) and Mayfield Heights, Ohio (Parker Hannifin). These northerners were invited to come to Jacksonville, and they have become part of the community. The City of Jacksonville purchased the Henry Farm property on the southern edge of Jacksonville in 1975. The Jacksonville Hospital, doctors offices, an Alabama Highway Patrol and driver testing office, a National Guard armory, a water tower, an airstrip, and a golf course and subdivision have been built on the Henry Farm property.

One night in the 1970s, during a home JHS football game, the crowd was startled to see the flames of a large fire that appeared to be on the square. The fire was in the Austin Auto Parts store on the corner of Ladiga and Chinabee Streets, and the fire department, located across the street, was able to contain the fire and save the library and recreational building.

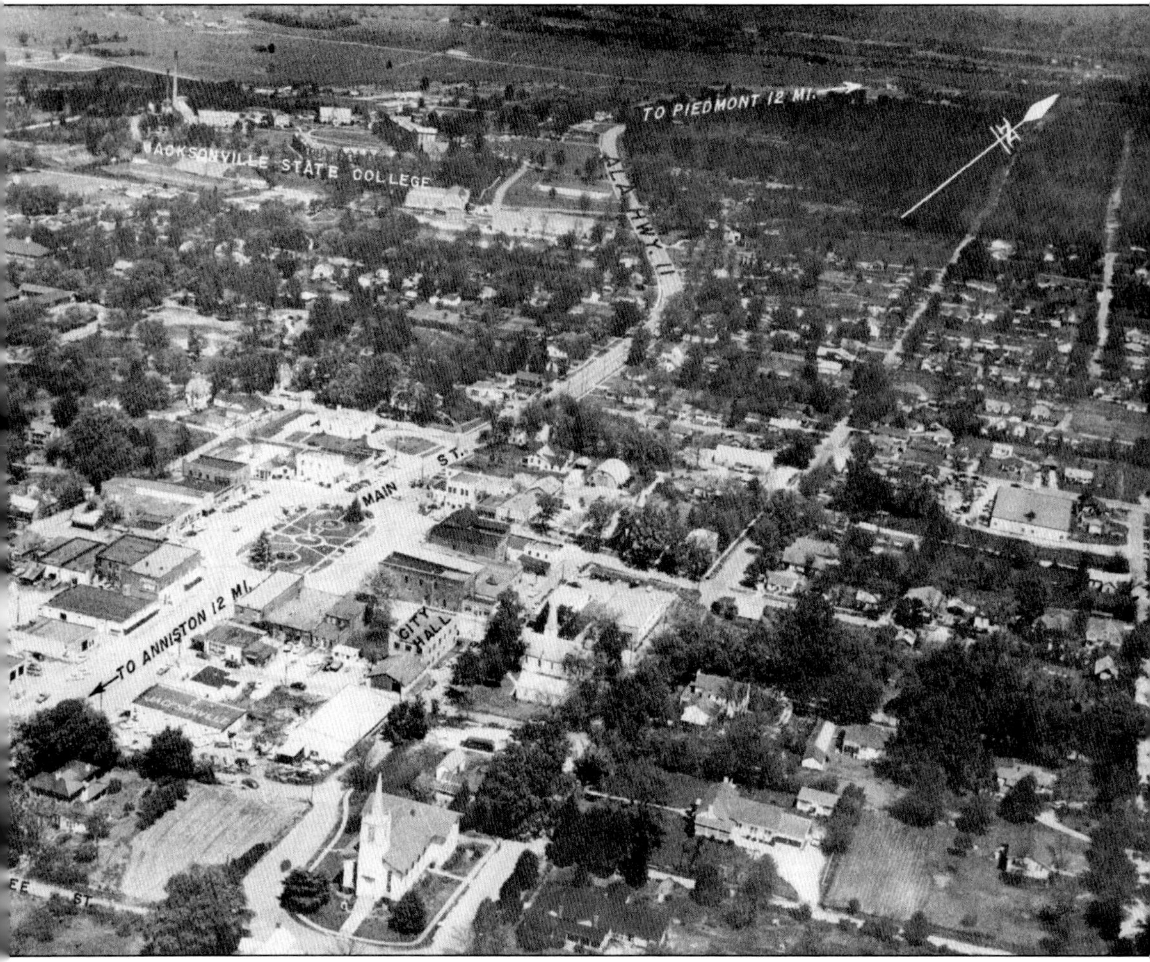

This aerial photograph shows 1950s Jacksonville. Note the First Baptist Church's unique driveway in the center foreground.

This 1950s postcard shows the Episcopal church and the new Billy Daugette memorial parish house. The parish house was dedicated on April 12, 1953. Daugette's parents, Rutledge and Mary Elizabeth, were instrumental in getting the structure built.

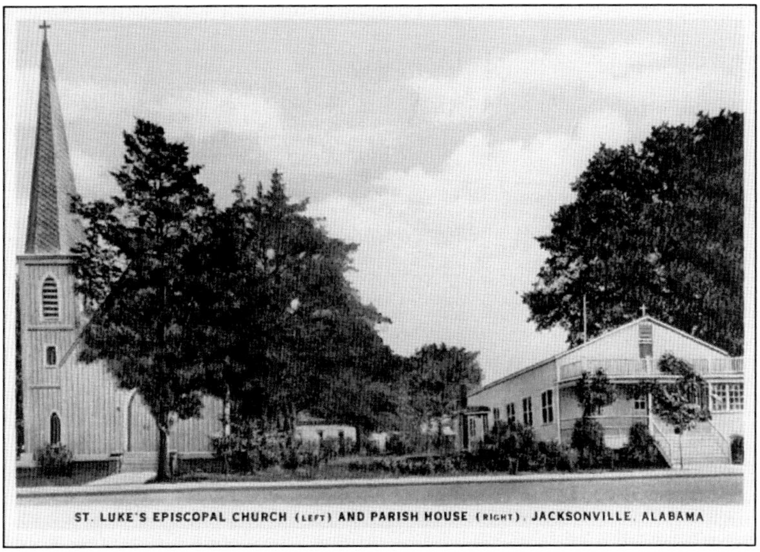

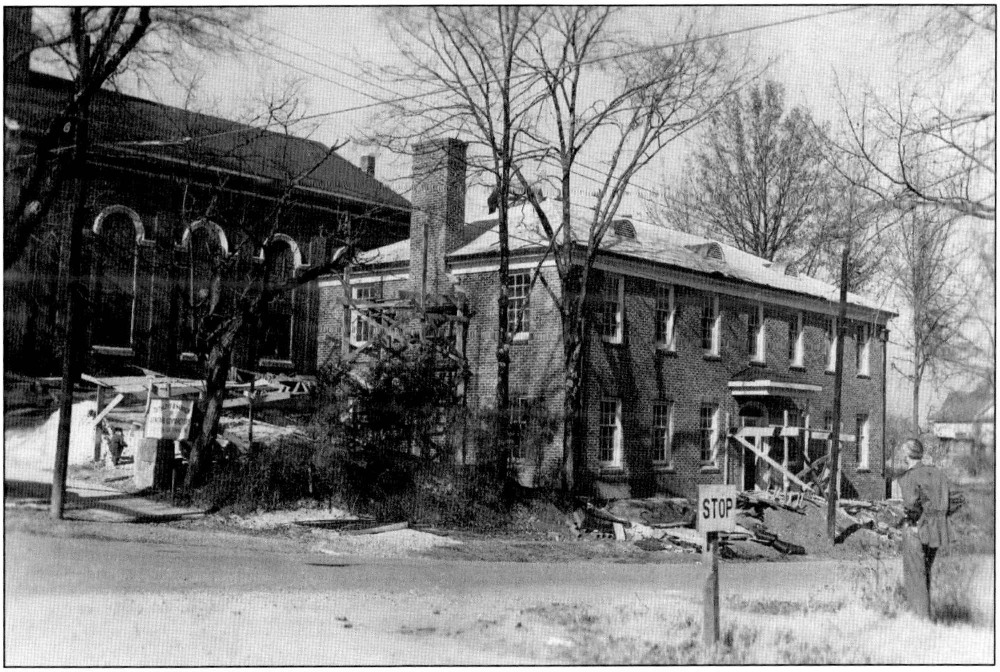

The educational building at First Presbyterian Church is under construction about 1952. Pastor Robert McCray (far right) observes the work. The seed money for the educational building came from a fundraising program that McCray challenged the congregation to a few years earlier, involving the parable of the talents from the book of Matthew. An article ran in the July 1950 issue of *Good Housekeeping* about how McCray challenged everyone in the congregation to take cash *out* of the offering plate ($10 for adults, $5 for children) and invest it using whatever "talent" the congregant had. Some raised chickens, one made corsages, one raised a calf, another cracked pecans. The fundraiser made $8,021 in eight months on an initial investment of $810. Most of the money went to put a new roof on the building and install an electric organ. (Courtesy of First Presbyterian Church.)

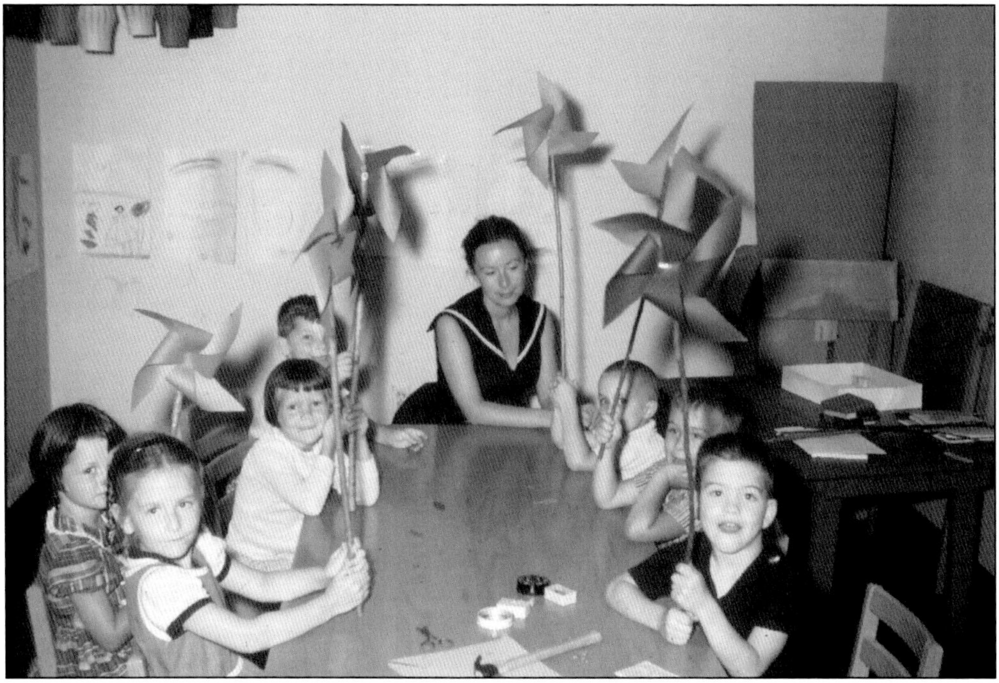

Children work on an arts-and-crafts project at a late-1950s Vacation Bible School at the First Presbyterian Church's educational building. Shown here are, from left to right, Erica von Spacovsky, Kathy Ward, Karen Barnwell, Danny Barnwell, Traudle von Spacovsky, Myron White, Hans von Spacovsky, and Theron "Tim" Montgomery. Traudle and her husband, Anatol, immigrated in 1951 to the United States from Germany, where they had met in a refugee camp after surviving the brutal winter of 1944 in Breslau. Anatol was in the camp after he fled the communist takeover in Yugoslavia. A former White Russian officer, he fought the Bolsheviks during the Russian Revolution and escaped in December 1919 by skiing hundreds of miles to Finland. (Nisbet family collection.)

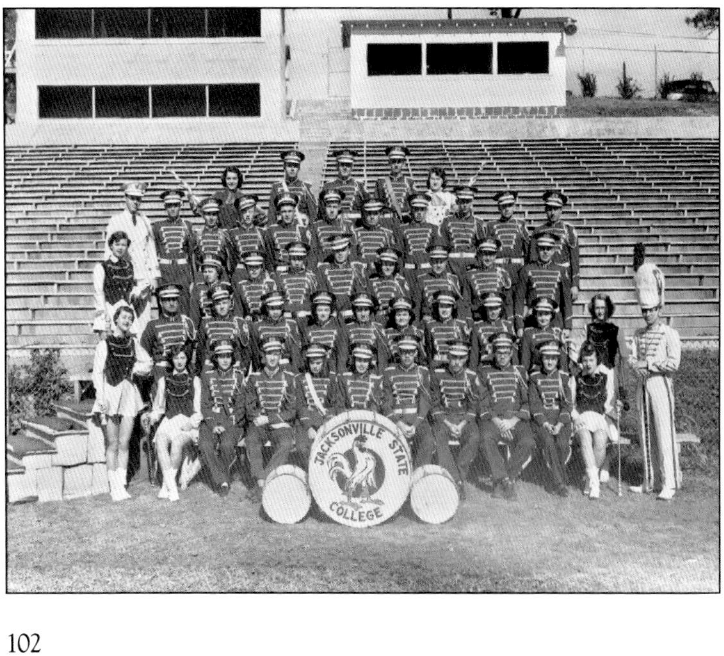

This photograph shows the 1952 Jacksonville State College marching band, the Southerners. Within a decade, the marching band had doubled or tripled in size, had become the Marching Southerners, and had added the Marching Ballerinas. (Courtesy of Jacksonville State University.)

Parades were a longstanding Jacksonville tradition. This photograph shows the Santa Claus float from the 1956 children's Christmas parade.

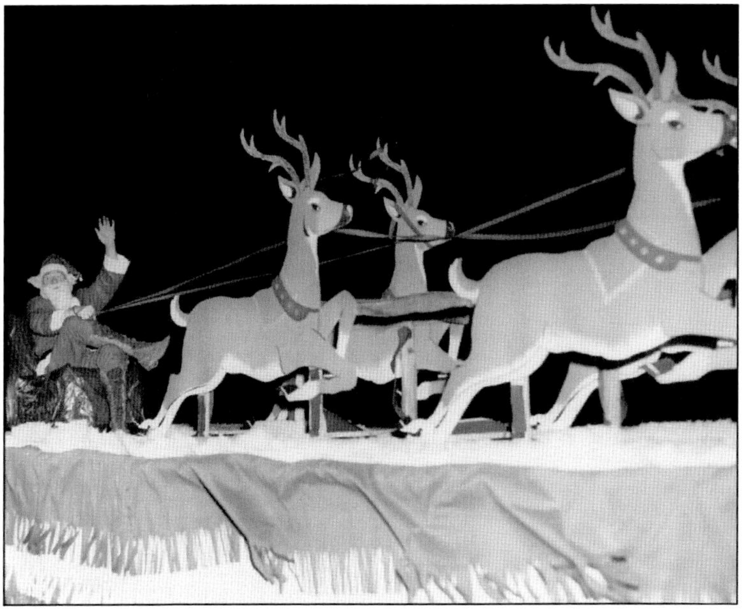

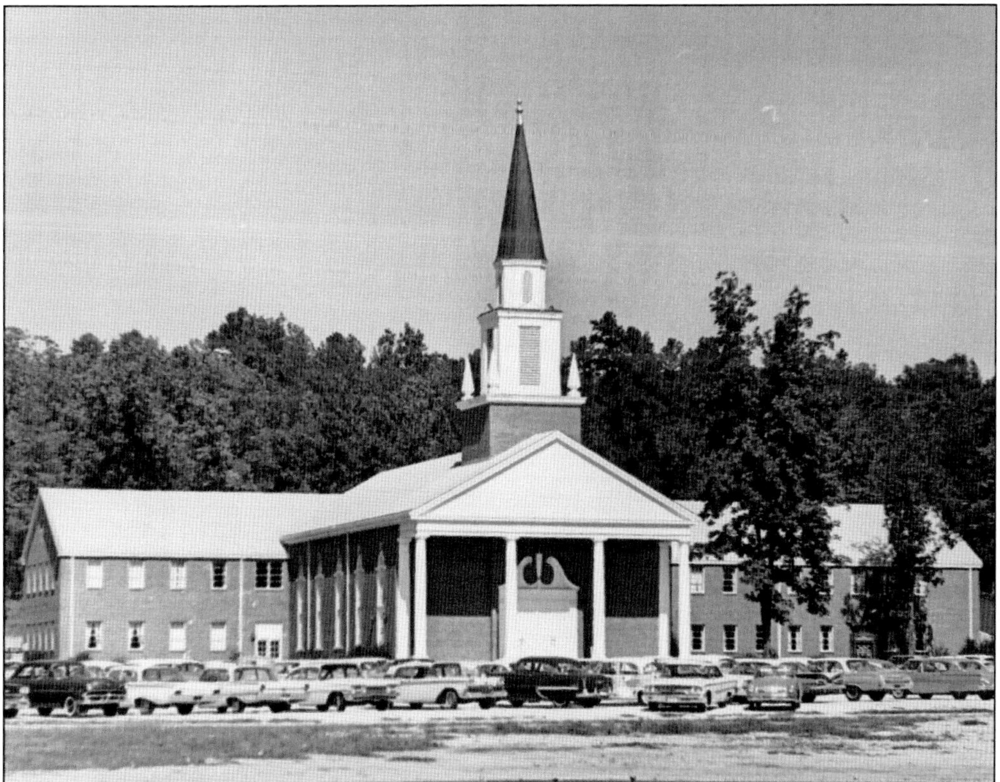

This is the new First Baptist Church building, located north of the square on Church Street between Sixth and Eighth Streets. The building, dedicated on May 3, 1959, has been enlarged several times since its dedication. (Nisbet family collection.)

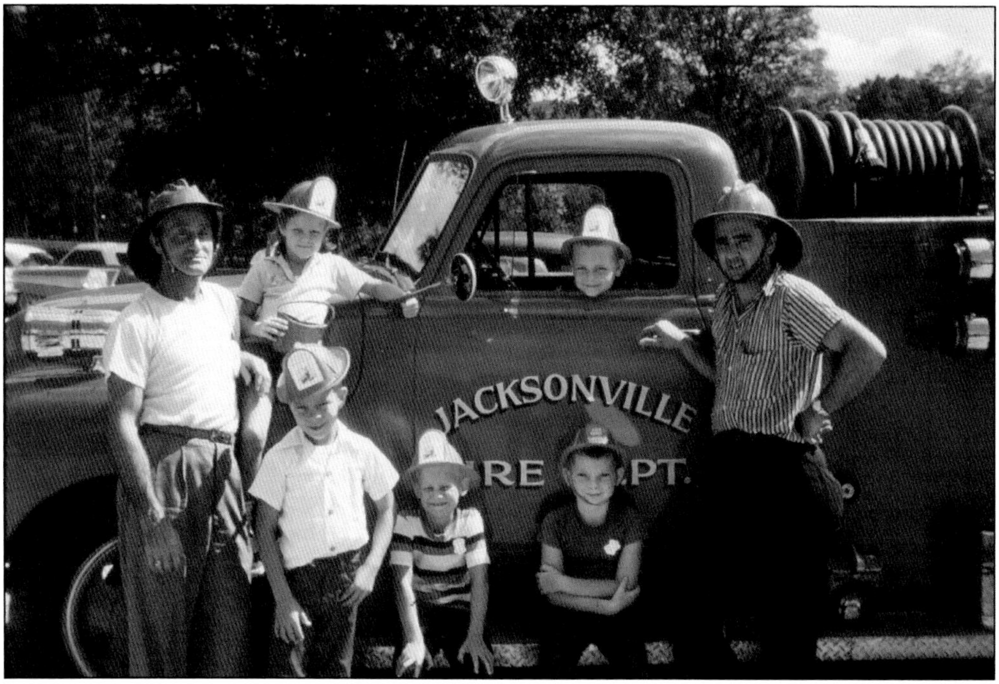

In the fall of 1959, J.B. "Buster" Pritchett (on right) and another Jacksonville volunteer fireman brought their fire truck to Jacksonville Elementary School for a demonstration. The lucky boys shown above got to sit in the truck. The boys' fire hats were furnished by an independent agent for the Hartford Insurance Company. Below, the volunteer fire department displays its fire truck to the first grade at Jacksonville Elementary. (Both, Nisbet family collection.)

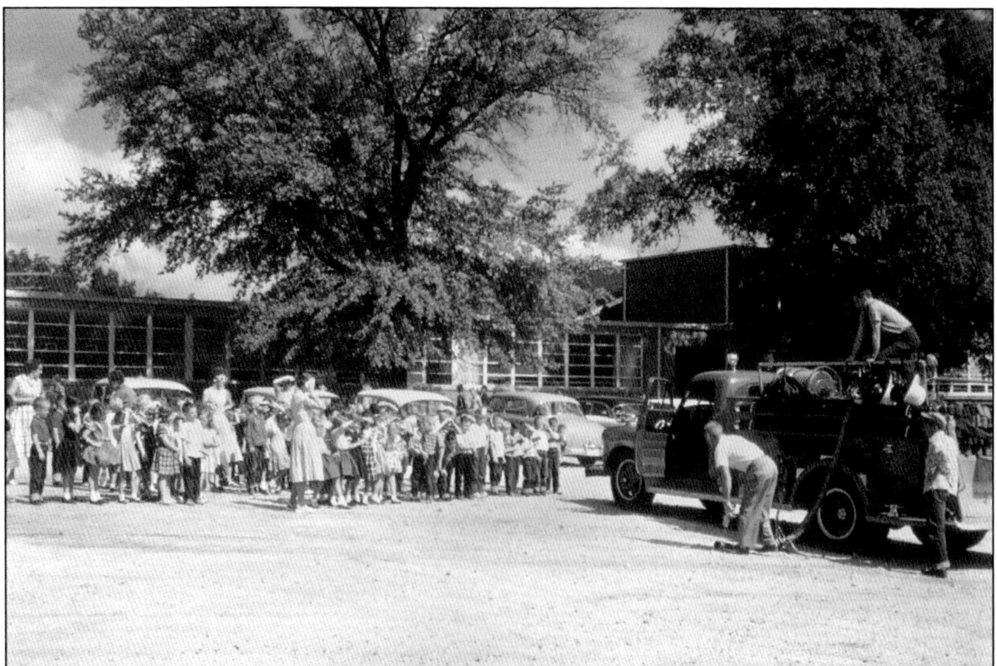

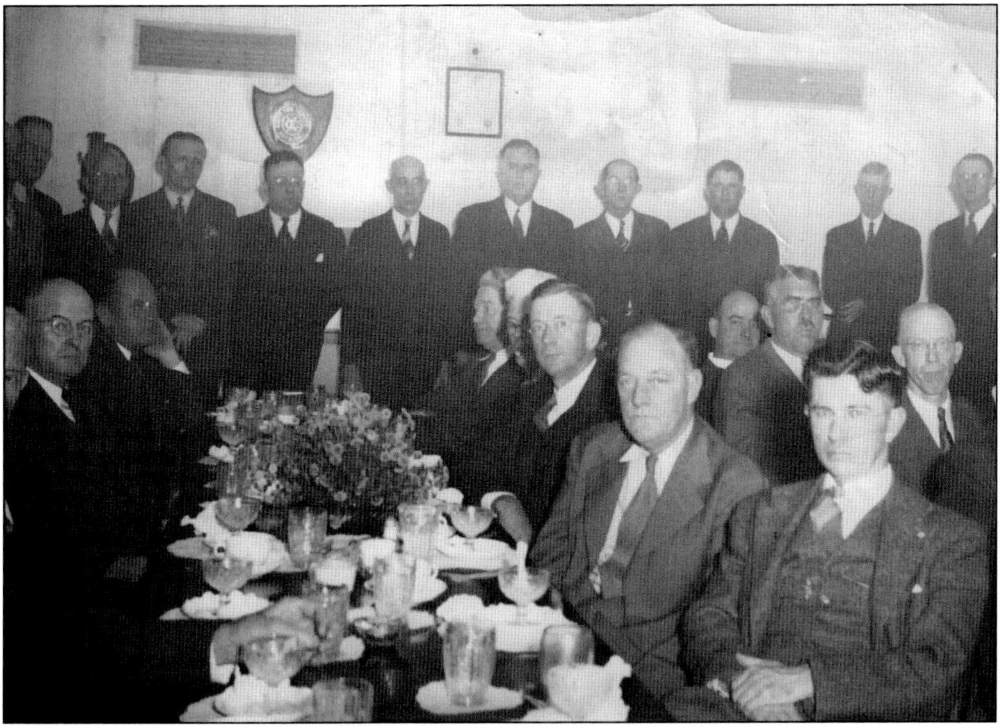

This is a 1940s meeting of the chamber of commerce. Some of the men in this photograph are, in no particular order, Dr. L.W. Allison, Grover Currier, Hubert Lester, and J.F. Gidley; R. Liston Crow, C.R. Wood, R.K. "Red" Coffee, and John B. Nisbet.

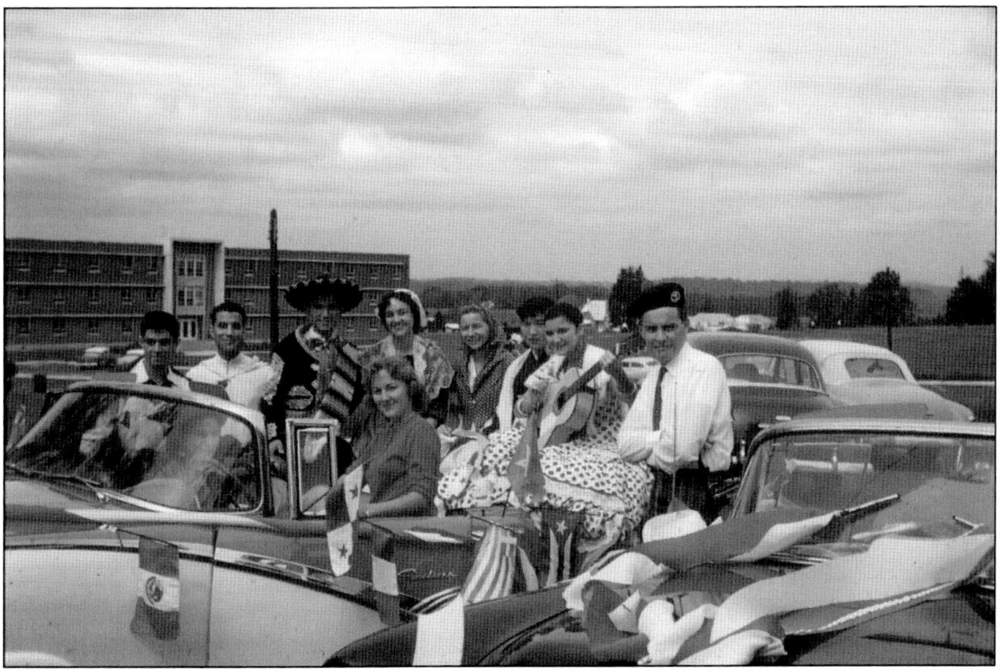

The students from the JSU International House are all dressed up for their participation in the 1957 Jacksonville High School homecoming parade. (Nisbet family collection.)

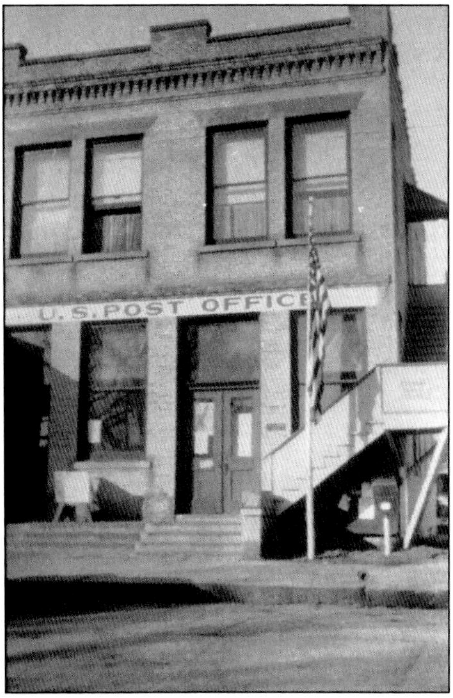

This large two-story building was erected in 1907 by Walter Dean. It is located in the northeast section of the square. In 1907, the first floor of the building was leased to the US government for use as a post office. The second floor housed the U-R Next barbershop and Dr. Rayfield's office. The steps were eventually modified to come straight down the side of the building to the sidewalk. Over the years, the front door and front windows have also been modified.

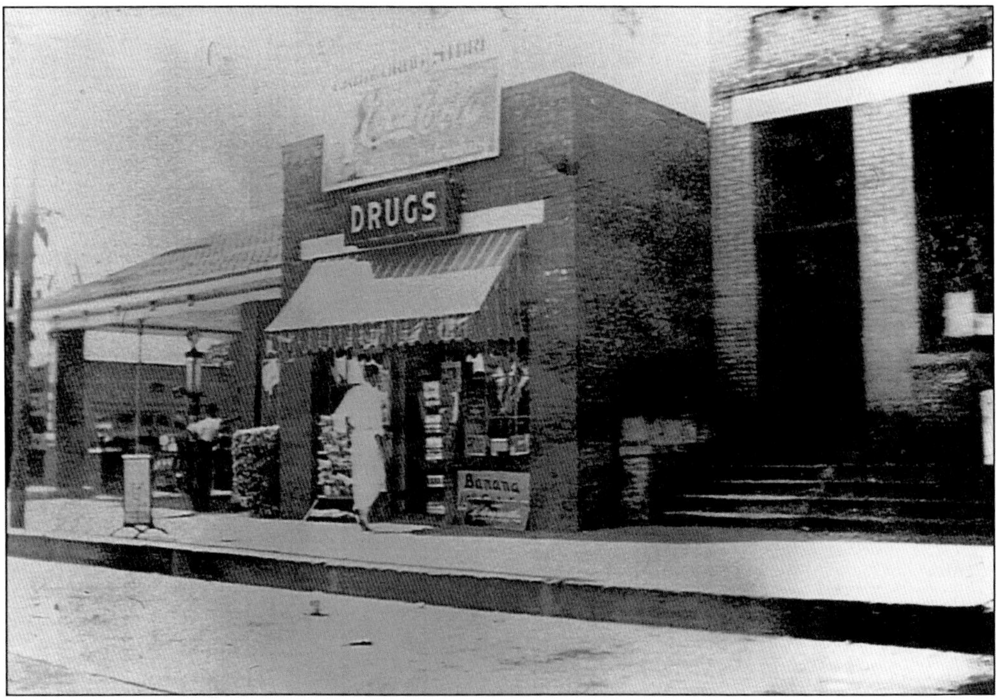

This photograph shows what the northeast corner of the square looked like in 1926–1928. A service station is seen on the far left. Note the glass containers on top of the pumps. The building at center is the original Crow Drug Store. The building on the right is the same as the one shown in the upper photograph. In 1936, Ralph Crow remodeled the post office space on the first floor and moved his drugstore into that location. (Courtesy of Mrs. Homer Barnwell.)

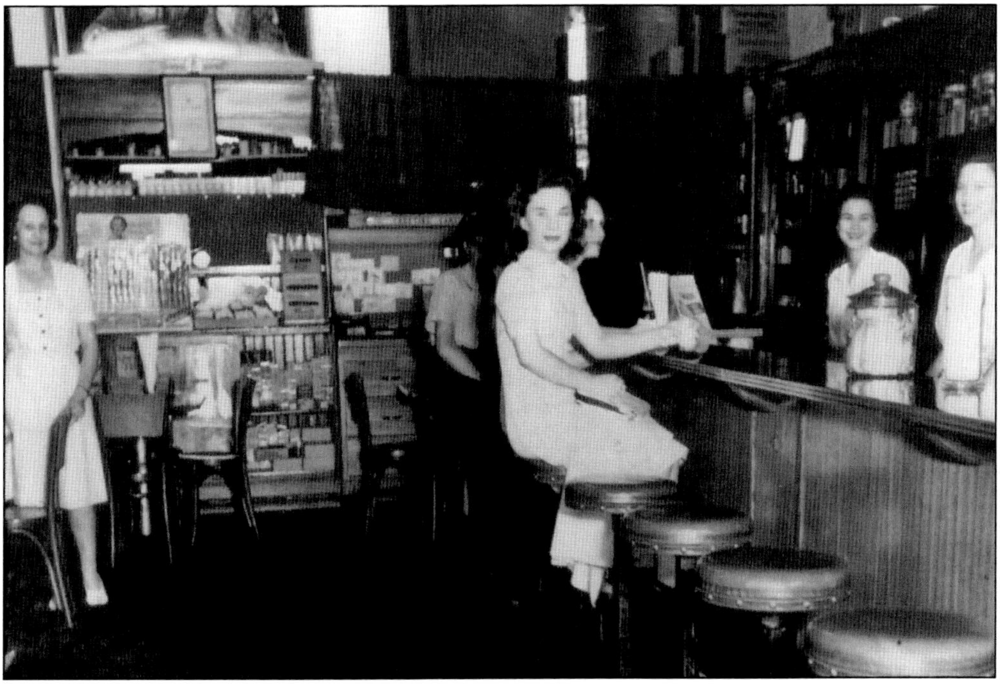

This 1940 photograph shows the interior of Crow Drug Store. In this photograph, in no particular order, are Mrs. Ralph Crow, Marjorie Pyron, Floy Burnham Driskell, and Virginia Fugua. This is the interior of either the original Crow store in the previous image (bottom of page 106) or the remodeled store shown in the photograph below. (Courtesy of Mrs. Homer Barnwell.)

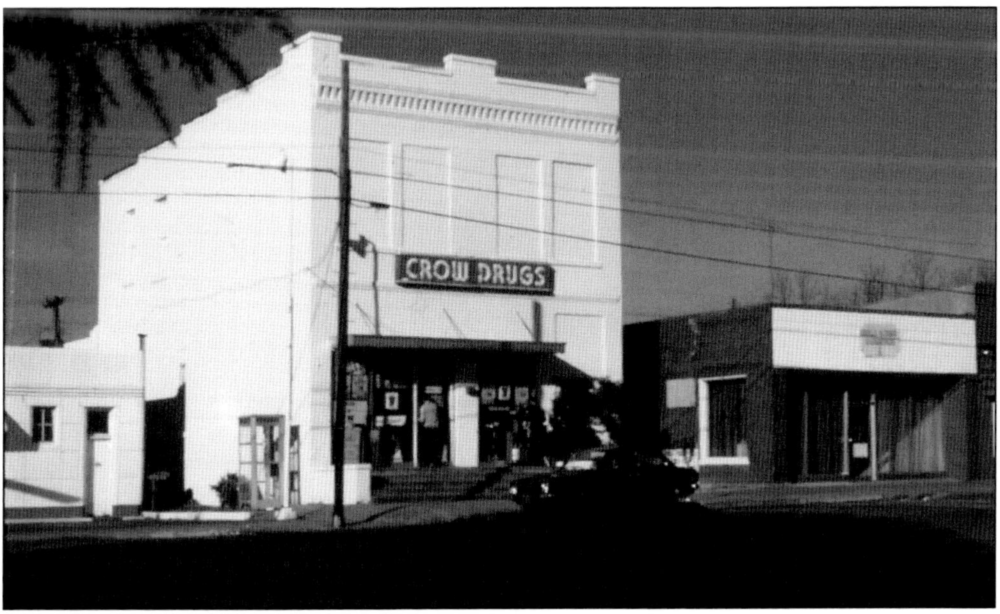

This 1970s photograph shows Crow Drug Store after it was sold to Darwin Hardison in 1960. Crow Drug Store remained in this building until the store relocated to the east side of the square in 1998.

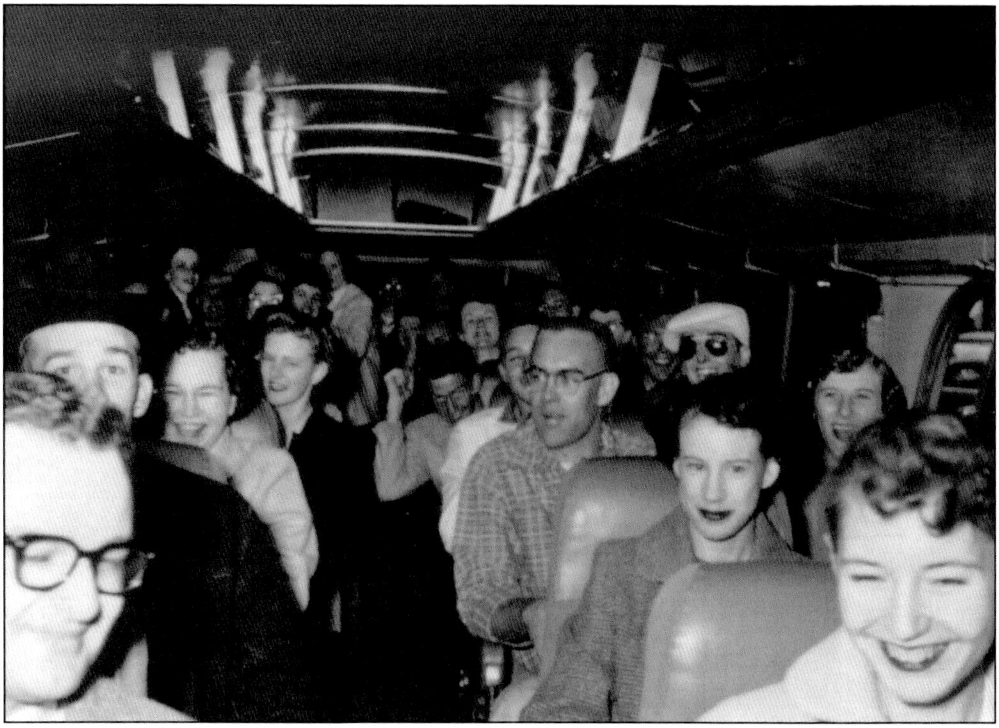

Starting in the late 1940s, it became a tradition at Jacksonville High School for the seniors to take a trip to Washington, DC, Philadelphia, and New York City. These students are taking the trip in April 1957. Pictured are, in no particular order, Harold Lee, teacher, Johnny Bullock, Carolyn West, Myrtis Whaley, Clarence Wood, Nette Marin, Janice Martin, Carolyn Knight, Bobby Henderson, Orval Motes, Lavon Jordan, Frank Pentecost, Erin Duggan, Bill Gardner (in hat and sunglasses), Minerva Wright, Ann Scroggin, and Ann Hudson. (Nisbet family collection.)

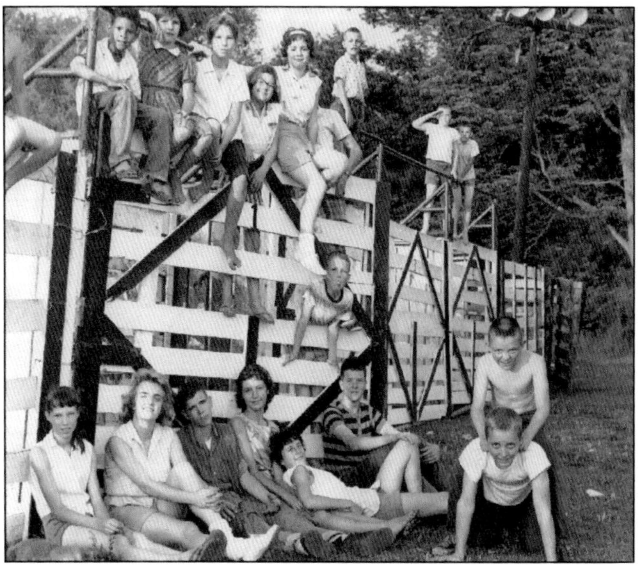

In the late 1950s and early 1960s, there was a small animal park, owned by the city, next to the (white) city pool, just down the hill from Forney Hall. The paddock pictured here held the riding animals. Some of these children have climbed the paddock fence for this photograph. Some of the children shown here are, in no particular order, Michaael Tony Ackley, Charlotte Spears, Lynne Spears, Shirley Willis, Randy Barnes, Glenda ?, Lynda Anderson Rochester, Doug Whaley, Helen Griffith Cochran, Bobbie Miller, Lynn Young, and Kevin Young.

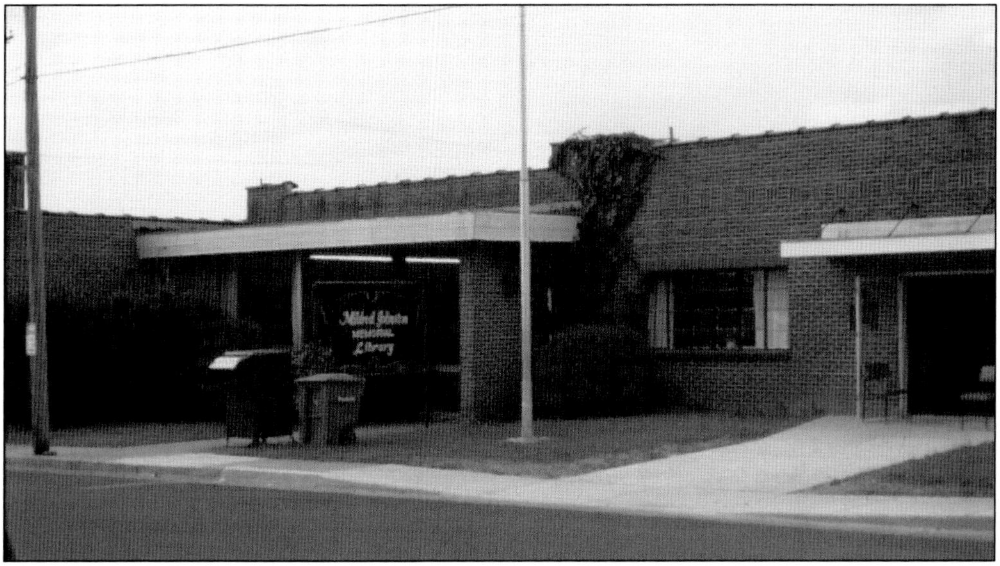

The above photograph shows an early location of the Jacksonville Public Library, with its original name, Mildred Johnson Memorial Library. Mildred Johnson was a librarian at Jacksonville Teacher College who thought a town the size of Jacksonville should have a public library. Johnson died in 1957 without seeing her dream fulfilled. The Jacksonville Public Library began in 1957 as a part of the Calhoun County Library system, when the Town and Country Realty Company provided an eight-foot-by-seventeen-foot space for the collection of books. A high school student was employed as a librarian and paid by the Jacksonville Book Club. In 1958, more clubs agreed to participate in a building fund and the library moved into city hall. In 1959, the library expansion continued with a move into the recreation center. In 1963, Mrs. A.C. Shelton was appointed librarian to keep the library open 20 hours per week instead of the previous nine. The first month that this "new" facility was open, 50 books were checked out. The below photograph shows the interior of the Mildred Johnston Library, with Margaret McEwan at the checkout desk.

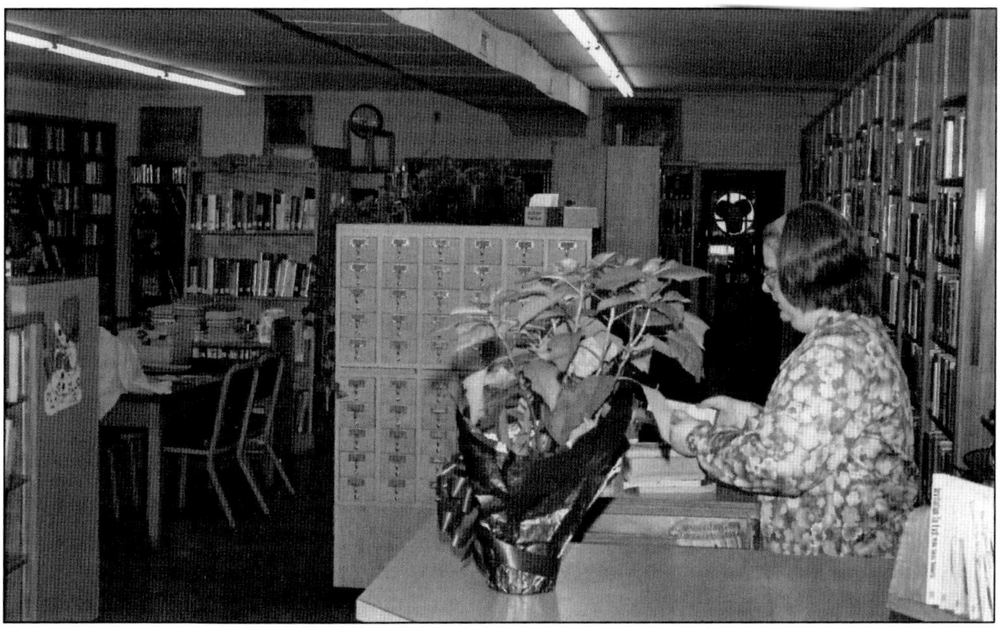

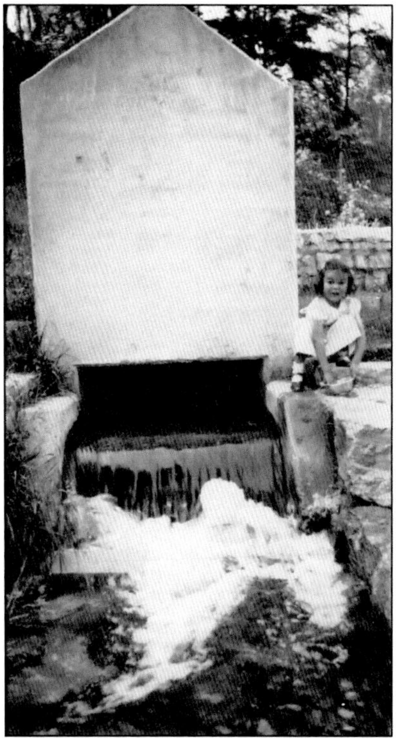

In 1846, Jacksonville had an underground water system that brought water westward from the mountains on the east side of town. This system cost $600 and used hollowed-out pine logs for pipes. The next attempt at a water system occurred in 1872, when a reservoir was built on the hill beside John Nisbet's home on Ladiga Street. This version used a system of wrought-iron pipes to bring water to the public square. This system's hydrants can be seen on the map at the beginning of this chapter. The second system fell into disrepair and, in the 1880s, was sold to an individual. The system changed hands several times; William I. Greenleaf eventually purchased the system. The photograph at left shows an unidentified child at the big springs off Spring Street. The photograph below is of the pump house over the springs at Germania Springs (north of town).

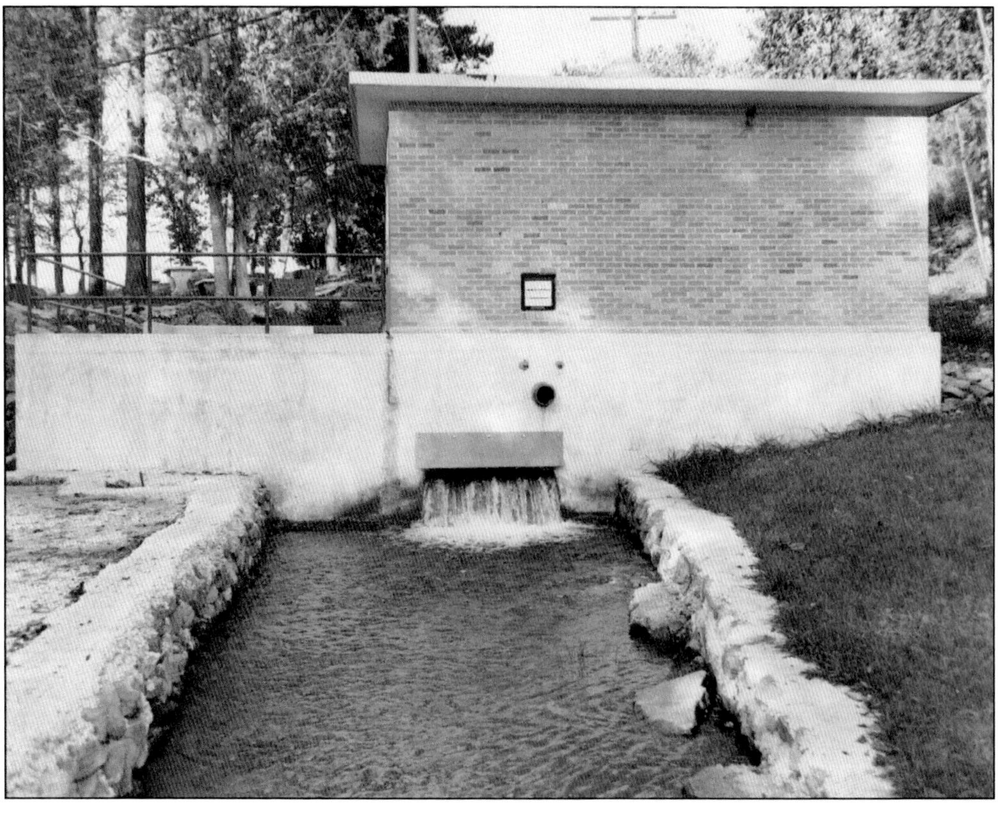

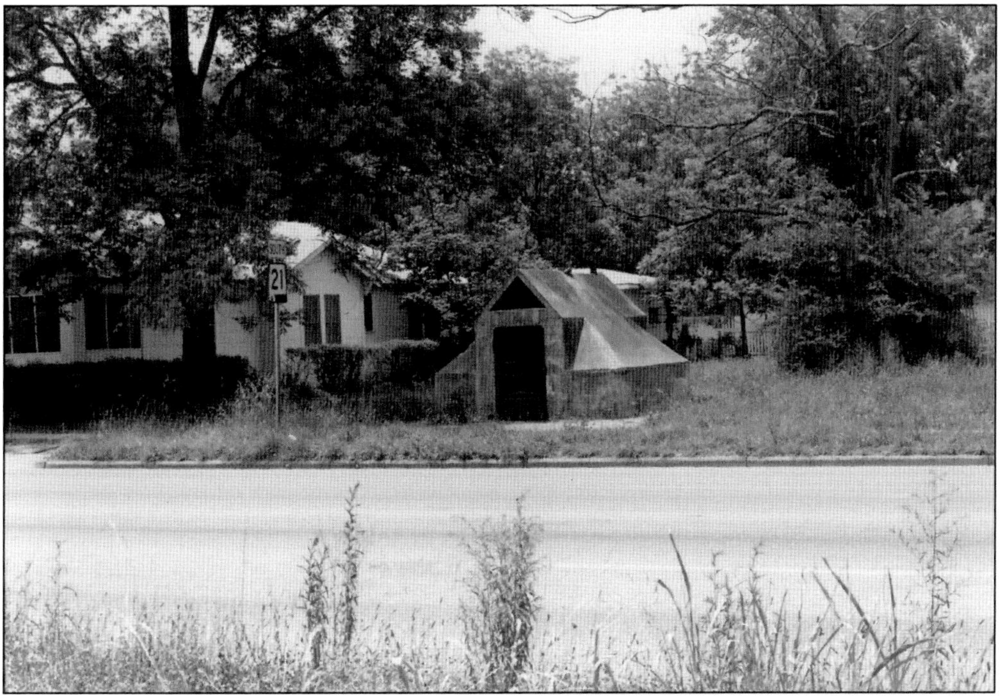

The concrete house-like structure shown above is actually the entrance to part of the Greenleaf water system. This system provided water to businesses and houses in Jacksonville as well as to fire hydrants. When the City of Jacksonville purchased the water system from Greenleaf in the 1960s, these Greenleaf system hydrants were painted black to indicate that they no longer provided water.

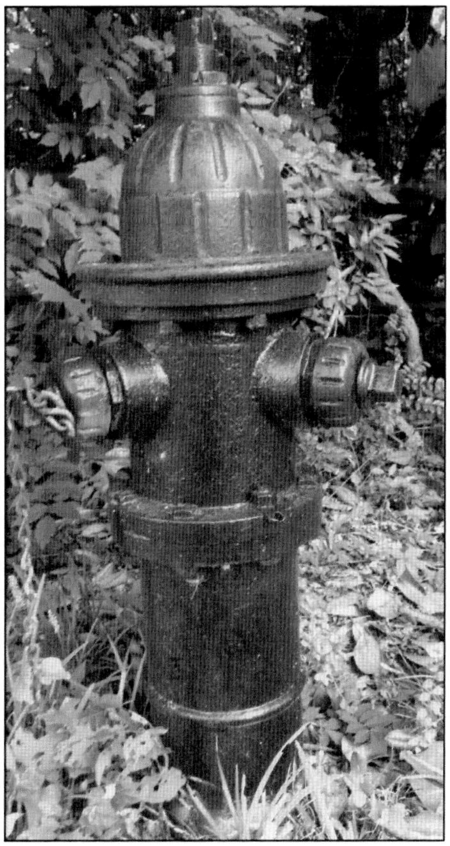

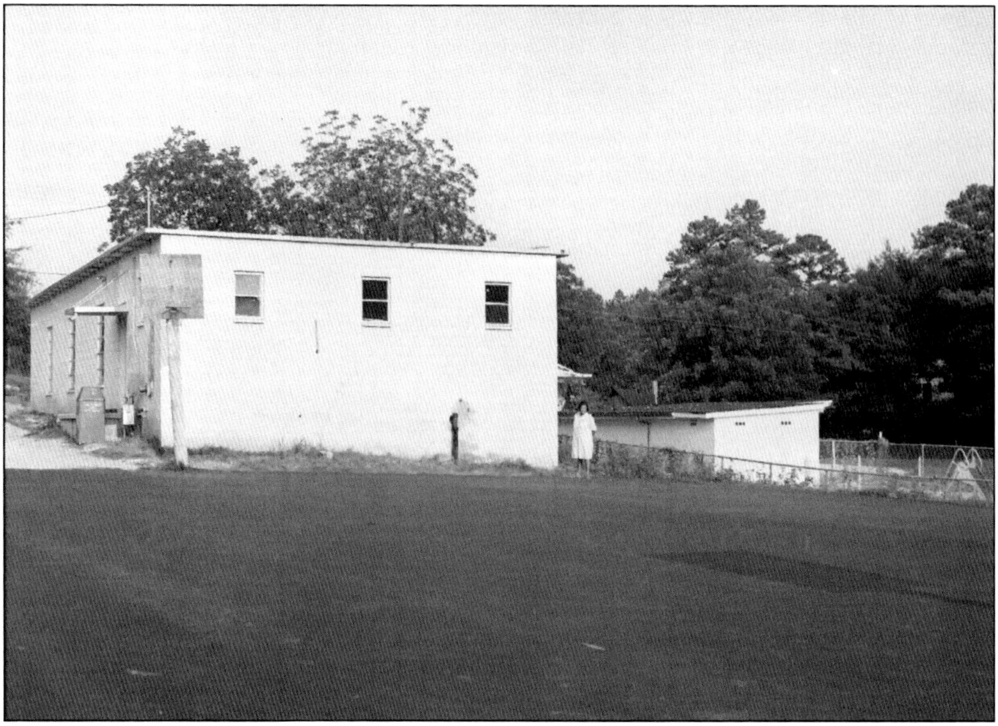

The above photograph depicts the back of Eastwood Community Center, with the Eastwood pool on the right. Although no longer in use, the center served the community from its dedication in 1965 into the 21st century. The dedication plaque (below) is no longer on the building.

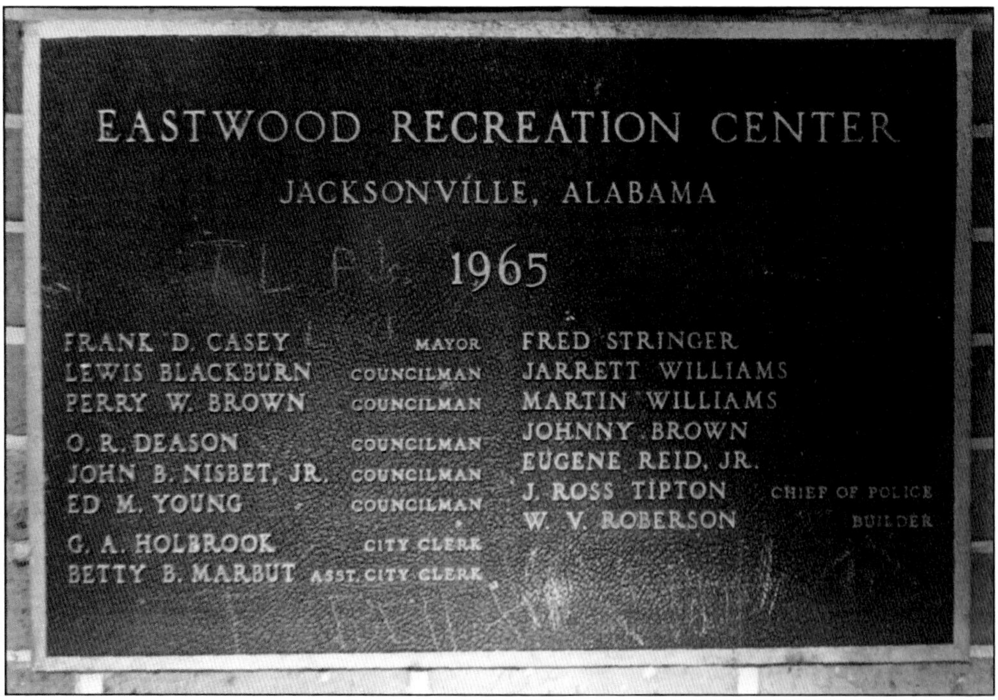

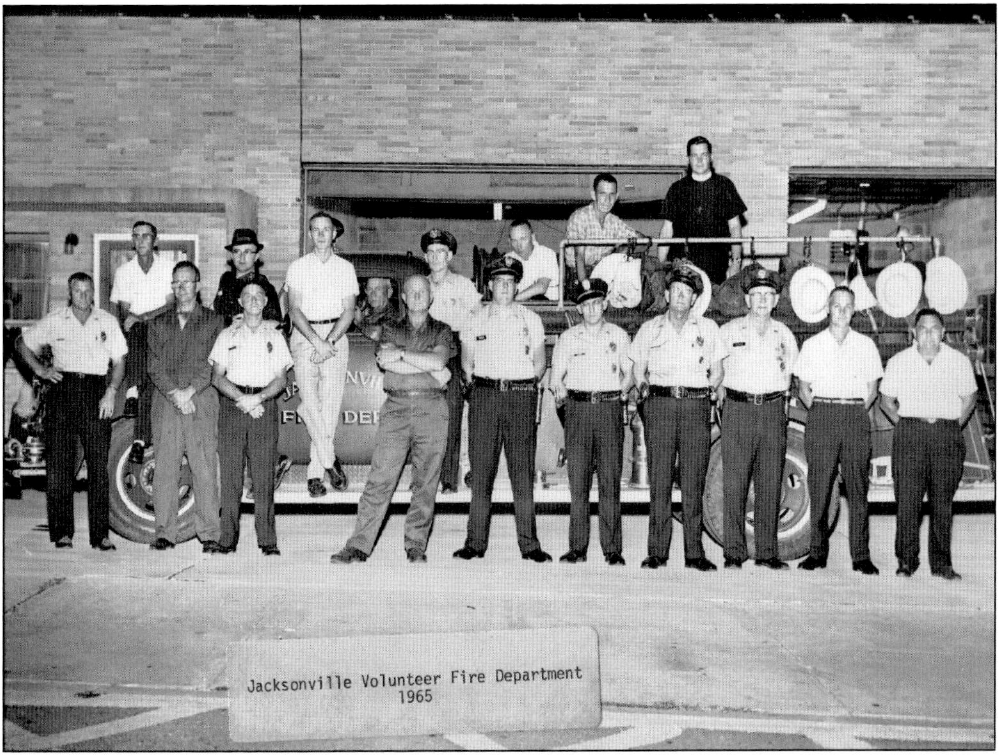

In 1965, Jacksonville still had an all-volunteer fire department (above). Below, the department shows off its newest fire truck in front of the station. With the purchase of a ladder truck a few years later, the bay doors had to be raised.

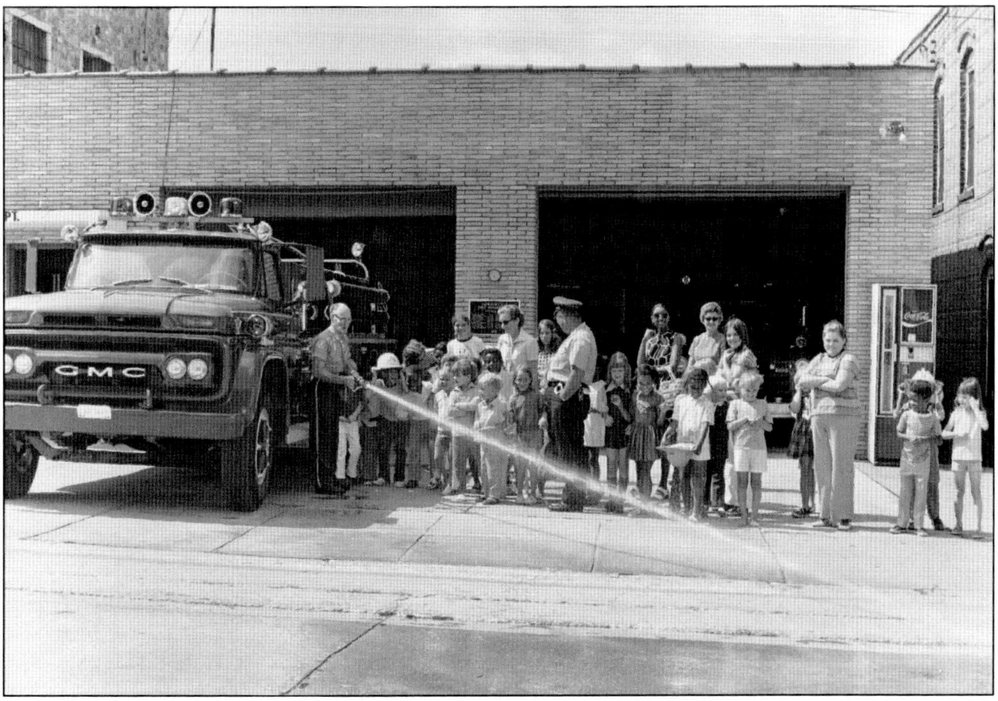

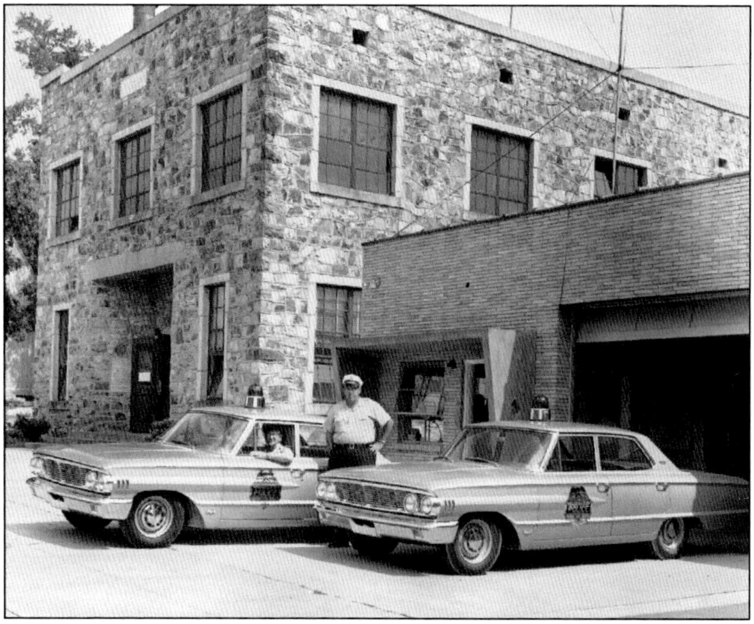

Standing in front of City Hall and the police station, Chief Ross Tipton shows off Jacksonville's state-of-the art police cars.

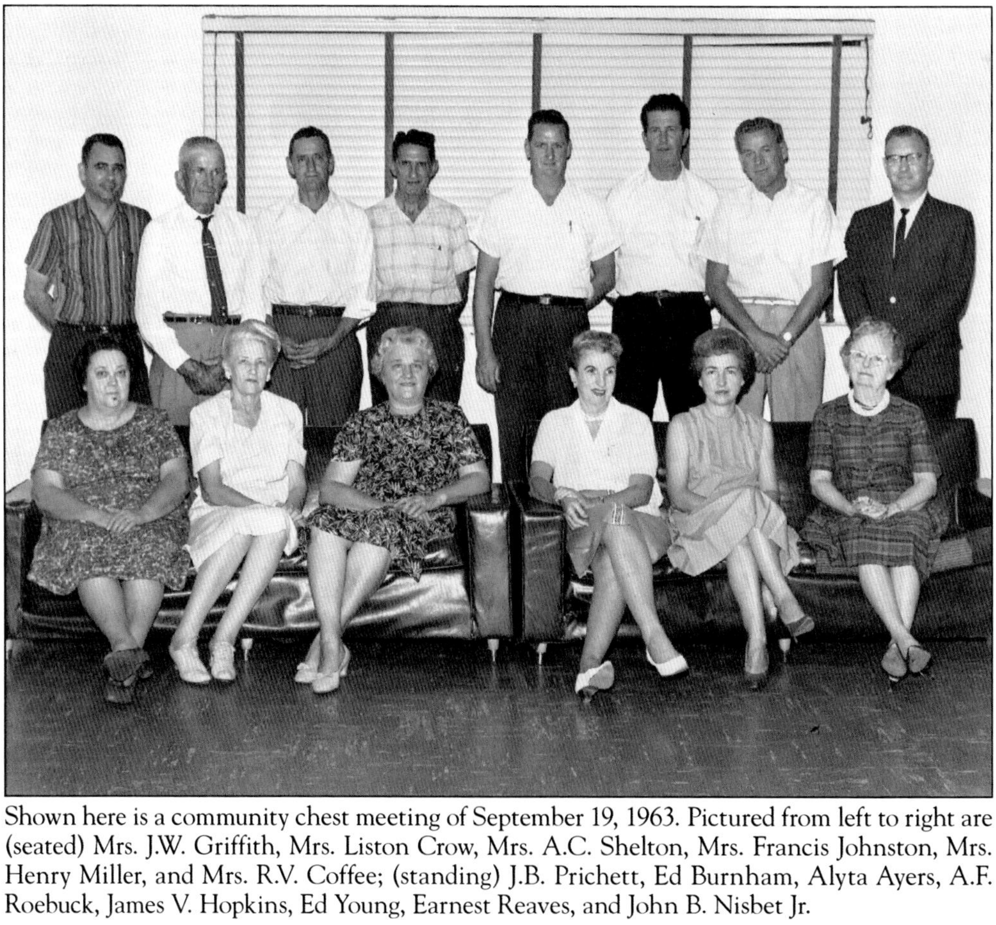

Shown here is a community chest meeting of September 19, 1963. Pictured from left to right are (seated) Mrs. J.W. Griffith, Mrs. Liston Crow, Mrs. A.C. Shelton, Mrs. Francis Johnston, Mrs. Henry Miller, and Mrs. R.V. Coffee; (standing) J.B. Prichett, Ed Burnham, Alyta Ayers, A.F. Roebuck, James V. Hopkins, Ed Young, Earnest Reaves, and John B. Nisbet Jr.

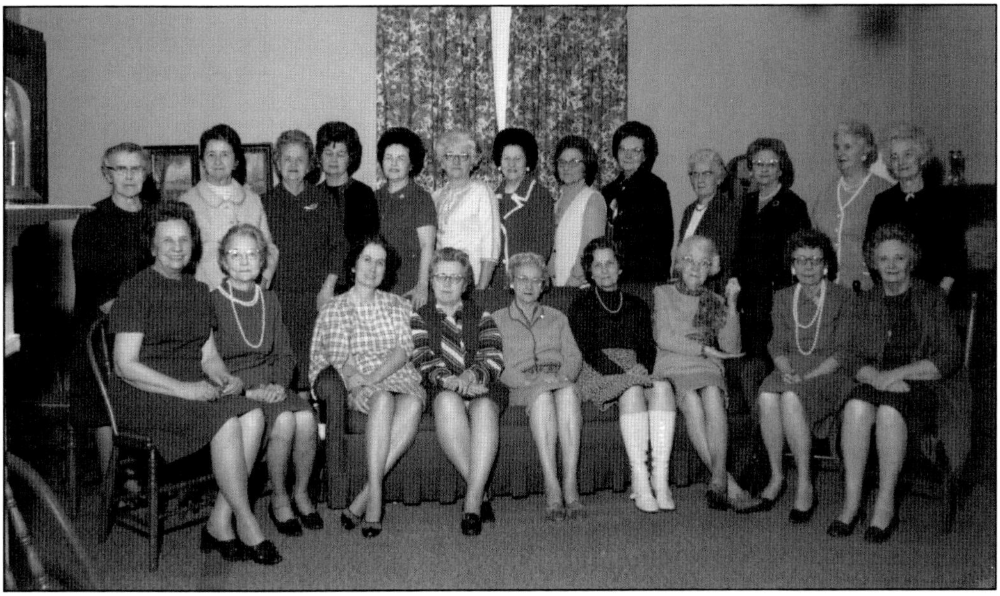

Pictured here is the Progressive Study Club in 1971. This club, along with a dozen or more other clubs and organizations, donated time and money to the Mildred Johnston Memorial Library. Pictured here from left to right are (seated) Julia Roebuck, Postelle Watts, Louise Windsor, Mrs. Ogilvie, Lucell Rowan, Mary Ed Hay, Miss Erie Currier, Mrs. A.J. Arnold, and Ester Mead Glazner; (standing) Mary Etta Stephenson, Annie Lee Williams, Edith Weaver, Annie Lee Williams, Lee Phillips, Sara Staples, Mary Shelton, Mary Beth Lowery, Mrs. Jerome Wilson, Kitty Stone, Sara Kate Morton, Mrs. Reuben Self, Mrs. Joe Harris, and Mrs. E.J. Landers.

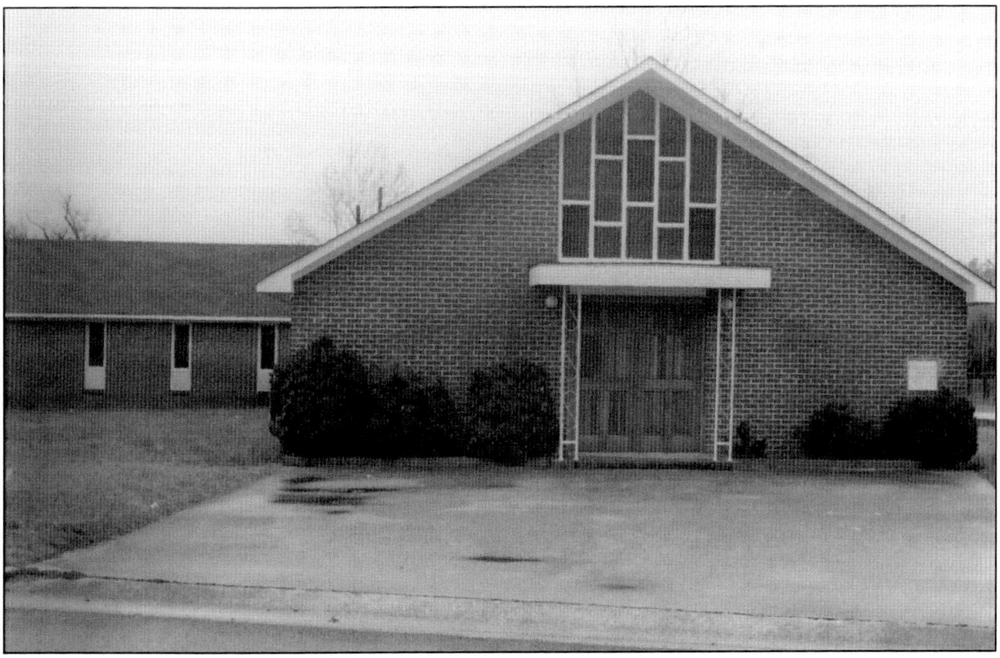

The Mill Village Baptist Church was organized in the building where the Mill Village School met in 1952. The school building was moved across the street and the congregation built its current structure (shown here) in 1971.

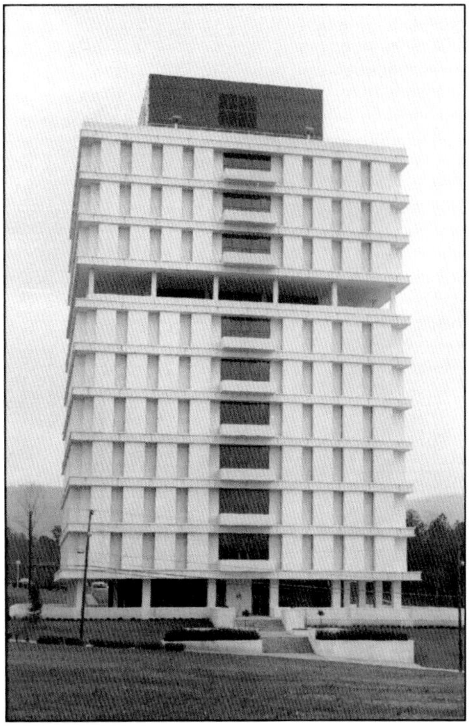

This 12-story library was completed in 1972 and dedicated on October 15, 1973. It was named for Jacksonville State University president Houston Cole (1942–1971). In 2002, the white marble facade was replaced with a red slate one.

This photograph shows St. Charles Borromeo Catholic Church. St. Charles, as it is known, was consecrated on April 16, 1972, by Bishop Joseph Vath. There was no real Catholic presence in Jacksonville from the closing of St. Rose of Lima Church in the 1930s until February 1960, when a small band of Catholics began worshipping in the recreational center on Ladiga Street. In June 1962, the diocese purchased a house on Seventh Avenue that served as a Catholic campus center. From 1962 to 1972, mass was held in a small chapel in that house.

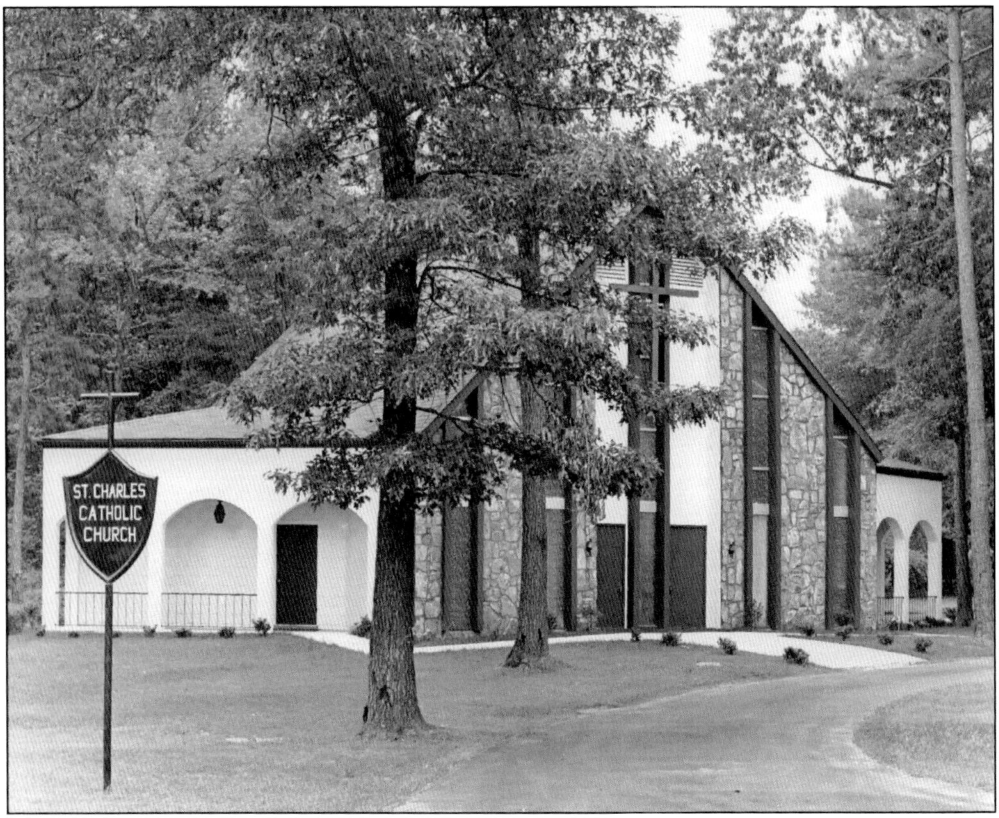

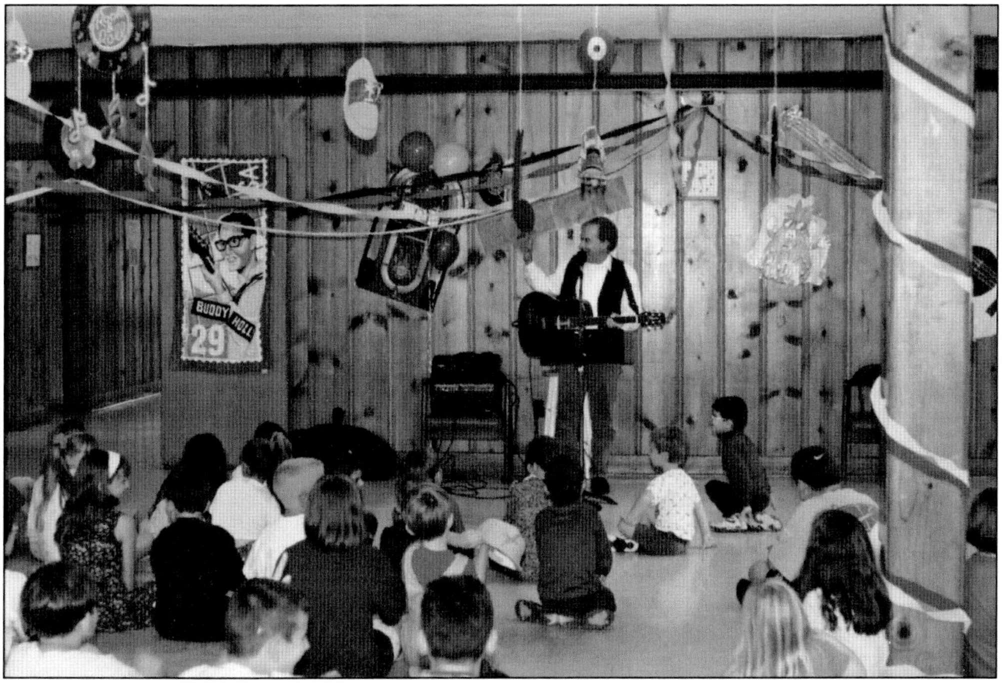

This photograph reveals the pine paneling of the recreational center on Ladiga Street. The facility was built to replace the federal recreational center that burned down. Here, a folk singer entertains a group of children.

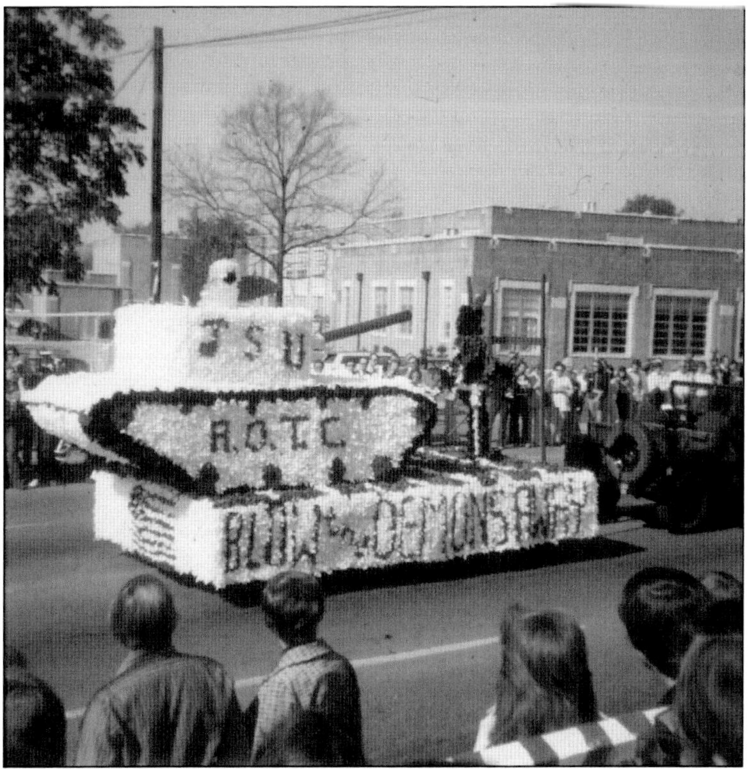

This 1970s photograph of the JSU ROTC program's float shows the Jacksonville High School library (formerly the cafeteria) at right. This parade marched north on Pelham Road. (Nisbet family collection.)

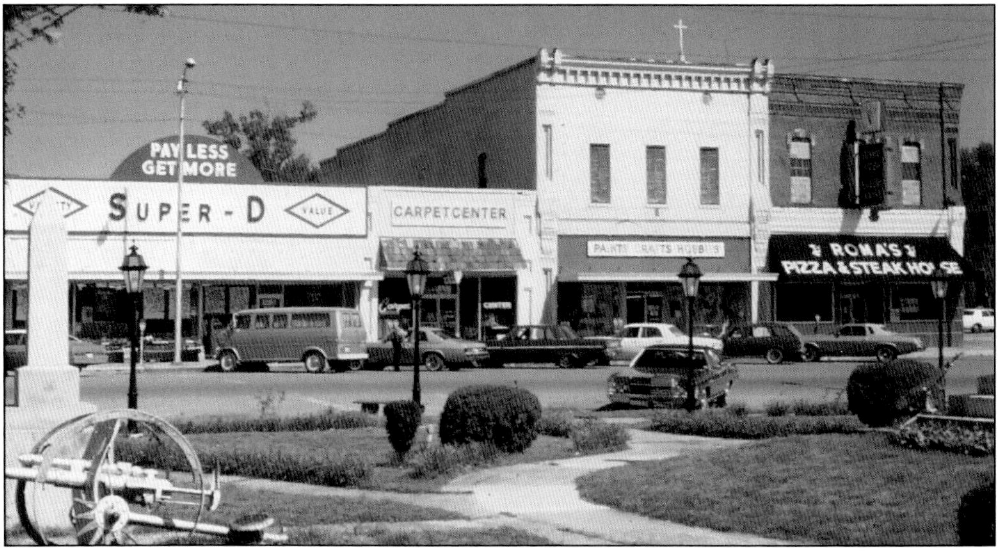

The east side of the square is seen here in the 1970s. Super D Drugs is in the building that now houses Crow Drug Store. The Carpet Center is now Java Jolt Coffee Shop. Paints Crafts Hobbies is in the building now occupied by Pointers. On the far right is Roma's Pizza and Steakhouse, which is still making the best pizzas in town. All of these buildings were rebuilt with brick after the fire of September 1883 destroyed all of the east side of the square. From 1900 to 1910, the post office was located in the carpet store building. That location served as a drugstore from 1910 to 1948, initially for Dr. J.T. Arberry and then for Dr. A.J. Kitchens. The 1883 fire started in William Milo Nisbet's drugstore, located in the right (southern) part of the Super D building.

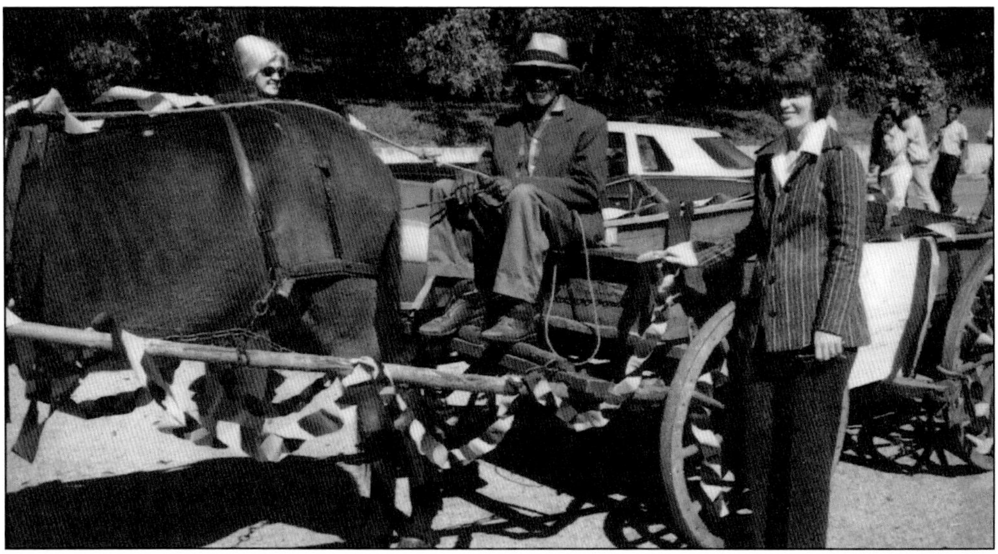

This photograph shows Henry Caldwell, a 20th-century Jacksonville institution. Caldwell, born in 1877, operated the first cement mixer at Camp McClellan in 1917. In the second half of the century, he was a jack-of-all-trades, driving his mule throughout the streets of Jacksonville. In the 1970s, Caldwell and the mule, Red, took granddaughters Lilla and Linda to the Jacksonville School each morning. Caldwell claimed that Red knew all the stop signs and could read traffic lights. At the time of his death, Caldwell was over 100 years old. Posing here with Caldwell and Red are Jean Johnson (left) and Dorothy Jane Nisbet (right).

This 1970s photograph shows the (white) Jacksonville city pool. The City of Jacksonville operated a second, smaller pool next to the Eastwood Community Center.

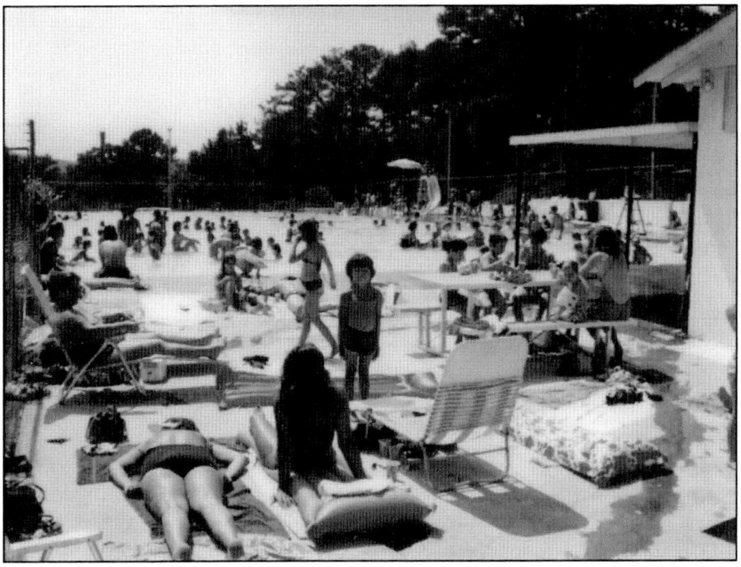

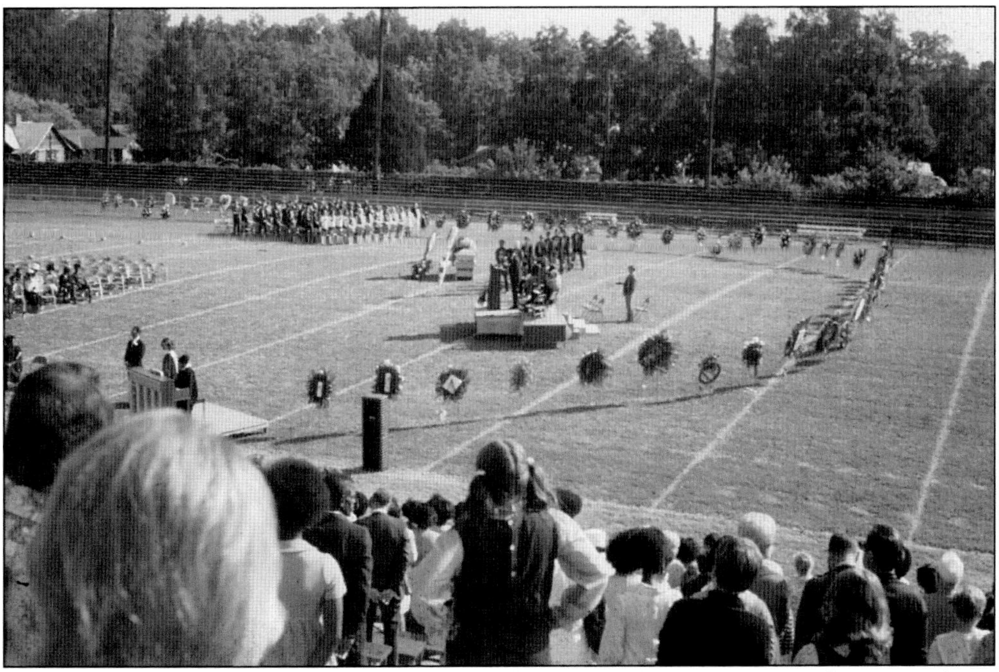

Shown here is the 1972 memorial service for Anthony "Speedy" Cannon at Paul Snow Stadium. Cannon was an African American young man who was killed while playing a high school football game between his team, Jacksonville High School, and Wellborn High School at Wellborn. His funeral, held in the First Baptist Church on Seventh Avenue, was attended by an overflow crowd. Wellborn High is two and a half miles from the location on Highway 202 where, in 1961, an angry mob attacked a Greyhound bus carrying seven Congress of Racial Equality (CORE) members, also known as Freedom Riders.

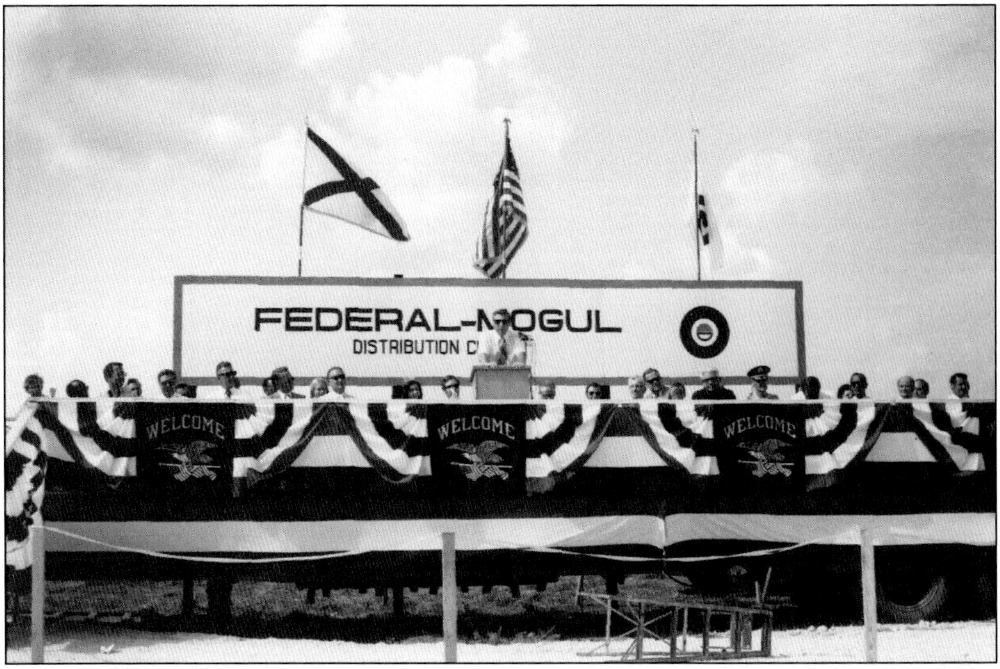

In the early 1970s, Federal-Mogul Corporation, headquartered in Flint, Michigan, decided to locate a distribution plant in Jacksonville. Shown above is the rostrum during the ground-breaking ceremonies on June 21, 1973. Numerous local dignitaries attended the event, and several spoke. The event featured the Marching Ballerinas, Boy Scout Troop 147, a picnic at nearby Germania Springs Park, Miss Alabama Jane Rice, and a ceremonial ground breaking with silver-painted shovels. The plant, completed in 1975, employed 500 workers. When the worldwide distribution center opened, the plant adopted cutting-edge technology, including a barcode system for inventory control, and invested in guided vehicles, handheld scanners, and computers.

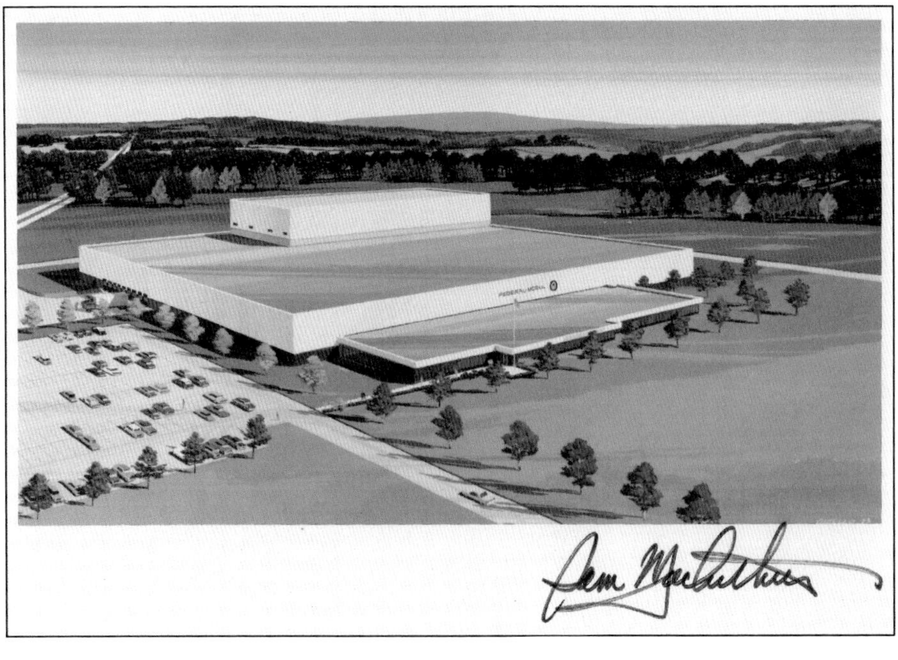

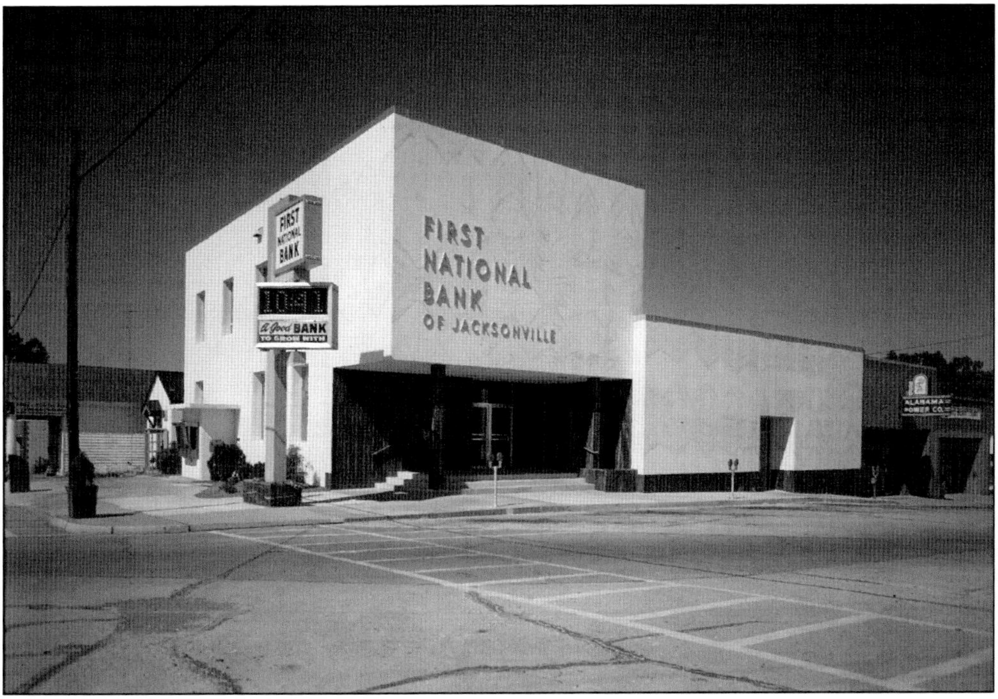

The above photograph depicts the First National Bank building after 1960s renovations added marble veneer. Dr. James C. Francis's office is in the background on the left. The last renovation, in 1977, to the First National Bank consisted of the two-story addition at the rear of the building and fluted columns with Ionic capitals (below). This renovation necessitated moving Dr. Francis's building. On July 6, 1985, the bank failed and was sold, with federal government financial assistance, to AmSouth Bank of Jacksonville. In 2014, this is Region's Bank.

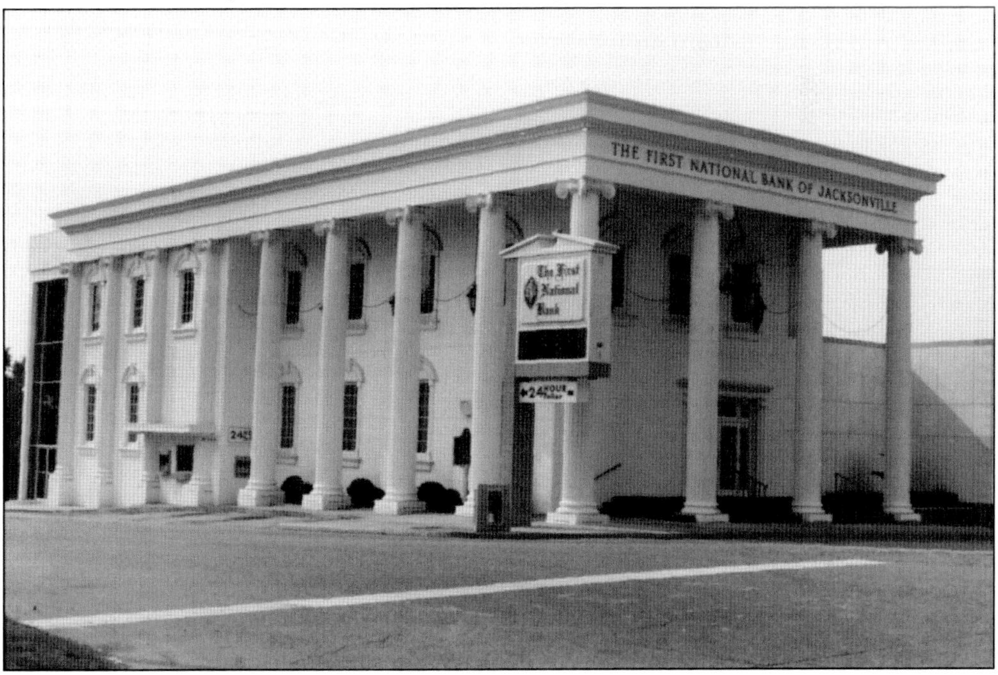

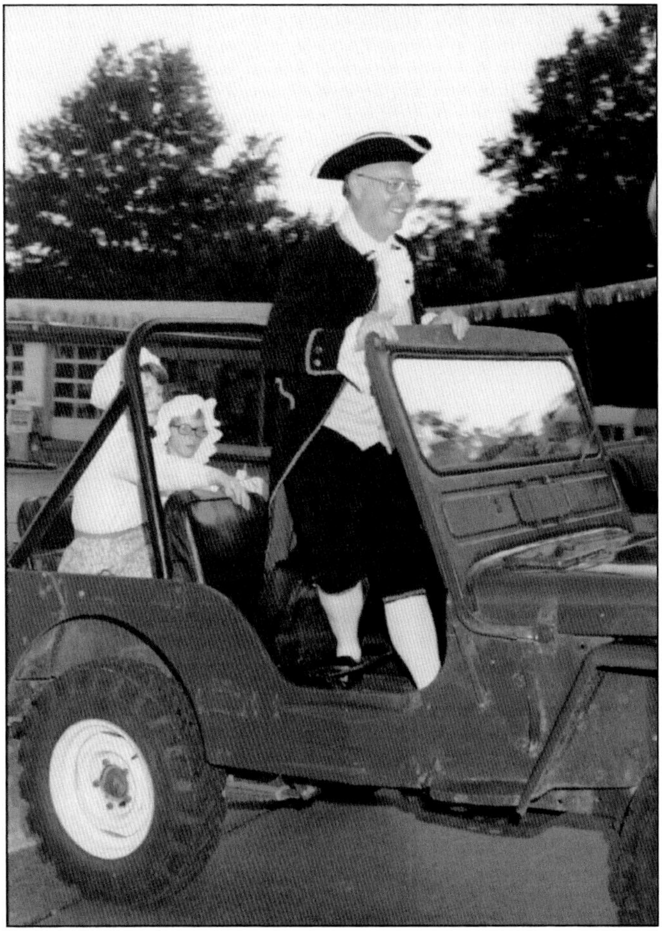

The country's bicentennial in 1976 was a big deal for Jacksonville. The town hosted a parade and a party on the square. In the left image, Mayor John B. Nisbet Jr. stands in a jeep, leading the parade around the square.

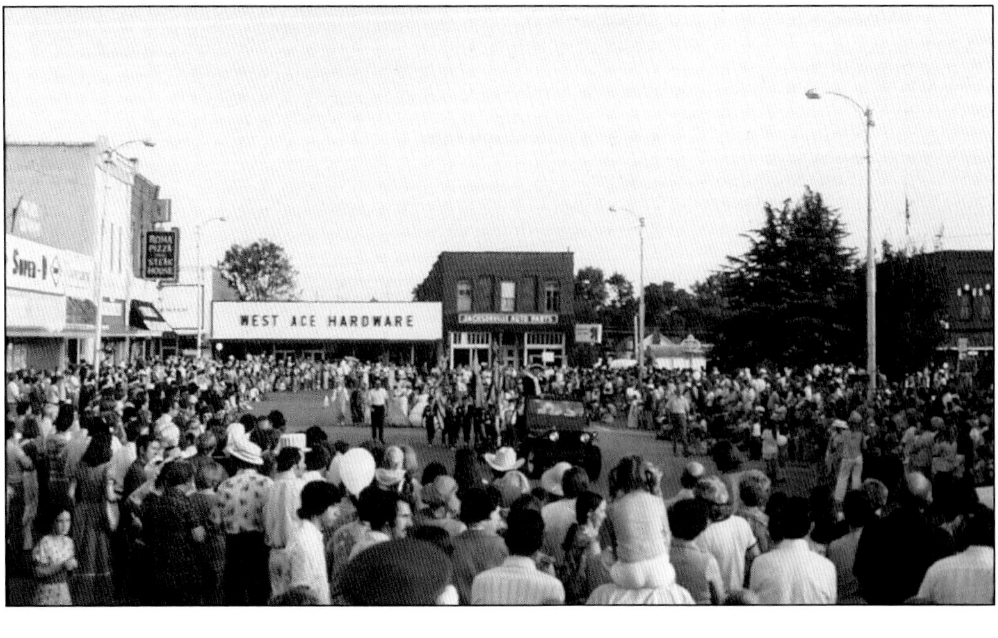

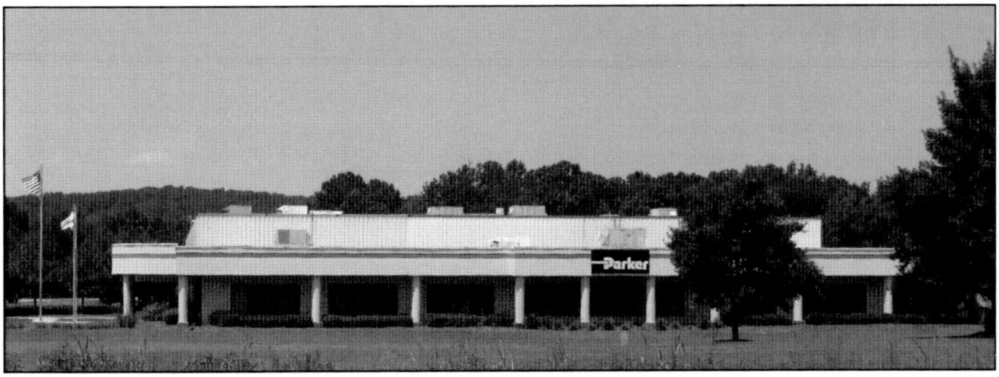

In 1978, Parker-Hannifin Corporation decided to locate an instrumentation valve plant in Jacksonville. The plant opened in 1979 or 1980 and employed 110 workers. (Photograph by Kenneth Record, used with permission.)

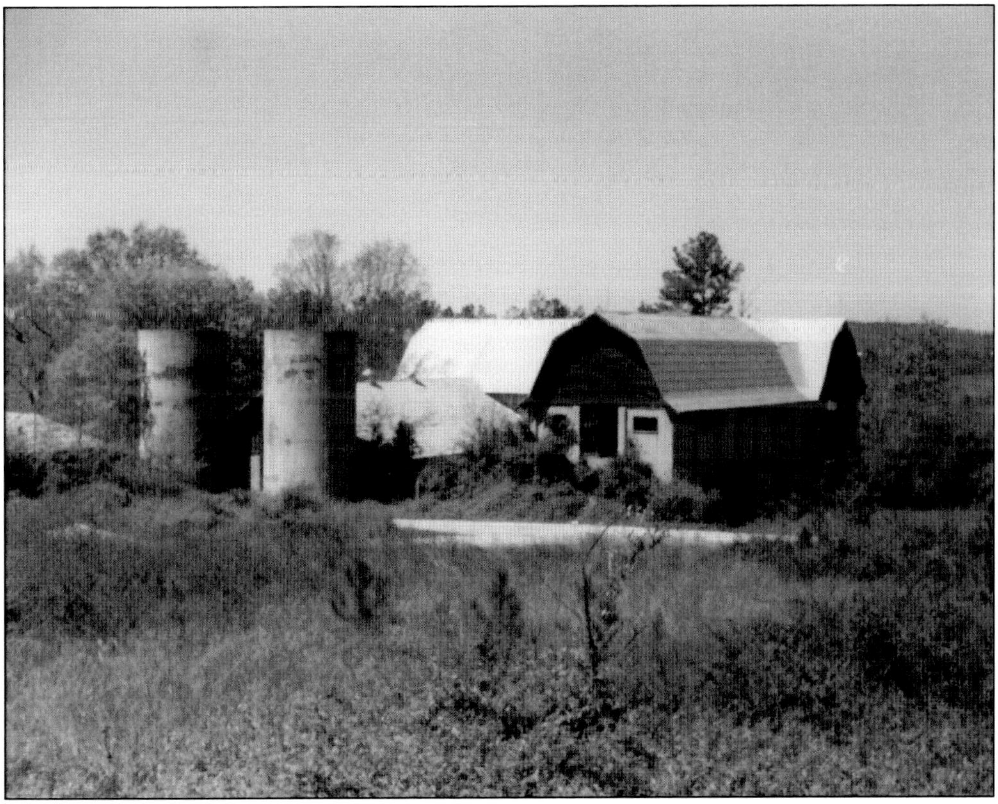

In the 1910s, about the same time that Charles Buck Henry purchased the Ide Cotton Mill, he also bought the former Stevenson plantation south of Jacksonville. Henry remodeled the 1856 house and added a state-of-the-art, 13,500-square-foot concrete dairy barn. The barn is shown in this 1970s photograph. The City of Jacksonville purchased the barn and 200 surrounding acres in 1975.

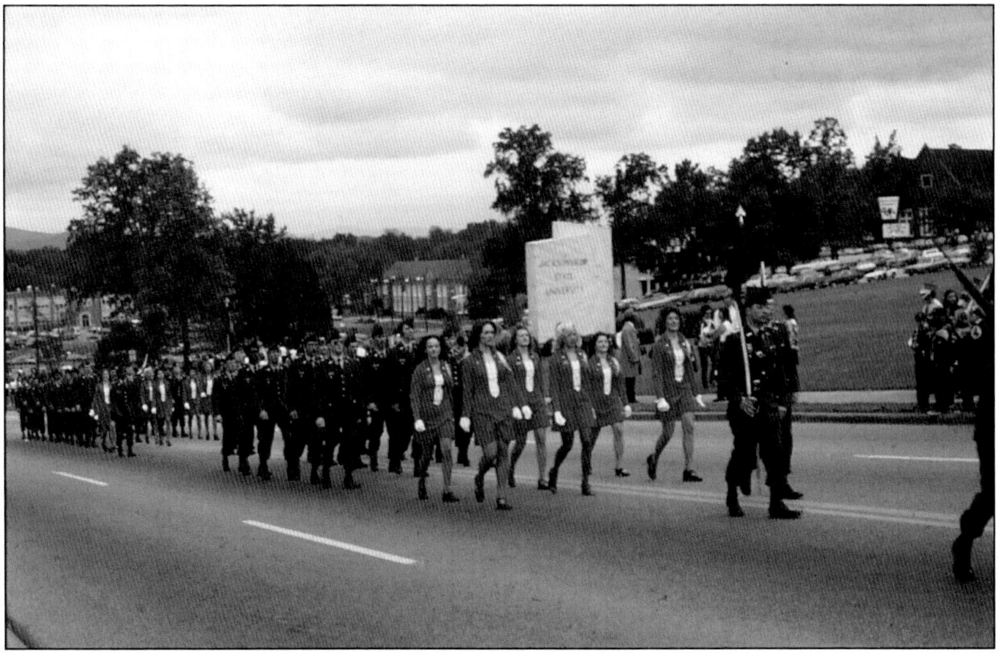

Sometimes, parades went up the hill, and sometimes, they proceeded down the hill. These 1970s photographs show homecoming parades. Shown above, marching in green uniforms, are members of the Jacksonville State University ROTC program. Their escorts are in bright red. Note the large marble JSU sign in the background. Below, the band in blue is the Jacksonville High School Marching Eagles.

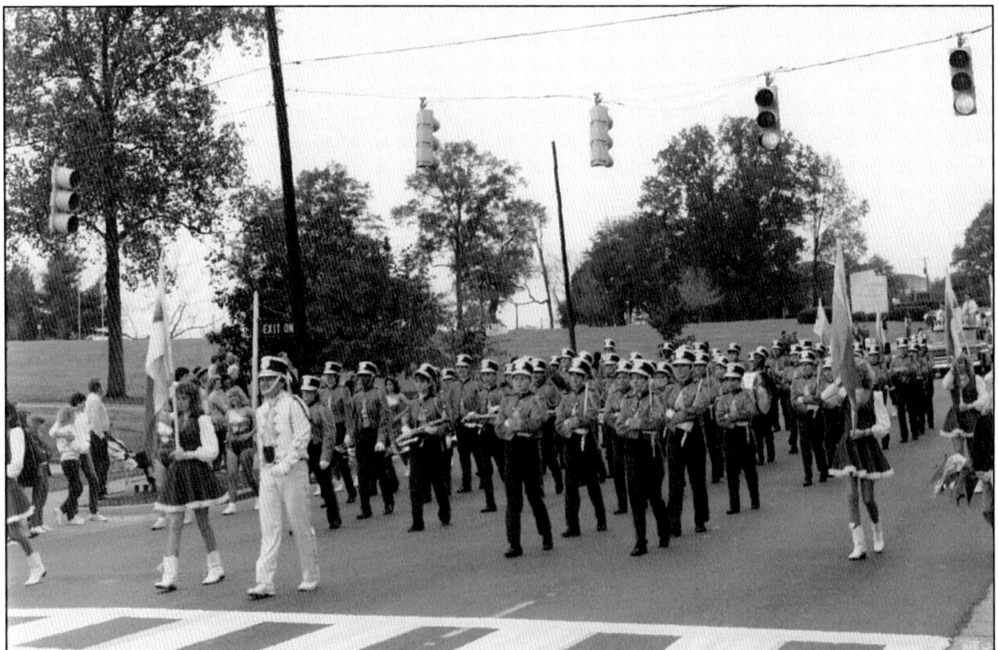

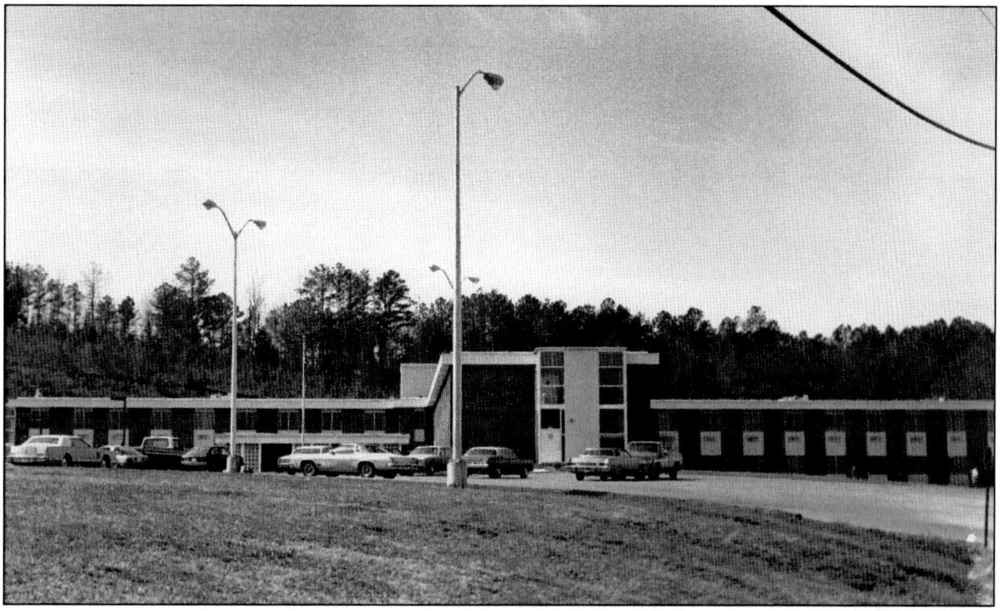

Owned and operated by the City of Jacksonville, the Jacksonville Hospital (above) was dedicated in 1976. It was built on city-owned Henry farm property. The city made $13.5 million in net profit when the hospital was sold in 1996. A portion of that money was used in 1998 to build a new Jacksonville High School sports stadium on another part of the Henry farm property. The dedication plaque (right) is no longer on the building.

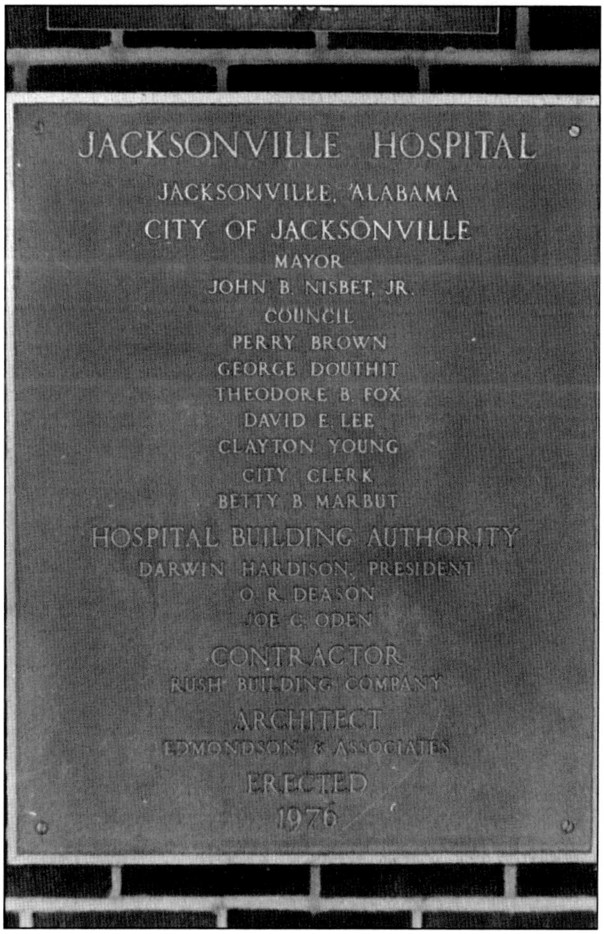

Bibliography

Boozer, Jack Dwight. "Jacksonville, Alabama 1833–1846" Master's thesis. University of Alabama, 1951. Unpublished: Available at Jacksonville State University.

Bragg, Rick. *The Most They Ever Had*. San Francisco: MacAdam/Cage, 2009.

———. *All Over but the Shoutin'*. New York: Pantheon Books, 1997.

———. *Ava's Man*. New York: Knopf, 2001.

———. *The Prince of Frogtown*. New York: Knopf, 2008.

Gates, Grace Hooten. *The Model City of the New South*. Tuscaloosa: The University of Alabama , Press, 1996.

Hollis III, Daniel Webster. *A History of First Baptist Church Jacksonville, Alabama 1836–1986*. , Self-published, 1985.

Howard, Gene L. *Death at Cross Plains: An Alabama Reconstruction Tragedy*. Tuscaloosa: The , University of Alabama Press, 1984.

Lake, Thomas. "The Ghost of Speedy Cannon," *Sports Illustrated Longform*.

Maxwell, Jerry H. *The Perfect Lion*. Tuscaloosa: The University of Alabama Press, 2011.

Moore, Albert Burton. *History of Alabama and Her People*. Chicago and New York: The American, Historical Society, Inc. 1927.

Nisbet, III, John B. "The Gallant Pelham," *New York Times Opinionator*, April 1, 2013.

Nixon, H.C. *Lower Piedmont Country: The Uplands of the Deep South*. Tuscaloosa: The University, of Alabama Press, 1946.

———. *Possum Trot—Rural Community*. Norman: University of Oklahoma Press, 1941.

Pate, James P., ed. *When This Evil War Is Over*. Tuscaloosa: The University of Alabama, Press, 2006.

Sawyer, Effie White. *The First Hundred Years: The History of Jacksonville State University*. Jacksonville, AL: Centennial Committee, Jacksonville State University, 1983.

The Heritage of Calhoun County, Alabama. Clanton, Al: Heritage Publishing Consultants, Inc., 1998

About the Organization

In 1984, when the library left the recreational building, the old name left as well; the library became the Jacksonville Public Library. By moving into the old post building on Pelham Road, the library doubled its floor space. In 1984, the library boasted a circulation of 39,112. In 2011, the library doubled its floor space again with the addition of an annex, which included a much-needed elevator. With the new space, the library began offering more classes and programs for all ages, in addition to the many programs that had been hosted off-site for 15 years.

The library has continued to grow. Programs often attract attendees from out of town and even out of state. In the last 10 years, the enrollment in the annual summer reading program has doubled, with 956 participants in 2014. Other program attendance has tripled; patrons read over 12,000 books each summer. Annual circulation currently hovers between 90,000 and 100,000 items. Approximate annual use of the library's computers for the Internet is 12,000, and free wireless Internet access is provided for those with their own laptops. The staff conducts free computer classes to keep citizens competent in new technologies.

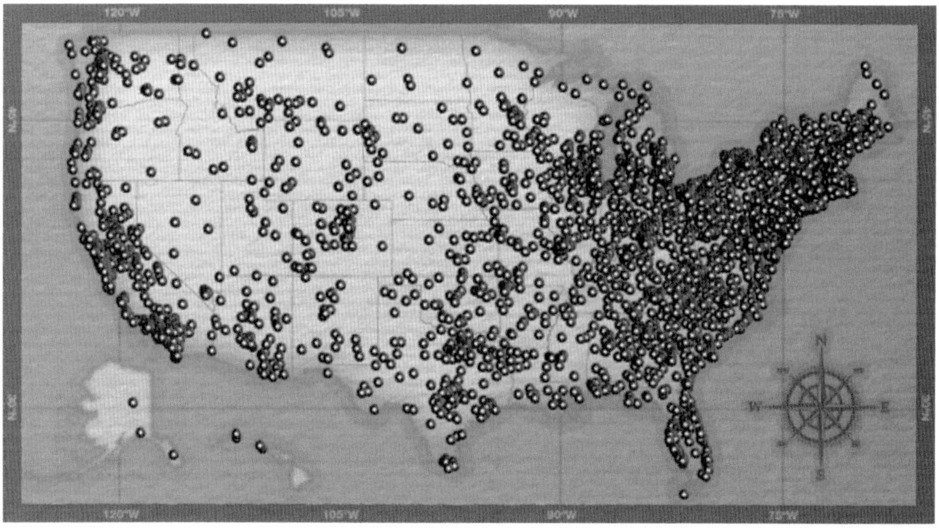